Principles of Social Change

Principles of Social Change

LEONARD A. JASON

OXFORD
UNIVERSITY PRESS

OXFORD

UNIVERSITY PRESS

Oxford University Press is a department of the University of Oxford.
It furthers the University's objective of excellence in research, scholarship,
and education by publishing worldwide.

Oxford   New York

Auckland   Cape Town   Dar es Salaam   Hong Kong   Karachi
Kuala Lumpur   Madrid   Melbourne   Mexico City   Nairobi
New Delhi   Shanghai   Taipei   Toronto

With offices in

Argentina   Austria   Brazil   Chile   Czech Republic   France   Greece
Guatemala   Hungary   Italy   Japan   Poland   Portugal   Singapore
South Korea   Switzerland   Thailand   Turkey   Ukraine   Vietnam

Oxford is a registered trademark of Oxford University Press in the UK and certain other
countries.

Published in the United States of America by
Oxford University Press
198 Madison Avenue, New York, NY 10016

© Oxford University Press 2013

Library of Congress Cataloging-in-Publication Data
Jason, Leonard.
Principles of social change / Leonard A. Jason.
p. cm.
Includes bibliographical references and index.
ISBN 978–0–19–984185–1
1. Social change.   2. Social action.   3. Community development.   I. Title.
HM831.J37 2013
303.4—dc23
2012024735

Over the past 200 years, people fighting for social justice have abolished slavery, provided suffrage to women, freed India from colonial rule, and ended apartheid in South Africa. This book is dedicated to the hundreds of grassroots organizations and community activists who have a proud legacy of instigating a more just, equitable, and humane world.

LAJ

CONTENTS

FOREWORD

Social movements, having left indelible imprints upon American and world history, are now rippling across the globe in ways that are profoundly reshaping our collective future. The successes and failures of organized efforts at social change leave many questions in their wake. How do regular citizens come to be positive agents of change? What distinguishes successful social movements from those that leave no lasting contribution? What are the core ideas and strategies shared by effective social change efforts? These are the questions central to Leonard Jason's engaging new book, *Principles of Social Change*.

In the pages that follow, you the reader will be thrust into a series of captivating stories about how ordinary people played extraordinary roles in changing neighborhoods, organizations, communities, countries, and the world. The book you are entering is in part a biography of social change, filled with such figures as Mohandas Gandhi, Martin Luther King Jr., Malcolm X, Jane Addams, Florence Nightingale, Mother Teresa, and Rachel Carson, to name a few. It is also the story of Leonard Jason's own career as a successful change agent. These historical and personal accounts alone are worthy of investing time in these pages, but there are two other qualities of this book that distinguish it.

First, Leonard Jason defines the DNA of successful movements aimed at everything from freeing neighborhoods of dog droppings to launching major public health and human rights campaigns. *Principles of Social Change* is in this sense a how-to manual for successful social action. The discussion of action steps alone will draw appreciative readers interested or involved in a wide spectrum of social causes. The discussion of the distinction between quick cosmetic change and the more complex and time-enduring processes of substantive change that elevate the quality of personal and community life is particularly valuable, as are Jason's five principles of social change that make up the heart of this book. The outline of successful change strategies and tactics also contains explorations of two rarely addressed issues: (1) the potential for harm in the name of help in the execution of social change efforts and (2) the need to anticipate and personally and organizationally manage the backlash that comes on the heels of social movements.

Second, *Principles of Social Change* ends with a reflective discussion about the deeper sources and solutions to the problems addressed by social movements. This final discussion is an exercise in connecting the small dots to portray a larger and previously unseen picture. Many readers will find this final essay both personally meaningful and a bit breathtaking. Leonard Jason's perception of patterns across social movements that reveal what is now slipping away or has been forever or long missing within our community life is itself a valuable contribution, as is his vision of how each of us can, as Gandhi suggests, become the change we wish to see in the world.

I have spent more than four decades studying and participating in a spectrum of social and public health reform movements. It would have been a godsend to have had this book as a guide from the beginning. I hope it will be of such value to you.

William L. White
Author, *Let's Go Make Some History: Chronicles of the New Addiction Recovery Advocacy Movement*

PREFACE

Connection: It's what makes for healthy relationships, strong families, and childhood bonds that turn into lifelong friendships. Yet if you look beyond your closest relationships—your spouse, your sibling, your best friend—these bonds begin to disappear. How often do you see strangers show compassion to another in need, rather than indifference or contempt? In a society that increasingly values individualism and success, we are taught to compete with one another rather than to appreciate our interdependence and the importance of community identity. This lack of connection in our communities and society is deep-seated, and the consequences dire.

For decades, growing inequalities—between the wealthy and poor, skilled and unskilled, blue- and white-collar workers—have threatened to push entire groups of people to the fringes of our society. As the gap widens, so does our sense of a separate self, further straining societal cohesiveness and our connections with others. Meanwhile, private and government institutions are facing gaping budget deficits and deep cuts, reducing the safety nets of those who are most vulnerable. In 2011, the Occupy Wall Street movement protested about income inequalities and regulatory policies that benefit corporations and the richest individuals at the expense of the average citizen. The movement was fueled by anger and frustration with the economic times, as many now feel that it is not possible to work hard, get a good education, and hold a decent job to support one's family. Something significant is needed to prevent whole generations from feeling hopeless and unable to effect change, with nowhere to turn for help. Yet, as we try to deal with these enormous and interconnected problems, organizations whose mission is to aid these populations neglect tackling the deeper, systemic issues that cause challenges within our communities, opting instead for easier, albeit short-lived, quick-fix solutions.

How, then, can the average person bring about social change when government and other large institutions have failed? This book is designed to address this question and provide practical solutions. History has shown that paradigm shifts rarely happen within established institutions in a society. It often takes a grassroots initiative that radically challenges the system or status quo. We need new ideas and fresh perspectives—as well as an understanding of historical and cultural influences that explain how we've arrived at this point—if we want to produce meaningful change and overcome seemingly insurmountable obstacles. Throughout history, it has been ordinary people, impassioned and driven by social justice, who have achieved meaningful, life-changing reforms, often starting in their own communities. These ordinary people then become iconic historical leaders who inspire future activists. Through first-hand accounts of modern-day agents of change, *Principles of Social Change* provides a road map for anyone committed to bringing about positive, long-lasting improvements in his or her community and society as a whole.

Activists usually organize in reaction to a problem in their community—whether it's a relatively simple need for a stop sign or, as I discuss later, a larger issue: preventing young people from becoming addicted to drugs. In many cases, once agents for change are successful in one campaign, they become committed to other larger causes. Some people may choose community activism as a career. For me, discovering the atrocities of the Holocaust at a young age inspired me to work for social change. That inspiration spurred me to volunteer for Lyndon Johnson's presidential campaign. It also led to my first deep disillusionment: President Johnson's stubborn refusal to end the war in Vietnam. A close-up view of the horse-trading and backroom compromises that are a part of lawmaking exacerbated my disappointment, turning me off to politics. Fortunately, I did retain a passion for activism and a fascination with psychology. I would never be a politician, but I would seek the changes I wanted for our society through a different route: by first understanding the people within our society and the systemic problems that shape their lives.

I enrolled at Brandeis University expressly to study psychology under Abraham Maslow, a legendary figure in the field and founder of the humanistic psychology movement (Maslow, 1962). As my education progressed, I met and studied under several other iconic figures, such as gestalt therapist Fritz Perls and sociologist Morrie Schwartz, who was featured in the book *Tuesdays With Morrie* (Albom, 1997). I began to develop a road map for understanding how seemingly intractable and insurmountable problems that condemn many people to a terrible sense of isolation can be solved by recognizing and acting upon the resources that already exist among people. Later, in graduate school, I discovered the field of community psychology, which seemed to be a perfect synthesis of my passions: the psychology of making a difference in the world.

Principles of Social Change offers a comprehensive guide to the development of community interventions and provides the tools and resources to initiate and sustain progress. I examine various strategies developed by community activists, coalitions, and social scientists to break down what motivates people. What worked and why? What can be applied to other scenarios? I also discuss practical solutions to complicated issues, such as protecting children's well-being, combating abuses of power, providing affordable housing, and cleaning up the environment. These ideas are designed to bring about enduring systemic changes at all levels of community life. Although activists such as Mahatma Gandhi, Mother Teresa, Saul Alinsky, Jane Addams, Malcolm X, and Martin Luther King Jr. have effected transformational change, everyday citizens and social entrepreneurs (Bornstein, 2004) have also made tremendously important and sustainable contributions. The five principles reviewed in this book can be used by anyone who wants to bring comprehensive, structural solutions to some of our most vexing social issues.

The five principles of social change are:

1. Determining the nature of the change desired: Is it a cosmetic, short-term fix, or does it address the root of the problem?
2. Identifying the power holders: Who are your influential friends and foes?
3. Creating coalitions: Identify and work with others who share your goals.
4. Learning patience and persistence: Small wins are crucial to attaining long-term goals.
5. Measuring your success: What have you accomplished? What is left to achieve?

Although this book offers innovative principles and simple instructions, the focus is on applying these principles to produce real-world change grounded in empirical data. Principles and strategies are provided within a theoretical model to demonstrate the role that the environment can play in promoting or resisting change. Perhaps most importantly, we need to recognize that many of our most complex problems can be tackled by community members themselves through identifying and taking advantage of resources that already exist.

As both an academic and a long-time activist, I have relied on my years of experience to find ways to solve some of the most complex and difficult problems that confront us. The issues addressed in the following chapters will hopefully help those seeking to bring about change in their communities or societies. These principles and strategies demonstrate that there is, in fact, a tangible way to achieve change—ordinary people throughout history have done it. This guide is intended for anyone with a desire to improve his or her community. It is expressly for activists with a wide range of causes, from changing environmental regulations to helping disadvantaged children, or other complicated social problems. The five principles described in this book are essential to solving these problems, and they carry the potential to influence new generations of engaged citizens, community activists, and students of psychology and related social sciences. By understanding these principles, community leaders and activists will be poised to bring about a more just and humane society.

ACKNOWLEDGMENTS

A number of people have, at various stages, facilitated bringing this work to fruition. I am deeply appreciative of the many current and former students who have helped me develop issues discussed in the book, including Darrin Aase, Monica Adams, Josefina Alvarez, Christopher Beasley, Michelle Beaulieu, Peter Bishop, Caryn Blitz, G. Anne Bogat, Blake Bowden, Abby Brown, Molly Brown, Radhika Chimata, Karina Corradi, Carol Cradock, Carmen Curtis, Lucia D'Arlach, Margaret I. Davis, Trina Davis, Julia DiGangi, Paul Dupont, Meredyth Evans, Andrea Flynn, Erin Frankenberry, Ben Graham, Brenda Greiner, David Groh, Ron Harvey, Jean Hill, Eve Holton-Walker, Elizabeth Horin, Bronwyn Hunter, Roy Jung, Joy Kaufman, Caroline King, Elias Kithuri, Cecile Lardon, Toni Lesowitz, Rich Liotta, John M. Majer, Francis Matese, Mike McCanna, Susan McMahon, Joel Minden, Sister Gloria Njoku, Thomas Olson, Mazna Patka, Bart Pillen, Steven Pokorny, Sharon Press, Olya Rabin-Belyaev, Karina Reyes, Jean Rhodes, Tom Rose, Doreen Salina, Jennifer Shlaes, Vicki Sloan, Sharon Song, Steve Spaccarelli, Edward B. Stevens, Mary Stockton, Daniel Tabon-Pierce, Renee Taylor, David Thompson, Susan Torres-Harding, Judith Viola, Lynn Wagner, Andrew Weine, Teri Williams, Mariya Zaturenskaya, Jennifer Zeisz, and Susan Shorr-Zoline. My thanks also to many colleagues for their insight related to the concepts and approaches discussed in this book, including Richard Contreras, Sheldon Cotler, Emory Cowen, Steven Everett, Joseph R. Ferrari, Karen Foli, Fred Friedberg, David Glenwick, Gary Harper, Daryl Isenberg, James Kelly, Christopher Keys, Ray Legler, John Moritsugu, Bradley Olson, Nicole Porter, Judith Richman, LaVome Robinson, Bernadette Sanchez, Roger Weissberg, and Edwin Zolik.

I would like to acknowledge and thank the following DePaul faculty and staff, without whom the changes at DePaul discussed here would not have been possible. In the 1970s, Edwin Zolik, Sheila Ribordy, John Reisman, and Sheldon

Cotler were among the faculty who helped create the Clinical Psychology doctoral program at DePaul University. In the following years, LaVome Robinson, Rod Watts, and Patrick Tolan joined the faculty and helped diversify the program. Many other faculty members contributed to the expansion of our Clinical Psychology doctoral program in the mid-1990s and into the 2000s. These scholars included Christopher Keys, Gary Harper, Susan McMahon, Bernadette Sanchez, Nathan Todd, Patrick Fowler, Brigida Hernandez, Gayle Iwamasa, Kathy Grant, Karen Budd, Jocelyn Carter, Jeanne McIntosh, and Antonio Polo. In the late 1990s, Joseph Ferrari and I felt that it was important to develop a Community Psychology PhD program that was independent of the clinical psychology program, with interdisciplinary courses and faculty. Consequentially, we created the stand-alone Community Psychology PhD program, which included eight clinical-community faculty, plus other scholars whose focus was on community-based research, such as Doug Cellar, Midge Wilson, and Howard Rosing.

Many of our undergraduates in the late 1970s were graduating without having acquired the clinical skills necessary to get a job. I was fortunate to have the help of Ernie Doleys, who worked with me to set up a human services concentration for our undergraduates. Since the mid-1990s, Sheldon Cotler and Bernadette Sanchez have done an excellent job of carrying on this program. I also want to thank Susan McMahon and Olya Rabin-Belyaev for collaborating with me in 2000 to create a Community Psychology concentration for undergraduates at DePaul.

Dozens of community partners worked with my team at DePaul University over the years. I am particularly indebted to Ed Anderson, Carol North, Tony LoSasso, Martin Perdoux, and Pam Woll. We were most fortunate to have the support of Paul Molloy, the founder of Oxford House, and Leon Venable, Richard Albert, Stephanie Marez, Rory Murray, Gilberto Padilla, LaRonda Stalling, Carolyn Ellis, Bertel Williams, Kathy Sledge, Robin Miller, Bill Kmeck, Makeba Casey, Lester Fleming, and Ron Blake. Additionally, I extend my gratitude to the members of the youth tobacco access project, including Buzz Talbot, Steven Pokorny, Monica Adams, Peter Ji, Charlotte Kunz, Yvonne Hunt, and Jeff Barr. Within the myalgic encephalomyelitis (ME)/chronic fatigue syndrome (CFS) world, I am greatly appreciative of help from Fred Friedberg, Pat Fero, Carole Howard, Connie Van der Eb, Ron Gilbert, Jill McLaughlin, Jeff Rabin, Rich Carson, Eileen Holderman, Staci Stevens, Matthew Sorenson, Morris Papernik, Judy Richman, David Lipkin, Morris Papernik, Kim McCleary, Nancy Klimas, Chuck and Darie Lapp, David Bell, Gudrun Lange, Ben Natelson, Lee Meisel, Rebecca Artman, Cindy Bateman, Suzanne Vernon, Art Hartz, Ken Friedman, Judy Mikovits, Chris Snell, Lydia Nelson, Martin Lerner, and Ron Glaser.

I also am indebted to Bill White for his insightful foreword, and his work has constituted an important part of the theoretical underpinnings of this volume.

I am most appreciative of Kimberly Beers and Joyce Sinakhone, who served as primary editors of this book and provided expert help and advice in the final revisions. Several individuals also have been extremely helpful in contributing to this book, in particular Ian Morris, Carol Sonenklar, Madison Sunnquist, and Nhim Michael Danh, who provided me with guidance and extremely helpful reworking of many chapters. My thanks also to Jessica Hart, Laura Hlavaty, Erin Clyne, Becky Brasfield, W. Keith Brown, Neetu Abad, Harriet Melrose, and Jo Ellyn Walker, who provided me with excellent feedback on particular chapters. I also thank Dorothy Wall and Meera Lee Sethi, who helped me with sections of chapter 2. I appreciate the writing contributed by Karen Foli for material within chapter 3.

In addition, I appreciate financial support received from the National Institute on Alcohol Abuse and Alcoholism, the National Institute on Drug Abuse, the National Center on Minority Health and Health Disparities, the National Cancer Institute, the National Institute of Allergy and Infectious Diseases, and the National Institute of Nursing Research.

Finally, I want to express my thanks to the editorial staff of Oxford University Press, and especially to Sarah Harrington, for the continuous support and invaluable guidance that she has provided.

Principles of Social Change

Changing the Rules of the Game

On Tuesday, December 2, 1997, I received a telephone call at my DePaul University office. It was not about my ongoing research or from a graduate student with a question. To my surprise, it was a congressional staff person from the Subcommittee on Health and Environment of the U.S. House Commerce Committee asking me to testify on teenage tobacco use. The staffer asked me to address prevention strategies, and in particular, issues involving teenagers' access to tobacco products at a congressional hearing the following week. The attorneys general from several states wanted to limit the once seemingly invincible tobacco industry; specifically, they wanted to bar advertising aimed at young people and reduce high rates of youth tobacco use. Each day, over 3,000 youths begin this deadly habit, and tobacco kills more people than all other types of drug use combined.

This topic had been a focus of my research, and I was honored to testify. Over several decades, many scientists had shown links between the dangers of cigarettes and the relentless efforts of the tobacco industry to encourage adolescent smoking. Finally, our efforts were coming to fruition. My comments could affect new tobacco regulations and help to restrict young people's access to it; my words could also influence public education, taxes, advertising, sales, and funding for science. These few minutes behind a microphone could be critical in promoting the meaningful social change for which I, and others, had been passionately fighting.

The next week, I arrived at the Rayburn House Office Building in Washington, DC, along with the other panelists, Michael Eriksen, the Director of the Office on Smoking and Health at the Centers for Disease Control and Prevention, and Howard Beales, an Associate Professor at George Washington University. The stately building, with its white marble façade, marble statues, and 40-foot ceilings, is home to congressional offices and much of our nation's history. If the building's aesthetics weren't enough, police officers, barriers, and other personnel signaled that this building was a place of great power. I found myself in the hearing room along with representatives, photographers, C-SPAN cameras, and about 100 audience members. Finally, in a blur of bright lights, shutter clicks, and noisy murmuring, the testimony began.

This singular opportunity—speaking out and encouraging large-scale social change—did not arrive by chance. My anti-tobacco journey began 22 years earlier, as an ordinary person at the beginning of a career. Change can be accomplished by challenging certain beliefs, laws, or decisions. It is absolutely possible, and you are the people to do it. But understanding how and why social change occurs, and the principles that guide it, is vital to success. Throughout history, the most powerful and effective agents of change have adhered to certain principles that helped them to accomplish their visions. This book will explore the five principles that have guided me through four decades of social activism and illustrate the gratifying path to creating positive change in your community.

Starting the Process of Change

What is change? There are a myriad of definitions. "Change We Can Believe In" was the campaign slogan a politician named Barack Obama used in 2008. The promise of change, and the feelings that it inspired, carried him into the White House and the nation's history. But as all too many Americans know, change is not always positive. Over the past few decades, many Americans have had to work harder and longer for less pay and fewer or no benefits. Looming budget deficits and cutbacks at the state and federal levels are making our lives even harder with reduced or eliminated social services. Yet, positive change arises from resilient, optimistic members of the community. Ordinary individuals who do not lose faith can overcome enormous odds to target the root of a systemic problem, instead of wasting time or money on simplistic or ineffective solutions. However, just like any journey, the road to becoming meaningful agents of change must begin somewhere.

We will explore five specific principles to approach problematic systems within our communities. The journey often begins with the recognition that something is fundamentally wrong and usually unfair. This recognition may take the form of an ache of compassion or a flash of outrage, but the feeling is clear: *This needs to change.* You may not even know why, but your intuition will steer you in the right direction. If you listen and watch closely, there are people and signs that will provide clues and direction; the key is to be open and receptive to them. Intuition, passion, knowledge, and understanding are crucial in creating a strategy for social change.

When I entered graduate school in 1971, I faced a situation in need of change. I was not, however, familiar with the basic principles of social change. During my first few months of school, I learned that many graduate students within my clinical psychology program were considerably dissatisfied. During several meetings with faculty, they vented some of their complaints. During one small group session, I had an epiphany, and the root of the dissatisfaction became crystal clear: The students lacked representation and wanted to influence how decisions were made in the program. It was as straightforward as that. I felt elated to have had the intuition to get beyond the small details and conflicts that clouded the fundamental issue. That insight emboldened me, and I shared it at the next large meeting of all faculty and students. The room became very quiet. I wondered if I'd said something inappropriate. Actually, I had stated a problem that many students believed, but had not wanted to confront, in direct defiance of the faculty. But this first realization was not enough. After several subsequent meetings, the effort to bring change—more student input—to the graduate program fizzled, and we went back to business as usual, following the faculty's dictates.

This effort for change had failed miserably. I learned, however, that power holders would not cede decision-making authority easily. As a lowly first-year graduate student, I felt inexperienced and underequipped to challenge the status quo. The professors had the authority to decide whether or not we stayed in the program. I needed to decide whether gaining more access to decision making was worth the risk of alienating the professors. At the heart of change lies this equation: determining the risk and benefit balance, especially in relation to people in power. I was not going to be there for long, and my heart was not fixed on making this a major issue in my life at the risk of my education. As a result, I did little to sustain this attempt at social change.

It was apparent that I needed to find something that I felt passionate about to stay committed to an issue over time. Therefore, I had learned a crucial step in the change process: choosing an area to which I was fully committed. If I didn't find the right issue, my chances of success would be negligible. With this in mind, I was ready for the next step: understanding the nature of the social change effort. The first principle of social change emphasizes the importance of determining whether the desired change is a short-term fix or an enduring solution that addresses the root of the problem.

First-Order Change

There are different ways to advocate for your cause, but not all are effective. Here, we will explore two drastically different approaches. These strategies are called first-order and second-order change (Watzlawick, Weakland, & Fisch, 1974). First-order change is a strategy that attempts to eliminate deficits and problems for individuals but rarely addresses the causes that contribute to those problems. To understand this distinction, consider this hypothetical scenario: Overlooking a beautiful lake with a long sandy beach are high cliffs where people often walk to take in a better view. One day, a person falls from the cliff and is flailing about in the water. The lifeguard spots him, quickly jumps into her boat, and saves the day. A bit later, another person wades too far into the water and panics. The lifeguard again dives into the water to save him. This pattern continues day after day—people are drowning; they need rescuing; and the lifeguard saves them.

Soon, the lifeguard realizes that she cannot keep rescuing every person that falls into the water or wades in too deep. In fact, she can't keep up with all of them, and some people have even drowned. The lifeguard feels overwhelmed by these problems. Trusting her intuition, she has a revelation: She could prevent people from falling from the cliffs in the first place and teach the rest how to swim.

Realizing that water safety is a serious issue, as drowning is one of the leading causes of death in the United States among children, the lifeguard wonders how to persuade local officials of the need for railings and swimming lessons. The lifeguard points out that 10 people drown each day, and of this group, children ages 1 to 4 have the highest drowning death rate (Centers for Disease Control and Prevention, 2012). During months of meetings with town officials, several powerful leaders do not want to spend the money to fund the needed changes. Through sustained community support, however, she is finally able to convince them that scrambling to save someone only *after* they start to drown is a dangerous policy. Finally, town officials budget the money to initiate swimming classes and install railings on the cliffs. The two measures save lives at the beach by altering both the environmental problem—the cliffs—and the individual problem—people's skill levels in water. Even after railings are built and classes are established, the lifeguard and community continue to monitor the situation and fine-tune improvements to include more people in swimming lessons and to ensure the railings are effective.

The process of change often requires new ways of thinking and a deep-seated commitment and passion for the issue. To bring about meaningful change, the lifeguard needed to identify a problem (people drowning), consider alternative ways of solving the problem (railings and swimming classes), confront powerful people who preferred to keep the status quo, and build consensus within the community to devote the resources to fix the problem. When you have that inner, nagging feeling that something is not right, listen to it. When you suspect the traditional approach isn't working, trust your instincts; you're probably correct.

In this scenario, first-order change involved the lifeguard repeatedly diving into the water and saving the drowning people. Second-order change involved making modifications to the situation, such as erecting barriers and establishing swimming classes. As a society, we often do not think in terms of prevention or changing risky environments. Successful change agents must have both knowledge and a sense of intuition and urgency to solve complex problems.

Here is a concrete example of a first-order intervention that you might see in a public school. A teacher perceived a student who consistently seemed bored and inattentive in class to be an underachiever. The teacher was frequently harsh and critical toward the child, hoping to motivate him to be more studious. This was a first-order intervention, as it aimed to modify the student's behavior without considering the circumstances that were causing him to be distracted. In fact, the student's lack of focus was not caused by laziness, but rather an environment that was not conducive to learning. The school was located in a gang-controlled area. Members were relentlessly trying to recruit the student, making him anxious and distressed. The student was overwhelmed and unable to concentrate in the classroom. As happens all too often, school officials found it easier to blame an individual rather than recognize and confront the real situational obstacles.

First-order change is cosmetic and only provides, at best, short-term solutions. Of course, some first-order interventions are appropriate and effective, such as setting a broken arm after an accident. However, the pressing and intransigent problems that face our nation require more comprehensive solutions. Sadly, most current interventions to solve these problems are first-order strategies. Herein lies the paradox: First-order change interventions are alluring because they promise to solve the most deeply rooted problems with simple solutions, yet they fail at the most basic levels. These types of interventions can render people powerless to overcome their oppression or unable to break out of a cycle of crime or addiction. We can see this more clearly by looking at total institutions and top-down strategies.

First-Order at Its Worst

Total institutions are places in which residents live under absolute control of authority figures and are separated from their families, friends, and natural environments. They are quite possibly the worst form of first-order solutions. Unfortunately, most of our resources are disproportionately poured into these types of institutions—prisons, mental hospitals, or other facilities that house some of our most vulnerable citizens. These institutions are the worst examples of first-order change; not only are they very expensive but also, overwhelmingly, they fail to provide rehabilitation for their inhabitants or teach the skills needed to live within the broader community.

Politicians usually claim success after putting criminals behind bars or finding shelters for the homeless. And while these "successes" make for great sound bites and campaign slogans, more often than not, they mislead the public into believing that these problems are solved. In reality, nothing could be further from the truth. Most inmates and those with mental health problems will eventually be released back into the community—at best, unchanged; at worst, bitter and more dangerous. Studies show that of a group of released offenders, 68% were arrested for a new offense, and 52% returned to prison on a new charge or parole violation within 3 years of release (Langan & Levin, 2002). As prison populations continue to rise at an annual cost of nearly $30 billion, the current system and its cycle of detention, release, and recidivism is both ineffective and costly (Stephan, 2004). The psychological impact on prisoners is even worse.

A famous prison study by Stanford psychologist Phillip Zimbardo (1971) provides insight into the poisonous environments that arise within total institutions such as prisons. During a 2-week experiment that explored human nature and how environments affect people's behavior, Zimbardo randomly divided a group of average male college students into two teams: One group played the inmates at a mock simulated prison; the other group played the prison guards. The prisoners were given the full inmate treatment: They were taken from their homes, arrested by actual police officers, and forced to live in cells for 24 hours a day. In contrast, the guards worked 8-hour shifts and then returned to their regular lives. Surprisingly, the personable boys who were given the roles of prison guards quickly asserted power over the prisoners and began to behave cruelly and sadistically toward them. The prisoners responded in kind: submitting to the authority, erupting in emotional breakdowns, or acting out in defiance. One participant who was assigned a prisoner role described the emotional turmoil after a "parole" hearing:

> I fell a long way down when ... I was not [released]. That one act worked its way into me and brought about an even heavier feeling of desperation. I broke as a result.... If prison is anything like what I went through here, I don't know how it could help anyone. (Zimbardo, 2007, pp. 161–162)

Zimbardo lost control of the environment in his role as superintendent, and in order to avoid serious emotional and physical injury to the subjects, he prematurely ended the experiment after only 6 days. While the ethics of this experiment have been rightfully criticized, the exercise was a stunning demonstration of how environment, job titles, and preconceived roles can dramatically influence the way we interact with others.

You might think that the Zimbardo study was just an experiment. Yet, we do not have to look far to see how real-world settings and roles can influence people to engage in exceedingly inhumane actions. For example, the environment of the Abu Ghraib prison in Iraq in the early 2000s led to the horrific torture and physical, psychological, and sexual abuse of prisoners committed by U.S. military personnel. As we will see in later chapters, the abuse of power often begins at the highest levels, although it is often very difficult to identify the source. The abuses at Abu Ghraib are not just a result of the actions of the soldiers at the prison; they can be traced back to the development of the Bush administration's legal opinions to disregard the Geneva Convention's definition of torture, allowing any type of "enhanced interrogation" as long as it did not risk organ failure or death. This directive was passed down the chain of command and encouraged personnel to extract information—giving prison guards free reign over prisoners whom they perceived to have no rights (Clemens, 2010).

It is important to realize that these prison guards, like the students in the Stanford prison study, neither were innately brutal nor had a history of violent behavior; their inhumane behaviors were encouraged and reinforced by the environment of total prison institutions. This learned behavior was shaped by norms within the system and a culture of war. The first time a prison guard witnessed an inmate being abused, he or she likely reacted with surprise and alarm. Yet, an inexperienced soldier will habituate to violence and can gradually descend into barbarically aggressive treatment of inmates if the guard is made to believe that superiors endorse such violent practices. This Iraqi prison was a total institution; guards were taught and encouraged to engage in these types of behaviors. Many of the guards (like the politicians who endorse total institutions) may have even thought that they were doing the right thing; this happens all too commonly in first-order change efforts. What occurred in the Zimbardo study and at Abu Ghraib suggests that even people with idealistic values can become abusive over time in these types of total institutional settings, leaving inmates traumatized and far from rehabilitated.

Prisons are certainly not the only places that influence our attitudes, behaviors, and interactions with others. These dramatic types of transformations occur more often than we might want to admit. I knew a college student who was a champion of social causes. In classes, he always argued for egalitarian and progressive solutions and he campaigned for liberal political candidates. After graduation, he enthusiastically elected to teach in a poverty-stricken neighborhood, hoping to tap into the positive potential of his inner-city students and alter the trajectory of their lives. Unfortunately, his school did not provide adequate preparation, training, or supervision. Students made no attempt to hide their boredom. Several fights in class broke out, and maintaining discipline became harder each day. In this increasingly stressful environment, the young teacher's attitudes toward his students began to shift. Sadly, his initial idealism was increasingly replaced by anger, cynicism, and outright disrespect toward his students and the school.

Far too many idealistic teachers become quickly burned out and disillusioned in settings that are detrimental for students as well as staff. Clearly, not all prison guards would torture an inmate, and many staff at total institutions maintain their values and idealism. Some young teachers do inspire and motivate their students in even the most disadvantaged schools. Nevertheless, first-order thinking does not enable the kind of meaningful change most communities need in order to overcome their difficulties at large. Because context and settings can enormously influence our behavior, interventions that are geared toward superficial solutions will most likely produce unsuccessful, or even destructive, results. Therefore, it is critical to consider the effect that roles, expectations, and environments have on us. Unless we go beyond the surface of a problem to its root, we are unlikely to be effective in our efforts to create meaningful change.

First-Order, Top-Down

Elected officials often impose first-order interventions through top-down strategies, in which the power holder attempts to solve a community problem but dis-
regards the needs and strengths of the community itself. For example, politicians
like to boast of a zero-tolerance stance toward drug use or of an abstinence-only
program in sex education courses. Taking a hardline stance may be good for
their poll numbers, but solutions that force students to take abstinence and anti-
drug programs simply do not work. The well-intentioned developers fail to real-
istically consider young people's norms and values that almost always reject such
simplistic messages and interventions (Kendall, 2008).

Social service agencies also struggle to enact meaningful change when using
top-down approaches. Again, although well intentioned, these efforts risk making
problems worse. Consider this scenario: A social service agency sent an outreach
worker to a low-income community. His aim was to bring needed services to
impoverished areas and include community members in the process. The agent
met with local leaders and proposed a number of actions to bring some improvements to the neighborhood, such as a job training course and an after-school
program. However, because the residents knew that the social worker was being
paid to offer help from outside, they were initially suspicious of him. Nevertheless,
with help from his agency, some new and important programs were created.
Unfortunately, a year later, the outreach worker was assigned to a new neighborhood and slowly, due to the loss of external funding, the new services and programs stopped. As you can imagine, the community members were very frustrated
with this outcome. They grew wary when the next person from a similar social
service agency entered the community to offer services. It's no surprise that people
become cynical in the face of these top-down, short-term, and often paternalistic
interventions. Successful and enduring change must engage community members
directly in initiatives, rather than thrusting new programs upon them.

The Influence of Environments

The discussion of total institutions like prisons and some schools sheds light on the
role of the environment in shaping and influencing our behaviors and values. All
too often, however, our tendency is to ignore or discount the importance of environments or the larger contexts within which we live, a term coined by researches
as "context-minimization error" (Shinn & Toohey, 2003). This is a grave error, as
research has taught us that the environment does play a significant role.

Developmental psychologists have pointed to the important effect of the
environment in shaping individuals. One study found that infants with prenatal

complications had few, if any, negative long-term effects if they came from intact families with high socioeconomic status. Conversely, children with the same complications who came from families of low socioeconomic status and unstable environments were more likely to experience academic and health problems later in life (Sameroff & Chandler, 1975).

It is important to look at both a person's traits and the environment, with the understanding that both factors change over time and affect each other. A downward spiral of negativity between individuals and their environments can lead to restricted opportunities and significant psychological and physical disabilities. First-order changes do nothing to break these destructive patterns. So, as neighborhood conditions have been linked to delinquency, personal distress, children's health, and academic performance, we need to work with both individuals and community contexts in trying to change complex social problems (Sandler, Gensheimer, & Braver, 2000).

Jim Kelly (1979), one of the founders of the field of community psychology, also spoke of the need to study both individuals and their communities. Over a 3-year period in the 1960s, Kelly studied the particular characteristics of two high schools. One school's administration conveyed clear norms, offered great flexibility, and encouraged students to be creative. The second school's administration took a more rigid, authoritarian stance but had less clear norms. This ambiguity produced tension among the students and staff. Kelly's later work showed the importance of understanding roles and expectations in schools and how some children flourish in one setting rather than another. I have known children who have failed miserably in traditional, authoritarian classrooms only to be transformed into highly motivated and successful students in schools that valued creativity and activities based on intrinsic motivation.

Whether it be during childhood development or within school systems or total institutions, it is clear that environmental factors can have detrimental effects on our growth and ability to flourish. Our first task in surmounting the destructive cycles that some environments perpetuate is to examine the nature of the particular social problems in order to discover real, enduring solutions to them. In so doing, we can understand the rich interconnections the world contains and pinpoint opportunities for pursuing social justice.

The First Principle: Second-Order Change

Second-order change, our first principle, focuses on change that influences the individual and his or her social network, as well as all other components of the environment that may contribute to the particular problem. Emory Cowen, my mentor in graduate school, taught me early in my career that there would never be enough mental health professionals to treat people in need of services. With budget cuts aimed at making a dent in our current $16 trillion deficit, it is safe to say that there will never be enough money to provide all types of social services for those in need either. Only through prevention and more structural interventions will we make a significant difference in solving our social problems. Second-order interventions direct precious resources in more productive ways; they go beyond a reactive response by enacting measures to avoid potential problems. True second-order change also involves altering shared goals, roles, and power relationships (Seidman, 1988).

One of the most influential social activists, known for bringing about long-lasting progress, is Mohandas Gandhi. He was a proponent of classic bottom-up strategies, organizing coalitions of people to achieve goals. As a young lawyer, Gandhi moved from India to South Africa and began fighting for the civil rights of Indian immigrants. Gandhi lived in the community for nearly 20 years and became familiar with the cultural, class, political, and religious institutions, allowing him to develop a detailed analysis of the societal infrastructure and tailor his nonviolent interventions to the needs of the people (Du Toit, 1996).

In the wake of World War I, Gandhi moved with his family back to India. He brought his experience with civil rights victories along with him and became a passionate advocate for India's independence from Great Britain. Many who deal with powerful institutions often try to accommodate, compromise, and appease their adversaries to little effect. Such a passive approach, however, never would have ended such a repressive system. Gandhi realized that for Indians to become emancipated and govern themselves, colonial rule had to end. Because the British had an insurmountable military presence, he drew on his second-order, bottom-up successes in South Africa to launch a series of nonviolent civil disobedience movements (Low, 1997). These involved nonviolent resistance to the government on specific economic and social issues. It also involved the creation of several propaganda campaigns at various times during his multiple imprisonments. His bottom-up approach welcomed the views of different religious and political factions within Indian society and worked for the needs of each group. Gandhi led operations that concentrated on returning economic power to the Indians and promoting the social welfare of all disenfranchised groups, such as the untouchables and other castes. He demonstrated that significant change takes long periods of time, and that many networks of people were necessary in challenging oppression. This second-order, bottom-up intervention stands as one of the most impressive victories that brought social justice to an entire nation.

In the United States, Reverend Martin Luther King Jr. used these same types of nonviolent resistance and bottom-up strategies to help win civil rights battles in the 1950s and '60s. Most Americans find it hard to imagine the extent of segregation that was commonplace just 50 years ago: The notion of "separate but equal" was the rule of law in places of learning, restaurants, doctors' offices, hospitals, retail stores, and many other settings. I remember as a child in the 1950s that African Americans were not able to use the same restrooms as Caucasians and had to sit at the back of the buses. Civil disobedience, legal challenges to discriminatory laws, and federal legislation were all used to bring about these structural and enduring changes, including voting rights and educational opportunities for African Americans. Both Reverend King and Gandhi gave their lives to these battles, proving that instigating second-order change can be a threat to those who want to maintain the status quo. Taking on widespread abuses of power is certainly one way of launching second-order change, but other small-scale and often less confrontational interventions starting at a community level can also be effective. Whether the movement ultimately leads to small- or large-scale change, it almost always begins with the community.

Finding the Root of the Problem

One well-known, second-order change effort involved a deadly epidemic that broke out in England in the mid-1800s. Cholera was killing thousands of people in London, and a doctor named John Snow began searching for a reason. At the time, germs and bacteria had not yet been discovered, and doctors and scientists believed that pollution, or a noxious form of "bad air," caused cholera and other diseases. Snow spoke to local residents and traced the source of the outbreak to a public water pump on Broad Street. Using a map, he showed that cases of cholera were clustered around the pump, suggesting a connection between the source of water and the illness. Snow immediately disabled the well pump by removing its handle. This simple action ended the outbreak despite the fact that no one, including Snow, knew the cause of cholera.

By using a second-order strategy, Snow was able to make associations between risk factors (the polluted water) and disease (cholera), which eventually led to the end of widespread infection (by removal of the pump handle). In short, although we will not always know the exact reasons for a social problem, we can still develop second-order change plans that successfully address the heart of the issue. If Snow had focused on first-order plans that only treated those who had the disease, he would have fought a losing battle to reach and treat people who continued to be infected by the polluted water. Thus, another key to second-order thinking is to get to the root of a problem rather than to treat the symptoms of the illness (Smith, 2002).

Efforts to bring about second-order change are often less specific and more complex than the example of Dr. Snow and cholera. Rather, they might involve the nature of community bonds, reminding us of our fundamental need for connection and the importance of environmental factors. Malcolm Gladwell's book *Outliers* (2008) described a small town in eastern Pennsylvania in which virtually no one under the age of 55 showed signs of heart disease, and the rate of death in all categories was 30% to 35% lower than the rest of the United States. Nothing about the population's diet, amount of exercise, or genetic makeup could explain these findings. But the people in the town did share one characteristic: They were deeply involved and invested in their community. They went to church together, formed organizations, respected and helped the elderly, lived in the same homes as their parents and grandparents, and frequently got together for backyard cookouts. As Gladwell said: "[You] had to appreciate the idea that the values of the world we inhabit and the people we surround ourselves with have a profound effect on who we are" (2008, p. 10). These high levels of protective support in the community seem to be the reason behind a healthier life. Thus, second-order interventions might engage environmental factors in order to enrich the lives of community members. So, our second-order actions can be as narrow as eliminating access to polluted water, as Snow did in London, or they may involve changing broad characteristics of community and neighborhood support.

In other parts of the world, the sense of connection and comfort we have to each other has actually been found to affect rates of schizophrenia. Murphy (1982, 1983) found low rates of schizophrenia in populations with high degrees of social harmony, such as in the Tonga Islands in the South Pacific and in a collectivist, pacifist Hutterite sect in western Canada. In contrast, cultures that extol the virtues of individuals over community support seem to foster high rates of schizophrenia. Richard Wilkinson and Kate Pickett's (2009) provocative book *The Spirit Level* puts forth the intriguing notion that in rich countries, many health and social problems are caused by large inequalities in the societal structure. Using plenty of supporting data, the authors theorized that these economic inequalities not only cause stress and anxiety but also lead to more serious health problems. These examples illustrate how important it is to look beyond the individual in exploring the basis of many of our social problems. Yet, when considering communities with less heart disease, lower rates of schizophrenia due to social support systems, or serious health problems due to income inequalities, it is challenging to think of what we can actually do to change the status quo.

Ordinary people have put second-order change strategies into practice. For example, in Geel, Belgium, people have taken an extraordinary approach to helping those with mental illness (Goldstein & Godemont, 2003). For hundreds of years, people in Geel dealt with mental illness in an unusual and deeply humanistic way: They brought people with mental disorders into their homes and considered them to be members of the family. No one in these families had any training on treating people with mental disabilities—they simply gave them meaningful work and responsibility. The entire town worked together to protect those with mental illnesses rather than fear and stigmatize them. Eventually, the people with mental illnesses were able to function independently, in spite of their handicaps, and became members of the community. The simple power of compassion, empathy, and supportive environments cannot be discounted.

Others have taken revolutionary approaches toward treating mental disorders through the creation of specific communities as opposed to institutions. For example, in 1964, Jean Vanier founded the l'Arche ("the Arch") community in France out of the need to provide a nurturing environment for people with mental disabilities (Dunne, 1986). Vanier had no formal training, so his idea and approach were free of preconceived expectations that professionals might have brought. Vanier's vision was to build a community of trust and interdependence by developing a more humanizing lifestyle that would dissolve the barriers that prevented people from communicating. At l'Arche, people with developmental disabilities and "normal" abilities lived together, following a pattern of work (gardening, housekeeping, or workshop), meals, and play, and members strived to grow in "their capacity to be more open and loving within the ideals of communitarianism" (Dunne, 1986, p. 47). Over the past 50 years, more than 1,300 l'Arche communities have been formed. This is a powerful demonstration that ordinary people can work together to create communities that are conducive to positive, second-order change.

Our discussions have revolved around second-order change and its focus on changing both individuals and social environments. We can encourage schools to foster supportive environments for learning and to work toward the creation of humanistic environments as in Geel, Belgium, or at l'Arche. But all of these laudable goals beg the million-dollar question: how? Most of us will not be the next Gandhi or King, but we can use their extremely effective strategies to work on important second-order change over time. For me, it took two decades of work to be called to testify on the tobacco settlement, but I took small, practical, and realistic steps that set the process in motion.

My Anti-tobacco Journey

Remember for a moment my failed attempt at producing change as a first-year graduate student. Despite the fact that I could see the root of the problem clearly—the power inequalities in our program—I inadvertently discovered the significance of the second principle of social change: identifying the power holders who oppose or support the desired change. It became apparent that I lacked several things: knowledge of the academic political system, support among my peers, and most important, the passion to take a significant risk by confronting the professors or the power holders.

However, I discovered I did have the necessary passion for another issue: antismoking campaigns. "During the 1940s and 1950s, cigarette smoking rivaled baseball as America's national pastime," researchers Robert Kagan and William Nelson (2001, p. 11) wrote. Growing up in the 1960s, it seemed that everyone I knew smoked, and as a society, we were inundated with advertisements that boasted the benefits of various cigarette brands (see Figure 1.1). The tobacco industry's reign over the American consciousness had to be challenged.

In the 1950s, the medical and scientific community began finding connections between smoking, ill health, and higher death rates (Feldman, 2004). Using research that tracked participants over many years, by the early 1960s, the famous Framingham Heart Study uncovered startling findings that smoking shortened human life, caused cancer, and led to heart disease, emphysema, bronchitis, and a number of other illnesses (Yach, 2010). Then, in 1964, the Surgeon General's landmark report stated the dangers of tobacco use and served as a critical turning point in America's smoking culture (Warner, 2006).

Figure 1.1 Advertisement on smoking.
Available at: http://lane.stanford.edu/tobacco/index.html

In 1967, lawyer John F. Banzhaf III orchestrated the first successful campaign that brought some balance to how television portrayed the glamorous life of a smoker (Feldman, 2004). He petitioned the Federal Communications Commission to require licensed broadcasters to give free airtime to opposing viewpoints on controversial public interest topics such as smoking, and for the first time ever, health organizations could run counteradvertisements (Miles, 1982). However, rather than allow anti-tobacco messages to increase along with tobacco ads on TV, the tobacco industry supported a total tobacco ad ban on TV, which forced antismoking countercommercials to cease. In the end, unfortunately, money that tobacco companies would have poured into tobacco ads on television was redirected to billboards, newspapers, and magazines (Feldman, 2004).

Even 7 years after the Surgeon General's landmark report stated the dangers of tobacco use, I could not find a nonsmoking professor with whom to do anti-tobacco research in graduate school, and I had to wait until graduation before I could pursue this passion. I knew that the tobacco epidemic was killing hundreds of thousands of people per year—more than the yearly deaths from illegal drugs, influenza, pneumonia, and auto accidents combined. Worldwide, smoking causes 4.9 million deaths per year (Falk, Yi, & Hiller-Sturmhöfel, 2006). Treating people with nicotine or alcohol addiction may be the most important policy measure to reduce mortality and morbidity (Peto et al., 1996; World Health Organization, 2010), not to mention the cost that treating smoking- and addiction-related illnesses places on our overburdened health care systems. Helping to prevent more deaths from smoking was a cause I deeply believed in. Yet, I was unsure how I could make a difference, particularly with my interest in second-order change.

For many beginning activists, the path toward second-order action is often uncertain. When Snow began documenting cases of cholera, he did not have a clue as to where his investigation might lead, but he was persistent in collecting data to ultimately find a solution. Determined to begin pursuing my passion, I began with two simple goals: helping other nonsmokers deal with an environment that was filled with second-hand smoke and preventing young people from picking up the habit. Using the principles in this book, I joined the effort to fight the formidable tobacco industry.

Upon finishing graduate school in 1975, I was relieved to finally have the opportunity to do research on smoking as an Assistant Professor of Psychology at DePaul University. Despite all of the gains made by anti-tobacco groups, cigarette smoking was still rampant throughout society. At this beginning point in my career, I was unsure of how to advocate for second-order change, so I started with small, manageable steps, such as learning about tobacco use in my immediate surroundings.

Even as late as the mid-1970s, smoking was still considered the norm. We all had ashtrays in our offices. Even I, a fervent antismoker, obliged smokers and let them smoke in my office. I decided to measure the amount of time I was exposed to smoke in my work setting over the course of a few weeks. Using a stopwatch, I was surprised to learn that I was exposed to about an hour of second-hand smoke each day (Jason, 1976). Then, I counted the number of cigarette butts in the ashtray on my desk for several weeks and was appalled at the findings. As a first course of action, I removed the ashtray. It proved utterly useless; not only did the number of cigarette butts deposited in my office stay the same, but also the level of smoking did not change. People simply left butts on my desk or in my flowerpots. Smokers believed that they could light up anywhere, and it was clear that a stronger intervention was needed to reduce my daily exposure to smoke.

My next effort involved placing a large "No Smoking" sign on a wall in my office. The sign made a big difference: It stopped people from smoking in my office. While the smokers complied, some took offense to my new policy or began to perceive me differently. One associate mentioned that I was less friendly for establishing anti-tobacco rules in my office. Nevertheless, this successful intervention encouraged me to seek out other places where smoke exposure could be limited, particularly where there was no authority figure like myself monitoring no-smoking areas (Jason, 1979).

My graduate students and I began a series of studies that gauged cigarette use in places such as barbershops, supermarkets, and elevators (Jason & Clay, 1978; Jason, Clay, & Martin, 1979–1980). Smoking restrictions were virtually nonexistent at that time in downtown Chicago. We discovered that someone was smoking one-third of the time in elevators of downtown office buildings. Although no-smoking signs worked in my office where I was an authority figure, they were less effective in public areas. We found, however, that most people, when asked politely to put out their cigarettes, did so. One of our successes was establishing a smoke-free area in the university cafeteria (Jason & Liotta, 1982).

Eve Holton, a graduate student at the time, and I then targeted restaurant owners to provide separate sections for nonsmokers. As an incentive, we offered 30 Chicago restaurants free publicity and a customer base of people from several organizations who wanted nonsmoking sections. After 3 months, only three restaurants set up smoke-free sections. This study proved to us that restaurant owners, like many other power holders when faced with a call to change, would not voluntarily designate sections unless compelled to do so, thus demonstrating the need for legislation (Holton & Jason, 1988). Advocacy groups such as ASH (Action on Smoking and Health) were also pushing for smoke-free sections in public areas. They helped to create nonsmoking sections on planes and public transportation (Miles, 1982). Local citizens in organizations such as GASP (Group Against Smokers' Pollution) used bottom-up, statewide strategies to promote nonsmokers' rights in public buildings, restaurants, and work areas (Kagan & Nelson, 2001). Change was occurring slowly, but the tobacco industry was still resistant.

While continuing to work on environmental change strategies and learn more about the community, I engaged in other ways to help educate the public. For instance, I debated on television with tobacco industry lobbyists who were representing smoking in a positive light. As my involvement in second-order efforts increased, more opportunities became available, and other like-minded organizations sought me out. Because of my work on creating nonsmoking environments in public settings, I was invited to serve on the Smoking and Health Committee for the Lung Association of Chicago. This opened up other avenues, such as documenting the prevalent practice of freely offering cigarettes to underage teenagers and children (Davis & Jason, 1988). Later on, I designed, implemented, and evaluated smoking cessation programs in media outlets. All of these significant policy interventions began with a simple act: removing the ashtray from my desk. With tangible progress made in my first goal, I turned my attention toward my second aim: preventing children from picking up the habit.

The Failures of Traditional Adolescent Smoking Prevention Programs

As I was working to reduce smoke exposure in the workplace in the 1970s and '80s, I was also designing and implementing school-based anti-tobacco programs (Jason, Mollica, & Ferone, 1982). Much like other health issues that plague our nation, the key to reducing prevalence rates is prevention. In a national representative survey of young people, 42% of ninth graders reported they had smoked cigarettes (Fryar, Merino, Hirsch, & Porter, 2009). In the United States alone, over 3,000 kids begin smoking every day (Schnupp, 2003). There are many school-based educational programs to prevent tobacco use; still, even well-controlled, evidence-based interventions fail to show positive, long-term outcomes (Peterson, Kealey, Mann, Marek, & Sarason, 2000; Wiehe, Garrison, Christakis, Ebel, & Rivara, 2005).

Obviously, these strategies were overlooking a critical factor that was undermining their efforts. First-order interventions that simply targeted individual children were not working; a new approach was needed. At one school, students told me that store clerks were freely selling cigarettes to them, and I realized that this sent a mixed message of adult approval of youth smoking and reduced the effects of our prevention strategies. In January of 1988, we confirmed that 80% of Chicago-area stores illegally sold cigarettes to minors. The students' information revealed a glaring problem in the environment that had to be addressed. In another part of the country, we learned that an 11-year-old was able to purchase cigarettes from 75% of the stores she visited (DiFranza, Norwood, Garner, & Tye, 1987).

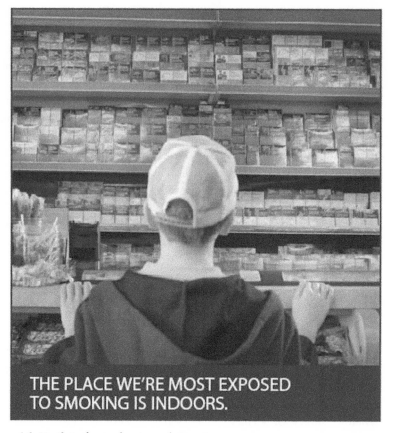

Figure 1.2 Youth in front of a store of cigarettes.
Available at: http://www.tbdhu.com/Tobacco/Protection/Tobacco+Vendor+Training.ht

But there was good news: Our study on minors' access to cigarettes garnered attention from the media, as well as members of the community. The benefit of the third principle of social change—creating coalitions with like-minded people to achieve a common goal—can be illustrated in a partnership that formed after we released our findings. Officer Bruce Talbot from the suburban town of Woodridge, Illinois, contacted me to say that his police department solved the problem of illegal tobacco sales to youth (See Figure 1.2). When I asked how, he said that the Woodridge chief of police sent a letter to store owners reminding them that it was against the law to sell tobacco to minors. I replied that this method probably would not work to reduce illegal sales; however, if he were interested, I would help him see if it made a difference. I knew that despite this letter-writing campaign, store owners were never actually caught selling to minors. A police officer would have to *see* a minor buying tobacco to issue the owner a fine; but if an officer were in the store, the clerks would never sell minors tobacco.

During my first visit to the Woodridge Police Department, I met Officer Talbot, an enthusiastic, dynamic man. As I was introduced to the chief of police and other officers, I was feeling a bit apprehensive; each one was twice my size, and at the meeting soon to follow, I had to tell them that I believed their letters to merchants were ineffective in reducing illegal tobacco sales. Surprisingly, the police agreed to partner with us and launch an alternate strategy that would help us determine who was complying with the law by regularly sending minors into stores to buy tobacco. After finding that the majority of the clerks still sold cigarettes to minors, we began to work on legislation to stop this problem. Woodridge's Tobacco Licensing and Enforcement Law, which required each merchant to have a license to sell cigarettes, passed on May 1, 1989. This way, Woodbridge police would be able to fine those who sold tobacco illegally and even suspend their licenses to sell tobacco products. We then continued to send underage minors into stores to see if they could buy tobacco illegally; if the merchants sold tobacco to youths, they were fined.

While it was important to hold vendors accountable, Officer Talbot also argued that if minors were caught with cigarettes, they, too, should receive a ticket, similar to a parking fine. He reasoned that because kids were not allowed to drink alcohol in public, they should not be allowed to openly smoke. Working at a junior high school, Officer Talbot felt powerless to stop minors from publicly smoking at school functions and in the neighborhood, which sent the message to other kids that smoking was "cool." I was skeptical of his idea of fining minors for tobacco possession, but after hearing these arguments, I decided it was important to have a combined strategy that focused on both store owners and minors.

After passage of the Woodridge law, our team sent minors into stores to monitor the extent of illegal sales, fined stores if they sold to minors, and fined kids if they were caught smoking in public. Woodridge was the first U.S. city to demonstrate that store owners could be stopped from selling cigarettes to kids, and that these actions could reduce youth smoking (Jason, Ji, Anes, & Birkhead, 1991). An editorial in the *Chicago Daily Herald* noted:

> According to a DePaul University study published in the *Journal of the American Medical Association* on Wednesday, the percent of stores selling cigarettes to minors dropped from 79% prior to the new law to less than 5% 18 months after its enactment. More important, DePaul reports that a "survey of junior high school students taken before and after the law revealed a 50% reduction in the rate of minors who had any smoking experience and a 69% decrease in the number of minors who smoked regularly.... True, such laws do not eliminate the chances of youngsters getting cigarettes. But evidence suggests they make it a lot harder for teens to take that first puff; to follow through on that curiosity that can kill them." (Teens and tobacco, 1991)

The tobacco industry, with its habit of discrediting its critics, portrayed our study in direct contradiction to my findings, indicating that educating merchants would stop them from selling tobacco to minors. This was not true, and our research had discredited this belief. Only fines for illegal sales would stop merchants from selling cigarettes to minors. Nevertheless, their efforts to deflect challenges to their power, even at the local level, were unsuccessful.

Word of our experiment spread throughout the country. People were impressed with the success of our collaboration and the achievement of reduced youth access to tobacco. Following the passage of the Woodridge legislation, Officer Talbot was contacted by dozens of communities interested in starting similar campaigns. He also presented our study during hearings at the 1990 national legislative initiative to reduce cigarette sales to minors, called the Synar Amendment. The Woodridge research was critical in the passage of this amendment in 1992, which required every state to provide evidence that it had lowered illegal sales of tobacco. But it was not until the late 1990s that the law was fully implemented.

Our victory in Woodridge also attracted the attention of a foundation, and they asked if I could produce similar effects in a larger metropolitan area. Still, change in Chicago would not come as quickly. The fourth social change principle of having patience and persistence proved to be highly valuable in our fight against those who represented the interests of Big Tobacco. For 2 years, my team worked with Chicago regulatory officials, showing them that fining merchants for illegal sales could reduce rates of illegal tobacco sales. When the results of the study came in, we scheduled a press conference with Mayor Richard Daley to introduce my successful findings to the city. I had been told that Mayor Daley was going to endorse our method for use with thousands of Chicago merchants. However, at the press conference, he shifted his support to merchant educational approaches, bowing under pressure from the Illinois Liquor and Control Commission, which was controlled by the governor and by tobacco retailers. This change of position was a complete shock to me. It was a much softer stance— merchants would not have to pay a monetary fine. At the press conference, I still addressed the key issues of what needed to be done in the name of the public interest and later wrote in an editorial in protest for the *Chicago Tribune*:

> The mayor has argued for continued merchant education programs, which are supported by the tobacco industry, the Illinois Liquor Control Commission, and the Illinois Retail Merchants Association. It's not surprising that such groups advocate for education programs because they offer few negative consequences for businesses that sell cigarettes to minors.... The question is whether our leaders have the courage and heart to enact the most potent and proven methods of attacking our youth's most deadly foe. There are powerful economic and political forces that will continue to thwart what needs to be done. (Jason, 1996, p. 123)

The mid-1990s was a tense time. Even Officer Talbot was shouted down by people funded by the Illinois Liquor Control Commission at a DuPage County meeting. Officials urged him to abandon fines for merchants and instead implement weak merchant educational approaches. Fines were considered antibusiness, and the town officials did not want any negative economic consequences to affect leading community figures, meaning that merchants would be able to sell cigarettes to youth with impunity. Officer Talbot and I knew that we were on the right side of this fight and persisted in our attempts to challenge vested interests in tobacco sales. Our diligence paid off. A few years later, to comply with the Synar Amendment that required officials to take actions that meaningfully reduced illegal tobacco sales to minors, the Illinois Liquor Control Commission would drastically change direction and would begin cooperatively working with our group.

I continued my research (Jason, Pokorny, Adams, & Hunt, 2008) and later found that our enforcement and reduction of accessibly to illegal tobacco may have even affected the environment surrounding illicit drug sales. If adolescents in a community were regularly fined for smoking, they were also approached significantly less often by someone trying to sell them illegal drugs (Jason, Berk, Schnopp-Wyatt, & Talbot, 1999). Over the past decade, we consistently found that a combination of tobacco possession and commercial enforcement laws was associated with a lower chance of young people supplying cigarettes to other kids (Pokorny, Jason, & Schoeny, 2006), a lower probability of a child having used drugs (Jason, Pokorny, Adams, Nihls, et al., 2009), less smoking on school grounds (Jason, Pokorny, Adams, Topliff, et al., 2009), and higher adoption of smoke-free areas (Jason, Hunt, Adams, Pokorny, & Gadiraju, 2007).

Several researchers suggested that these types of efforts should be abandoned, as they waste antismoking resources (Glantz, 2002), but a study by DiFranza, Savageau, and Fletcher (2009) found that because of the Synar Amendment and state efforts to reduce youth access to tobacco, there has been a 21% decrease in the odds of tenth graders becoming daily smokers. DiFranza's work showed that our research had made a difference. There is now a global consensus that sales to minors should be prevented, illustrated by the Framework Convention on Tobacco Control (2003). This framework was unanimously adopted by the World Health Assembly and has since attracted more than 172 member states, representing almost 90% of the world's population.

The Tobacco Settlement

Since the 1950s, the tobacco industry had been able to dodge implications of health dangers, lawsuits filed by people suffering from smoking-related illnesses, and regulation from the government. In the 1990s, a small army of defectors from tobacco companies began to emerge. Some of the first exposés aired in 1993 and 1994 on ABC and caught the attention of the government. On April 14, 1994, seven top executives from the largest tobacco companies testified before the Subcommittee on Health and Environment claiming that they did not believe nicotine was addictive (Brandt, 2007). This old tactic eventually became a public relations nightmare and pushed some additional former insiders to become informants. One of the whistleblowers, Jeffrey Wigand, told Mike Wallace of *60 Minutes* that the executives committed perjury when denying the addictiveness of nicotine. The former biochemist described a number of practices, including the development of a genetically engineered tobacco, that quickly delivered twice the amount of nicotine to a smoker's system (Brandt, 2007).

As more people filed suits for damages to their health because of smoking, a group of trial lawyers began to investigate new ways to initiate legal action. Many smokers were suffering from tobacco-related illnesses and relied on Medicaid to cover their medical expenses. Attorney Mike Lewis realized that states might be able to sue the industry for health care costs borne by Medicaid; a plan that he and his colleagues initiated in Mississippi was later joined by other states. This eventually created the Tobacco Settlement of 1998 (Brandt, 2007).

During the settlement hearings, my testimony in front of the House Commerce Committee, Subcommittee on Health and Environment was a critical culmination of the years I had spent on adolescent tobacco prevention research (Jason & Fricano, 1999). In deciding which topics would best encourage progress in the anti-tobacco movement, I used the fifth social change principle: measuring our success in what has been accomplished and what is left to achieve. I stressed that my research demonstrated that it was possible to reduce the number of young smokers. The findings from Woodridge, Illinois, were presented, showing that to reduce the availability of cigarettes, the sales of tobacco to minors needed to be reduced to 10%, rather than the 20% or less figure that they were considering. I also discussed ways to deal with issues that the settlement did not address. For example, the $500 million for antismoking ads, as proposed in the settlement, was sorely inadequate if the tobacco companies increased their advertisements commensurately. Also, while the federal government provided leadership on programs to reduce tobacco-related disease and death, it should not manage state or local campaigns. Instead, bottom-up, grassroots efforts needed to be encouraged.

For the next hour and 15 minutes, each representative of Congress—alternating Democrats and Republicans—had 5 minutes to ask questions of the speakers. I was asked about youth access to tobacco. One southern congressman was concerned about the placement of cigarettes behind counters to prevent them from being stolen. He felt that this would hurt the sales of lesser known brands. If minors did not steal cigarettes, he felt there was no reason to put them where customers couldn't reach them. When this issue was posed to both

Dr. Beale (a lobbyist for the tobacco industry) and myself, we both wanted to have the last word. We exchanged glances several times, hoping the other would comment first. Finally, I extended my open hand to him, giving him the signal to proceed. Dr. Beale stated briefly that placing cigarettes behind the counter was unnecessary, as he felt that minors did not steal cigarettes, although he had no data or experience on the subject. In my response, I described that findings from studies over the last 10 years showed that placing cigarettes behind counters was essential: As more and more stores stopped actively selling cigarettes to minors, some minors would be tempted to steal them. The southern congressman seemed swayed by my answer and nodded his head in agreement.

Following my testimony, Ms. Pat Kobor (Director for Science Policy) and other members of the American Psychological Association's Science Directorate were thrilled with how the hearing had gone. Along with a commentary in *USA Today* (Shapiro, 1997), I was quoted in an *Associated Press* article: "'There is no single magic bullet,' DePaul University psychology professor Leonard Jason told the House Commerce Subcommittee on Health and Environment. 'The best approach is a combination of tools, including restricting access and advertising, school-based programs, and price increases'" (Burrell, 1997).

The tobacco industry settled with the attorneys general of 46 states for $206 billion (four states had already made separate settlements). These settlements were part of an agreement that would recoup the costs of treating Medicaid patients for tobacco-related illnesses. In addition, tobacco companies were only allowed to sponsor one major annual event promoted on billboards and merchandise. The settlement also established a national foundation to develop prevention and cessation programs, as well as a mass anti-tobacco media campaign. Unfortunately, only a small part of these funds have been used for anti-tobacco activities, but at least the tobacco industry faced severe consequences for its immoral business practices. The battle continues as public interest groups monitor the tobacco companies' marketing strategies.

Within a few months, a person who was working with a large tobacco company contacted me. On their own initiative, the tobacco company had contracted with a public relations firm to develop youth smoking prevention ads; this included an 800 number for parents to receive a free booklet on how to discuss cigarette use with their children. He asked me to help write this booklet, which would be distributed nationally, but I was not convinced that this plan would be effective. I knew that one-shot training programs generally did not work, and despite the fact that I was told that the company's goal was to stop kids from using tobacco, years of experience with the industry had suggested that they instead sought to promote tobacco use under the guise of education. Was this just a thinly veiled effort to take heat off of the companies or to allow them to continue youth marketing research? In the end, I told them I would bring together a group of well-known scientists to work on the project with me on one condition: The materials I created could not be vetoed or altered in any way. They never called back, demonstrating that, for the industry, it was business as usual: The conniving and obfuscation that had gone on for decades would continue.

Lessons Learned

As we have seen, second-order change is very different from first-order efforts. First-order interventions offer cosmetic changes that are short term at best. Second-order interventions, though often more complicated, can be implemented by anyone who has the passion, intuitiveness, endurance, and understanding of the principles of social change. Conflicting points of view can challenge an activist's ability to recognize what a second-order intervention is. This is where intuition comes into play. Trust your instincts when you sense imbalance and discrimination in a system or that people are being treated unfairly. Next, sustained and systematic strategies are needed to realize your vision. The second-order changes described took years to accomplish. In summary, each of the five principles of social change applied to the substantive progress we made in tobacco prevention over the last half century.

Principle one: Focus on second-order change. For me, this involved reducing levels of tobacco through restrictions on where people could smoke and making it more difficult for minors to obtain tobacco. Major successes have occurred in both areas over time.

Principle two: Identify and weaken the power holders. In this case, it was easy to spot the goliath we were up against: a multibillion-dollar industry with a vested interest in getting kids hooked on tobacco. Other power holders such as local police departments, media outlets, and eventually, congressional leaders became allies, strengthening our cause.

Principle three: Involve courageous citizens and organizations to create coalitions. We were not alone; hundreds of activists worked on legislative and judicial strategies to push for change in a variety of arenas, such as targeting tobacco advertisements, substantially increasing the price of cigarettes, and reducing the access of tobacco to minors.

Principle four: Remain persistent, patient, and willing to do what is necessary over the long haul. We savored small victories to maintain enthusiasm and motivation for our change efforts. Activists used scientific findings dating back to the 1964 Surgeon General's report to spread information about the real dangers of tobacco and kept continuous, intense pressure on the tobacco industry.

Principle five: Constantly evaluate and refine strategies and tactics to find the most effective means of bringing about change. When my efforts to encourage restaurants to establish no-smoking sections were not successful, we realized that legislative strategies were necessary to reduce second-hand smoke.

All five principles of social change were used in this long-term effort to confront and counter the powerful tobacco industry. Although my work started modestly by documenting my own exposure to second-hand smoke, each subsequent action—following second-order principles—led me closer to my goals. By examining nonsmokers' exposure to cigarettes, I pushed for no-smoking sections in public settings. By working on nonsmokers' rights, I caught the attention of the local lung association, and together we were able to launch media-based tobacco cessation efforts (to be described in chapter 5). With each step, I accumulated momentum and experience that prepared me for the next, larger one. Case in point: My initial work with young people that focused on smoking prevention soon transformed into a 20-year effort to stop merchants from selling cigarettes to minors. And Officer Talbot, a key ally of mine, became a national figure who helped pass national legislation to reduce statewide illegal sales of tobacco.

Through this experience, I learned that resistance to widespread change—especially from well-financed, organized power holders—is never to be underestimated. In addition to the tobacco industry, I encountered local sources of opposition, from both the governor's and mayor's offices. The tobacco industry's manipulation of both government officials and my research findings reinforced the scope and breadth of its power. During all this, I tried to remain true to my values. Like many social change interventions, our success relied on partnerships with allies, and together we significantly reduced merchant sales of tobacco. In Illinois in the 1980s, when we began our work, close to 80% of merchants sold tobacco to minors, but by 2010, that number had dropped to 10%. There is still more to be done, but this change is an enormous public health victory.

One of the most important lessons we learned from these efforts was that no matter what the change objectives may be—a local or a large-scale societal problem—activists must listen closely to what community members are saying. If we are open to their suggestions, we might be able to think of second-order solutions to deal with the sources of the problems that they are confronting. By including the community's perspective, I was able to uncover aspects of a problem that otherwise would have been overlooked. For example, the students in the community were the ones who pointed out the contradiction between tobacco prevention messages and community merchants who openly sold cigarettes. Based on this knowledge and our collaboration with Officer Talbot and the Woodridge Police Department, we developed a second-order change intervention that reduced rates of illegal tobacco sales and eventually became a prevention model used across the United States.

Additional Resources

As a senior in high school, I helped craft legislation to start a research institution to study the effects of drugs at a mock congress at the New Jersey state capital. At the time, we knew little about the effects of these drugs, particularly LSD, on individuals. Although I had never tried this drug during these turbulent times, I thought we needed more data on its effects on individuals. My early efforts at activism with the writing of this legislation and several letters I received are available in the at this site: https://docs.google.com/file/d/0Bz4gyjhP7mm3UmxyUzZiQXJTQUU/edit

Society for Community Research and Action is the international organization devoted to promoting health and empowerment and preventing problems in communities, groups, and individuals. For more information visit this site: http://www.scra27.org/

To see Abu Ghraib and pictures of the guards and prisoners, visit this site: http://www.youtube.com/watch?v=LZ_Vxoyu8zY

For a report of 170 allegations of sexual abuse occurring at U.S. immigration detention facilities, visit this site: http://www.pbs.org/wgbh/pages/frontline/race-multicultural/lost-in-detention/how-much-sexual-abuse-gets-lost-in-detention/

Examples of other inappropriate tobacco commercials of the 1940s to 1960s can be found at these sites:
http://www.youtube.com/watch?v=gCMzjJjuxQI&feature=related
http://www.google.com/search?q=vintage+tobacco+ads&hl=en&qscrl=1&nord=1&rlz=1T4ADFA_enUS445US445&biw=853&bih=461&site=webhp&prmd=imvns&tbm=isch&tbo=u&source=univ&sa=X&ei=gNS_TtzsKsSW2AWdqO35Bg&sqi=2&ved=0CCwQsAQ

To see footage from the tobacco executive testimony, go to this site: http://www.jeffreywigand.com/7ceos.php

For more information on the continuing epidemic of tobacco use among youth, go to to this site: http://blog.myctb.org/?p=1501

Bernie Sanders, an Independent Senator of Vermont, has proposed true second-order interventions to solve some of the United States' most pressing issues. He advocates for publicly funding presidential and congressional elections, as well as overturning the Citizens United Supreme Court ruling that allows special interest groups to spend without limit in elections. His innovative solutions for saving Social Security, Medicaid, and Medicare are discussed in his interview with Bill Moyers at this site: http://billmoyers.com/segment/bernie-sanders-on-the-independent-in-politics/

2

Challenging the Status Quo

As I approached my 40s, I was healthy and took care to stay that way. I swam a quarter mile three times a week and made sure I had a healthy diet. However, I noticed that over the period of a few years, I was developing colds and sore throats more frequently—and having difficulty getting over them. I'd always been very productive, so rather than slow down, I ignored these warning signs from my immune system and continued my busy workload.

During the first week of August in 1989, I developed a persistent sore throat. By October, my sore throat worsened, and I was prescribed antibiotics by my physician, which proved ineffective. I started having trouble keeping up with my work schedule, which required me to take trips out of town that month. At the beginning of November, I realized that I was dealing with more than just a bad sore throat. When I was diagnosed with mononucleosis, I decided to finally stay home and get well.

After resting for 3 weeks, I followed my doctor's recommendation and returned to work. After being at the office for only an hour and a half, I would come home exhausted. Whenever I talked on the telephone for more than 2 hours, I was considerably weaker the following day. By late November, I could not write for more than 10 minutes without collapsing from fatigue. Soon, other troubling symptoms began to emerge: Insomnia kept me awake most nights. I developed an acute sensitivity to light, which prevented me from using my computer. I felt nauseated and began losing weight (20 pounds over 4 months). My tongue turned white, and my lymph nodes swelled. My concentration began to fail me. Along with my general physical discomfort, I was too weak to perform simple chores, such as grocery shopping.

Weeks passed without any signs of improvement, and I realized that I had an illness more serious than anything I had ever imagined. No amount of rest seemed to bring relief, and I became increasingly desperate for solutions. I saw my doctor and tried meditation, humor, and even spiritual tapes, but my condition continued to worsen.

When I shared my situation with friends and colleagues, they were perplexed by this mysterious illness. One friend even asked me if I was going crazy.

I was not. Someone else thought I looked too healthy to be ill: "Everybody gets colds and sore throats," he said. "What's the big deal? Why can't you do more?" Others pronounced me agoraphobic because I never left my apartment. People advised me to get some therapy, see a psychiatrist, or go on disability. "Why do you sleep so much?" a friend asked suspiciously. "It's all in your mind," another assured me. Some blamed me for my condition, lamenting that someone with my interest—and experience—in psychology had obviously not practiced what I preached. The support of my friends was gradually dwindling.

Experiences such as these are common to sufferers of chronic fatigue syndrome (CFS). Not only must they endure a crippling illness, but also they are met with skepticism from friends and coworkers. In addition, they face resistance from government officials, who for many years refused to acknowledge the devastating nature of CFS or how widespread it was among all segments of the American population.

Imagine suffering from a debilitating physical condition that is even more incapacitating than congestive heart failure, multiple sclerosis, adult-onset diabetes, or the final stages of kidney disease (Anderson & Ferrans, 1997). Envision symptoms so unrelenting that they consume your body and dominate your thoughts—a lack of deep sleep, exhaustion after even minimal activity, severe muscle and joint pain, headaches, persistent nausea, recurrent fevers, shortness of breath, and a heavy mental fog that affects reading and even the ability to compute simple sums. You may have once prided yourself on your robust physical stamina, but suddenly washing the dishes demanded an incomprehensible investment of energy, leaving you weak for hours afterward.

I would later meet the person charged with overseeing research into CFS at the Centers for Disease Control and Prevention (CDC)—someone with the power to channel millions of dollars into finding the cause and cure for an illness that has devastated so many lives. When I met this highly trained public health doctor, he was a little unsteady on his feet and explained that he was recovering from a broken leg. Then he looked me in the eye and said something completely astonishing: In the process of rehabilitating his broken bone, he claimed he had finally come to understand what people with CFS suffer. Recovering from the illness requires time and effort, like recovering from an injury, he explained. If patients were willing to push through the pain and work to rehabilitate themselves, they—like him—would completely recover. His comment made it clear that even those at the top levels of research on CFS held common prejudicial misconceptions about the disease and those who suffer from it—that it is a mainly psychological issue and that patients are simply too weak-willed to recover. You can imagine how a person with cancer or AIDS would have reacted to these comments.

Patients with CFS suffer from an illness that, at best, is misunderstood and, at worst, is met with disbelief. According to numerous studies, more than three-quarters of patients with CFS have experienced disrespectful treatment at the hands of health care providers (Anderson & Ferrans, 1997). Virtually every sufferer who seeks medical treatment for this condition has reported feelings of estrangement or alienation (Green, Romei, & Natelson, 1999). Seven out of 10 people report that those around them attribute their symptoms to psychological causes, leading to condescending and even offensive encounters with friends, colleagues, and family members (Johnson, 1996). These figures were more than just numbers to me; they were my reality. After years of battling the illness, I became one of the fortunate few to be able to return to work on a part-time, and eventually full-time, basis. When I did, my personal experience with the illness fueled a new passion for social change: reducing stigma and improving treatments for people with CFS. From what I had learned first-hand about the medical community's views and the public's perceptions of CFS, I also realized that understanding issues of power would be critical to my efforts.

Any change agent must be armed with a keen knowledge of the power system he or she is attempting to reform, the principal players, and the environment in order to continuously monitor and fine-tune strategies. In this chapter, I examine our second principle of social change (identify the power holders) through an account of a 20-year effort to change perceptions of CFS within the power structure at the CDC. I describe techniques that were invaluable for collaboration with other vested interests, as well as sustaining our commitment.

What Is Power?

There are many ways to understand power. It can be seen as a negative and corrupting force or as a useful resource to accomplish social justice objectives. Power is often used to control resources (who is hired or provided funding), to restrict channels for participation in community decisions (dictating meeting agendas), and to shape the definition of a public issue (censorship or discrediting a group's views or beliefs; Kloos et al., 2012). Most incarnations of social inequality are caused or exacerbated by an underlying abuse of power. Redistributing power is often a crucial component of a successful large-scale, second-order social movement.

When trying to understand power, the norms and values that exist within different communities are also an important part of the picture. For example, certain neighborhoods may have dramatically different social capital and, therefore, must have a sense of trust that the benefits one gives to others will be repaid in the future (Putnam, 1993). In communities with higher amounts of social capital, citizens are more likely to work together and cooperate for the collective benefit of the inhabitants. In areas with less social capital, citizens may trust their neighbors less and be more likely to either withdraw from others or use hierarchical solutions, such as coercion and exploitation, to maintain order. Therefore, if the social context of a community is poor, if people feel powerless and disconnected, and if there is lower involvement in civic associations, reforms aimed at rebalancing power might have more difficulty succeeding than in regions with higher social capital.

In addition to the influence of social capital, our notions of power are also heavily influenced by our current and past experiences. For example, children can learn to feel powerless when they are taught in schools to be passive when working on meaningless tasks and to be pleasing and obedient to authority figures (Purpel, 1989). Children are often raised in families in which parents exert absolute power, and adolescents are taught about democracy in school settings where they rarely have the opportunity to give input. Also, many young adults in the workplace are given little opportunity to influence decisions and provide input to authority figures. Our society reveres the revolutionaries who challenged the authoritarian policies of King George III, but we are surrounded with hierarchical institutions that contradict the very democratic foundations of our Constitution.

Who Abuses Power?

We are surrounded by people who seek power. It comes as no surprise that their actions are many times destructive for those involved, including the instigators themselves. McClelland (1979) found that those who relentlessly strive for more personal authority suffer more bouts of illness than their less driven counterparts. Plenty of people you know, and most people in a position of relative power, have probably been guilty of exercising inappropriate uses of their power at some point or another. They may give constructive feedback in a harsh or unsupportive way, set expectations that are beyond reach, or make divisive comments in front of others. These are all examples of power abuses. Some organizations have a progressive record regarding dealing with issues of social justice, but their leaders are arrogant, unsupportive, and condescending to their staff. When frequent, this kind of power abuse needs to be addressed and corrected.

History has repeatedly shown us the horrific nature of the absolute power held by despots like Adolf Hitler, Joseph Stalin, and Pol Pot. These men alone were responsible for the death of over 28 million people. Although it was clear that Hitler was a murderer who held absolute power, it took a worldwide alliance and the loss of many lives to stop him. Some unlimited abuses of power are even more difficult to change—Stalin's reign of terror only ended when he died of natural causes.

It is easy to identify these archetypal abuses of power in our history. However, others in recent years are cloaked in secrecy and more difficult to identify, such as President Bush's dismantling of the Geneva Conventions for handling prisoners of war. Power abuses can be hidden or they can arise unexpectedly. A person could have a stellar reputation for years, only to cause grave abuses later under new contextual pressures. Take Hubert Humphrey, who had a distinguished record of civil rights legislation throughout his career and was a critical player in passing the landmark 1964 civil rights bill that ended a hundred-year system of segregation. Yet, when it came to issues involving the Vietnam War, Humphrey backed President Johnson's disastrous pro-war policies. Initially, Humphrey strongly opposed President Johnson's strategy, but after being rebuked by Johnson, he became an avid supporter of the Vietnam War to regain the good graces of the president. This decision contributed to the prolongation of the war, led to the loss of thousands of soldiers' lives, and shows that complex motives can compel people or organizations to shift their policy positions. A political figure may have a record of supporting progressive policies, but under certain circumstances, he or she can endorse deeply harmful positions on other critical issues.

The 2010 British Petroleum disaster in the Gulf of Mexico was an example of how corporate greed created the worst oil leak in our history. In efforts to increase profits, British Petroleum had sacrificed safety measures to increase its bottom line for many years. These actions had resulted in prior explosions and oil leaks in Texas and Alaska. Yet, this company that had sacrificed safety for profits in the past was given permission to search for oil in some of the most ecologically vulnerable underwater sites in the world. On closer inspection, the abuse of power in this case was diffusely spread across multiple organizations. The combination of irresponsible business practices by British Petroleum, Transocean, Halliburton, and other subcontractors, as well as inadequate U.S. government oversight, caused this oil spill. The labyrinth of blunders, gross incompetence, and capitalist efforts to save money at the expense of safety among the groups involved makes it challenging to identify a single guilty party.

Another power abuse that frequently occurs in the business world is bribery—a form of power exertion. As we know, bribery is still common in government and industry, driving an enormous network of illegal cash payments. For example, BAE Systems, a major multinational organization, was accused in 2007 of paying billions to a Saudi prince in exchange for lucrative contracts to build military aircraft for Saudi Arabia (Michaels & Bryan-Low, 2010). Bribery exists on all levels of dealings, from the international to the local. A colleague told me about a school he visited that had one large classroom jam-packed with new, unused, and unneeded desks. The school superintendent, for political reasons, had pressured the principal to purchase the desks from an influential local company. It was also clear that this inner-city school had many unmet needs for new educational materials and personnel. Those who control valuable resources must be identified in order to confront the absurd decisions that are sometimes made.

Within organizations and coalitions, the power brokers sometimes have unexpected and unassuming roles. I have worked in school systems for most of my career, and early on, I presumed that the principal was always the primary power holder. Over time I learned that those who wielded the real power were often secretaries, influential teachers, or even, in one case, the janitor. These individuals had been in their schools the longest and many times had more knowledge and power to get things done or to set policies than the principals had. Although they are rarely seen at important public functions—such as meetings with superintendents or parents—these "second-level employees" frequently understand the setting's dynamics and can be either allies in bringing about change or obstructions to it. Power abuses can occur in very subtle ways. Therefore, it is imperative to know who holds power and what type of resources they control.

Confronting Abuse

Breaking free of repressive practices begins by questioning the established conventions by which we live. David Purpel (1989) encourages us to find answers to our most difficult questions: Who are we? What is important to us? What stirs us to make a commitment? How do we learn about the world and find meaning in it? What is worth fighting for? These are the essential questions that every social activist must ask.

We must also ask ourselves: Who are the power holders? Some might argue that second-order change can only occur when activists have a clear understanding of the power structure involved, such as when a country rises up to oust an abusive dictator. But as we have seen, the causes of abuse and underlying power structure may be difficult to see clearly. In asking these questions, your instincts may be your most powerful tool to uncover the veiled power abuses that need to be challenged.

We must use the same passion and intuition that help us see the path toward effective change to identify and analyze the distribution of power. The simplest and most convenient attribution of blame is sometimes not the correct one. In the case of CFS, it is much easier to dismiss the legitimate claims of patients than to understand those who control the way in which stigma and bias have perpetuated inaccurate myths about patients with CFS. In my antismoking campaigns, the power structure was much clearer: Our efforts needed to challenge those within the tobacco industry who profited from cigarette sales to minors.

I knew in the mid-1970s that the tobacco industry was responsible for enticing young people to begin smoking and actively fought attempts to limit smoking in public places. At first, I was unsure of a clear strategy to attack these problems, so I started with a smaller, less daunting action: collecting information on my own smoke exposure. I achieved small victories in my efforts to reduce smoke exposure by setting up no-smoking sections in several areas, including the DePaul University cafeteria. You might wonder if these are first-order change techniques, as they did not threaten the power of the tobacco industry at the local, state, or national level. However, I firmly believed that protecting nonsmokers' exposure to smoke in one area could lead to changes on a larger scale. My school-based prevention programs that aimed to prevent young people from gaining access to tobacco eventually did influence a paradigm shift: a federal amendment that led to states curtailing, for the first time, illegal sales of cigarettes to minors. In other words, small victories can directly lead to substantive higher level change. My efforts finally were able to address the power structures involved, challenging the tobacco industry's formidable resources to manipulate American youth.

Unlike the fight against Big Tobacco, sometimes it is possible to reach mutually agreeable solutions on issues of power through dialogue and compromise. However, the more important the policy implications, the less likely it is that power holders will be amenable to compromise unless they are challenged by coalitions that also hold leverage. One strategy often used by those in power is to appoint lower level committees that make inconsequential recommendations in order to appease dissatisfied groups. These minor concessions do not threaten the power structure itself and represent a deflection of true challenges to power. It is essential for change agents to recognize these types of barriers to second-order change.

Some of our change strategies can be traced to our intellectual heritage—to the ancient Greeks' passion for freedom of inquiry and tolerance for different points of view. Socrates believed that we should critically examine conventional thinking. Admitting ignorance and being willing to consider alternative possibilities is the first step. We can also look at our own tumultuous history in the fight for democratic principles. Government that requires the consent of the governed was designed to affirm the dignity and autonomy of the individual.

In *The Four-Fold Way,* Angeles Arrien (1992) describes how we might also learn from the ancient wisdom of indigenous people. She describes the several archetypal paths of the warrior in these cultures: the teacher, the healer, and the visionary. When dealing with power abuses and second-order change, the spiritual path of the warrior demonstrates how leaders can epitomize traits that empower others, such as the use of just power and solving problems with effective and well-timed communication. The path of the teacher emphasizes the need to be open, flexible, and objective to various outcomes. The goal of the healer is to listen to guidance from within and promote meaningful and loving interactions. Similarly to the philosophies of the Dalai Lama, the values of the healer underscore the power of gratitude, acknowledgment, and compassion to oneself, others, and the environment. Finally, the path of the visionary involves having the capacity to dream, to be intuitive, and to envision revolutionary goals or plans unfettered by the constraints of old paradigms.

The use of these concepts can help end practices that perpetuate violations of basic human rights, such as modern-day slavery, exploitation, discrimination, and abuse. Liberation theologians, such Dom Helder Camara of Brazil, Gustavo Gutierrez of Peru, and Juan Luis Segundo of Uruguay, interpret the Christian Gospel as a call for justice against oppression. Best known among influential theorists is Paulo Freire, an educator who believed that no change efforts are neutral, but rather that they can be used either to domesticate or to liberate (Hope & Timmel, 1985). For Freire (1970), change begins by helping people to identify the issues about which they have strong feelings and to search for solutions to their problems in an active way. He believed that everyone in the community can and should participate in the transformation of power.

For over 50 years, a community psychologist named George Albee (1996) wrote and argued that society will always have excessive amounts of mental illness as long as exploitation, imperialism, extreme concentration of economic power, and nationalism exist. His studies in the 1950s suggested that powerlessness, poverty, discrimination, sexism, racism, and ageism, to a large degree, are responsible for mental illness. Because no psychiatric disorder had ever been treated out of existence, he argued for more efforts directed at prevention. Another influential community psychologist, Isaac Prilleltensky (2008), also argues that change must occur by addressing issues of power, oppression, and liberation.

Abusers of power, whether it is the tobacco industry, a corporation, or a politician, commonly hold considerable resources and support to maintain the status quo. For individuals with a passion for changing this status quo, the task can be daunting—akin to the biblical story of David and Goliath. Greatly outmatched in size, David used a slingshot to bring down the 9-foot soldier, hitting him squarely on the forehead. Social activists must search for similar tools and strategies when faced with Goliaths who hold significantly greater power and resources.

Frustration can set in when comprehensive reform is needed but the necessary skills, resources, or networks are not available. Targeting abuses of power when considering poverty, for example, is a daunting challenge in terms of conceptualizing second-order change and determining who is responsible. Such large-scale objectives will not be reached without the mobilization of community groups and development of a long-term time perspective—our third and fourth principles, respectively. Successful change agents select targets for change that are appropriate for the available resources and the timing in the maturation of the social movement. Certainly, I would not want to discourage activists from taking on large-scale, transformative change projects, as Gandhi did when he sought to liberate his country from one of the most powerful countries in the world, but dealing with these larger types of second-order change often takes years of dedication. Quick-fix efforts without community support to change power relationships rarely work.

Some people may be more prepared and ready to confront issues of power than others. According to Rod Watts and Jaleel Abdul-Adil (1994), as people progress through their lives, they go through different stages of sociopolitical development that involve varying levels of readiness to engage in social change. In the *acritical* stage, people feel powerless and inferior and believe that they deserve their low societal status. In the *adaptive, precritical,* and *critical* stages, people gradually learn about social and historical roots of injustice and oppression. Finally, in the *liberation* stage, they are ready to engage in social action and community development. Our task as change agents is to help people and coalitions move through these stages, as each is critical to being able to challenge power to produce second-order change.

Governments have often failed to deal with concentrated power; it is often ordinary citizens who provide the leadership and innovation to correct social problems by confronting the status quo. Bornstein's 2004 book, *How to Change the World*, describes people who used new models to redress many social ills and promote social well-being. Florence Nightingale (Bostridge, 2008), for example, known for her activism and pioneering nursing work during the Crimean War of 1854, changed the way medical facilities are run. After British soldiers were dispatched to the Black Sea to support Turkish opposition against Russia, Nightingale left London to oversee nursing at the overwhelmed military hospitals. Upon her arrival, she found over 2,400 wounded soldiers housed in filthy conditions. Barracks were infested with insects and rodents. She realized that disorganized and squalid housing was causing heavy death tolls and immediately had the wards and soldiers' clothing cleaned. She also used political tact and private fundraising to bring much-needed supplies to the hospital. Within 1 year, the death rate in the hospitals dropped from 43% to 2%.

Her activism did not end when she returned to England. She collaborated with a leading statistician to write a book providing an extensive statistical analysis of the causes of soldier death and illness, highlighting the need for change in the British Army. Nightingale later founded the first secular nursing school and is credited with transforming nursing into a modern, respectable profession. Her lobbying efforts shaped worldwide standards for sanitation and hospital management (Bornstein, 2004). However, Nightingale suffered from an affliction that was still largely unknown and makes her accomplishments all the more heroic: She suffered from a chronic fatigue–like illness that left her weak and sick after returning from the Crimean War. In spite of her affliction, she spent the rest of her life tirelessly fighting to improve medical care for others. Chronic fatigue syndrome and fibromyalgia support groups commemorate her sacrifice and selflessness every year around the world with an awareness day on her birthday.

Jane Addams was also a pioneering social activist who is best known for the opening of a settlement house in an underprivileged area of Chicago (Addams, 1930). She raised money from well-to-do families to provide kindergarten classes, club meetings for adolescents, and a night school to improve conditions for low-income workers. Soon, more improvements were made, such as an art gallery and studio, a public kitchen, a coffee house, a gymnasium and swimming pool, a music school, a circulating library, and an employment bureau. She also led investigations into narcotics consumption and sanitation conditions. Her work showed that long-term investment to build trust in a community is key to tackling larger, second-order issues within the environment.

Other activists have been inspired by religious traditions. Mother Teresa, for instance, founded the Missionaries of Charity in Calcutta, India (Spink, 1997), which helped victims of HIV/AIDS, leprosy, and tuberculosis. Slowly and patiently, over many decades, she built a movement that significantly improved levels of care among disenfranchised people who previously had no access to even basic rights. By the late 1990s, 600 of her missionaries were operating in over 100 countries.

Gandhi's beliefs were also strongly influenced by religious ideas from the Bhagavad Gita. He believed that the war stories in this sacred text were not affirmations of war but rather allegories that each person and generation must interpret in relation to their circumstances (McCann, 1991). From these teachings, Gandhi derived the core tenants of his pacifist movement for social change. Martin Luther King acted within the Christian tradition and also preached nonviolence. King's methods are frequently contrasted with those of Malcolm X (1965), another change agent who was not content with the status quo of life for African Americans. Stressing that Blacks were oppressed by racist violence and murder, he, unlike King, advocated for aggressive self-defense "by any means necessary." After Malcolm X's assassination in 1965, activists who advanced Black Power continued his legacy of activism. The Black Panther Party for Self-Defense and Justice was founded, and students fought for Black Studies departments on college campuses.

Although legislation in the 1960s was effective in eliminating the most glaring signs of discrimination and segregation, more insidious versions still exist. For example, some inner-city schools that are composed largely of racial minority students continue to receive dramatically lower funding amounts than schools in more affluent suburbs. This funding disparity contributes to unequal educational attainments and subsequent opportunities for well-paid jobs. These are examples of education and job discrimination—more subtle than disenfranchisement or outright segregation—within a power structure that serves to maintain insidious cycles of poverty and inadequate education in the so-called land of opportunity. The level of inequality along with racism likely contributes to the fact that African American males are 7 times more likely to be incarcerated than Caucasian males (Prison Policy Initiative, 2005). Attention and intervention to eliminate this discrimination is as needed now as was the landmark civil rights legislation of the 1960s.

Mother Teresa, Jane Addams, Florence Nightingale, Mahatma Gandhi, Martin Luther King, and Malcolm X were exemplary social change agents who brought about second-order change. They focused on abuses of power, mobilized community groups and coalitions, had the patience to stay committed for extended periods of time, and constantly assessed their strategies.

Not all social movements, however, have been spearheaded by a charismatic leader to bring about change.

The disabilities rights movement involved a group of activists who suffered from many different kinds of impairments. There was a time when society did not provide support, job opportunities, or hope to people with disabilities. Those who were disabled also had to overcome barriers that prevented them from enjoying basic essentials that others took for granted every day, such as having easy access into stores or public transportation. Activism for persons with disabilities began in the 1960s, when Edward Roberts and other activists confined to wheelchairs focused on helping people with disabilities live independently. They fought tirelessly for the passage of the (American) Rehabilitation Act. When the bill became law in 1973, it guaranteed equal opportunity for people with disabilities and allowed them access to federal services, as well as other programs receiving federal funds. Even so, for years, guidelines to implement these regulations stalled; in 1977, Frank Bowe and the American Coalition of Citizens with Disabilities mounted a nationwide sit-in of government buildings operated by the U.S. Department of Health, Education and Welfare (Bowe, 1980). Other activists demonstrated with protests. They demanded the signing of regulations for the Rehabilitation Act of 1973, and protests were also staged in front of the home of Secretary Joseph Califano, the person responsible for signing the regulations. In San Francisco, a sit-in demonstration went on for 25 days. Eventually, Califano signed the regulations for the Rehabilitation Act of 1973, making these protests a celebrated success.

In 1969, the gay rights movement began in reaction to the New York police's regular harassment of transsexuals, lesbians, drag queens, and gay male patrons inside bars. The "Stonewall Riots" occurred when patrons inside a bar resisted a police raid. It signaled the beginning of a very important revolution; for the first time, the gay community fought back rather than silently being arrested and taken to jail. Riots followed the next night and people in the gay community began to organize, taking a more open and unapologetic stance about their sexual orientation. Soon after, the Gay Liberation Front and the Gay Activists' Alliance were formed. A year later, a hundred people assembled on 6th Avenue in New York City and proudly marched through the streets in commemoration of the Stonewall Riots. Soon, the riots became commemorated by annual marches across the nation, which became known as gay pride parades (Duberman, 1993). In the past, no one had dared to organize such protests. What began as police harassment and a subsequent riot in New York led to the gay and lesbian community taking an activist position around the country to proclaim their rights.

In the same way, no charismatic leader headed ACT UP, an action group committed to ending the AIDS crisis. Rather, the organization existed as a diverse group of chapters, spin-offs, and affiliations all over the world. Over 25 years ago, these activists learned that being polite was not going to change discrimination toward those afflicted with HIV (Rimmerman, 1998). To get their voices heard, ACT UP protesters chained themselves to the desks of drug company executives, poured buckets of fake blood in public places, mounted protests that closed tunnels and bridges, tossed cremated ashes of dead bodies onto the White House lawn, and held regular demonstrations at the Food and Drug Administration, the National Institutes of Health, and the White House. In one particularly provocative display, they draped a giant condom over Senator Jesse Helms's house. These activists forced pharmaceutical companies and the government to develop and disseminate drug treatments that were used to fight against HIV/AIDS. Ironically, their actions eventually paved the way for these activists to serve on the committees they had previously picketed. ACT UP changed the landscape of how patients with HIV/AIDS are perceived and treated in the United States today. They made a dramatic difference in the world by focusing on clear second-order change objectives and successfully confronting the power structures that stood in the way.

All of these agents of change succeeded because they were specific in their demands for basic human rights. More importantly, they were persistent in keeping pressure on those who were unwilling to change the status quo. They stayed focused on critical issues and made it clear to those in power that they would not be defeated. Ultimately, those in power realized that these tenacious activists would not relent until real second-order change was achieved.

Chronic Fatigue Syndrome

We are usually not cognizant of how much our daily satisfaction and happiness are determined by our good health. We quickly recover from bouts of the flu or minor injuries like a broken arm. However, illnesses including sleep disorders, pain, and depression can have profound, long-term effects on our quality of life and happiness. Over 63 million Americans suffer from multiple chronic health conditions (Vogeli et al., 2007). I am one of over a million people who suffer from chronic fatigue syndrome, a condition that led me to challenge the status quo to improve outcomes for others who suffer from this illness.

My experience of falling gravely ill with CFS is not unique; it afflicts all kinds of people at any stage in life. The devastating nature of CFS can be illustrated by the story of one 11-year-old girl, Kate. In September of 2004, Kate was an outgoing honor roll student who ranked in the top 10 in her state for competitive swimming. After one swimming competition, however, Kate complained of sinus-related symptoms and uncharacteristically slept for the rest of the day. For the next few months, she experienced unrelenting periods of complete exhaustion for several days followed by a few days of normal functioning. Test results by numerous specialists offered no diagnosis, and by December her symptoms worsened. On nights that Kate was actually able to get to sleep, she woke up feeling like she hadn't slept at all. While attempting to go Christmas shopping, she begged to use the store's motorized carts and even added "wheelchair" to a birthday wish list. She began to stay in the car while her family shopped. Her parents, in hindsight, realized that they should have allowed her to use the carts.

Almost 1 year after Kate's health began to deteriorate, her parents were conflicted about whether she should begin home schooling. She missed 20 days of the first semester in seventh grade, and the school staff began questioning the existence of her illness. What they did not see, however, were her worst days at home when the extreme fatigue and pain kept her in bed. On one drive to the doctor and again a few days later, Kate said, "Mom, I want to die. I don't want to live my life like this." By the spring of 2006, she was finally diagnosed with CFS.

Some patients have experienced terrible indignities, such as being denied basic medical care or being placed in mental institutions (Lost Voices, 2008; Ryan Baldwin Returned Home, 2010). At a conference in Great Britain, I met a woman whose son was so seriously ill with CFS that he had trouble moving and needed to use a wheelchair. The state had placed the boy in a mental hospital where the psychiatric staff—believing that he only "thought" he lacked energy—tried to shock him out of this delusion by racing his wheelchair down a hallway and suddenly stopping it. The staff expected the boy to instinctively grab the arms of the wheelchair to resist flying out of it; instead, he fell hard onto the floor. Even after this incident, the staff remained so convinced that he simply needed motivation to break a psychological condition that they dropped him in the deep end of a pool. He quickly sank to the bottom.

Offenses like these, though demeaning and excruciating for patients, make sense within the social context that causes them: Many people believe that the disorder is all in the mind. When CFS was first identified, several prominent scientists in the United States and Europe insisted the disorder arose primarily from psychological factors (Johnson, 1996). In 1991, two researchers described the disorder as nothing more than "a culturally sanctioned form of illness behavior" (Abbey & Garfinkel, 1991, p. 1638). A year later, another pair of scientists claimed that fatigue was among the least medically important symptoms a person can present (Lewis & Wessely, 1992).

Some experts have adopted an approach to understanding fatigue and CFS that tries to integrate the biological and psychological aspects of illness, but many continue to believe CFS is a mental disorder. One research group from the Netherlands maintains, to this day, that people with CFS are preoccupied by their physical limitations and simply do not get enough exercise (Vercoulen et al., 1998), as if this relatively trivial reason causes their bodies to fail. Other scientists have said that CFS symptoms are inappropriate reactions to childhood stressors or are linked to childhood traumas (Heim et al., 2006). Few illnesses have caused such a schism between opposing "psychological" and "biological" views as CFS (Jason, Richman, et al., 1997). The strongest force of opposition to the psychological view of CFS held by many physicians, policy makers, and the general public has come from patient-activist groups.

For over two decades, two key groups have squared off over the issue: the CDC and a large patient organization known as the Chronic Fatigue Immune Dysfunction Syndrome Association (CFIDS Association). These two entities held the power to define the way CFS was portrayed, understood, and treated. Like many controversial but important causes, the interactions (sometimes collaborative, other times contentious) between these two groups played out amid a dynamic and complex landscape of contradictions, misinterpreted information, and changing alliances (Jason, 2011).

Over the course of 20 years of work, important change has occurred in this area. Each of the five principles for social change—engaging in second-order change, identifying power holders, creating coalitions, staying committed over long periods of time, and measuring success—was used with patient advocacy coalitions to effectively achieve social change (Kroll-Smith & Gunter, 2000).

A "Yuppie Flu" Illness

In the early 1990s, when I began reading CFS articles, I realized that the CDC was underestimating the prevalence of the disease. In addition, the name given to the illness by the CDC trivialized and stigmatized it, and the CDC's case definition of CFS was not well defined. Tests used to diagnose CFS were biased toward finding psychiatric problems, and treatment approaches were potentially harmful. I was well aware of my challenge: The CDC is one of the most powerful regulatory institutions in the country. Its pronouncements on disease define medical standards and the treatment patients receive throughout the United States. CDC protocols set the bar. I was unsure of where to start to help change the myths about CFS. How could I begin to work on second-order change regarding the debilitating effects of this disease from which I and thousands more were suffering?

**Examples of Books, Journal Articles, and Articles in the
Popular Media That Promote the Stigmatization of CFS**

- The term *yuppie flu* is first popularized and reflected a stereotype that
  CFS affects affluent "yuppies"
  - *Newsweek* cover story, November 11, 1990
  - Available at http://www.thedailybeast.com/newsweek/1990/11/11/
    chronic-fatigue-syndrome.html
- "The suffering of these patients is exacerbated by a self-perpetuating,
  self-validating cycle in which common, endemic, somatic symptoms are
  incorrectly attributed to serious abnormality, reinforcing the patient's
  belief that he or she has a serious disease": A quote from a scientific article
  describing CFS and other similar conditions by Barsky and Borus (1999)
- "Hystories: Hysterical Epidemics and Modern Media: Alien Abduction,
  Chronic Fatigue Syndrome, Satanic Ritual Abuse, Recovered Memory,
  Gulf War Syndrome, Multiple Personality Syndrome"
  - Book title by Showalter (1997)
- "Childhood Trauma May Lead to Chronic Fatigue Syndrome in Adulthood"
  - Asian News International news article, January 6, 2008
  - Available at: http://www.thefreelibrary.com/Childhood+trauma+may+
    lead+to+chronic+fatigue+syndrome+in+adulthood.-a0212307657
- "Chronic Fatigue Syndrome Stigma Hurts Patients"
  - John Schieszer, Reuters Health, January 31, 2001
  - Available at: http://www.me-cvs.nl/index.php?pageid=4585&printli
    nk=true&highlight=illness
- "Depression, Not Virus, Causes Fatigue"
  - *Palm Beach Post,* July 4 1990
  - Available at: http://www.lexisnexis.com/lnacui2api/auth/check-
    browser.do?rand=0.034634112093286484&cookieState=0&ipcou
    nter=1&bhcp=1
- "The Top Health Stories for 1991; 'Yuppie Flu'—The Fatigue That Never
  Ends"
  - *The Washington Post,* January 1, 1991
  - Available at: http://www.lexisnexis.com/lnacui2api/api/version1/
    getDocCui?lni=3S8H-3560-000F-G226&csi=8075&hl=t&hv=t&hns
    d=f&hns=t&hgn=t&oc=00240&perma= true
- "CHRONIC FATIGUE SYNDROME: Illness Forces Many Workaholics
  to Take a Much-Needed Break"
  - *The Capital,* January 28, 1998
  - Available at: http://www.lexisnexis.com/lnacui2api/api/version1/
    getDocCui?lni= 3T29-49Y0-0093-53WC&csi=145224&hl=t&hv=t
    &hnsd=f&hns=t&hgn=t&oc=00240&perma=true

Social activists are often faced with a similar dilemma: where to start in the face of seemingly insurmountable or multiple abuses of power. The activist must have the endurance and resources to achieve the small wins needed to sustain a long-term commitment. Intuition steers us through the maze of misleading information, paradoxes, and obstacles to decide on a course of action. I concluded that as long as scientists and the public perceived CFS as a relatively rare and purely psychological condition, they would never give it the attention it needed. I decided to focus my initial work on determining the most accurate number of people who had CFS, as well as their characteristics.

In the 1990s, investigators at the CDC published research that portrayed CFS as a relatively rare disease, affecting only about 20,000 people. Patients were characterized as predominantly European American, middle- to upper-class women (Reyes et al., 1997). These findings perpetuated a myth that CFS was a "yuppie flu" disease, affecting middle-class and affluent people. As long as scientists and the public perceived CFS as a rare illness of middle-class housewives, it would be difficult to garner the needed attention and resources to develop a better understanding of it or to provide help to those in need. The CDC prevalence studies were based on a method that relied on physician referral of CFS patients (Reyes et al., 1997). However, if physicians did not believe the illness really existed or if some patients did not have a physician, many people with CFS would not be counted in the study.

Representing the patient community, the CFIDS organization with Kimberly McCleary as CEO confronted the CDC about the inappropriate and biased research it conducted. I approached McCleary in the early 1990s, and her organization was able to provide funding for a pilot study at DePaul University. Our research team randomly selected and telephoned a sample of people in the community. During the call, we asked questions that determined whether the person had several CFS symptoms. If so, that person was brought to a medical setting and given a complete medical and psychiatric examination to determine if he or she actually had CFS. Thus, this research differed from the CDC prevalence study in a critical way: The CDC's methods used physicians' referrals of possible CFS cases, while our methods involved directly assessing the general population to identify people with this illness.

The small pilot study involved calling a random sample of about 1,000 people in Chicago (Jason et al., 1995) and suggested that the number of people who had CFS was much higher than the CDC had previously estimated. Based on these results, we applied for federal support to conduct a larger study of over 18,000 people that would allow us to determine whether our initial estimate of higher prevalence was correct. Even though we had pilot data that challenged the misconception that CFS was rare, federal grant reviewers maintained that there was no need for us to do any further research. They told us that the CDC had already proven that prevalence rates were very low. We spent several years submitting and resubmitting grants, trying to obtain funds for our study, and eventually challenged the review process itself. To truly work for second-order change, it was essential to challenge the misguided estimates of the CDC and other federal officials with a large-scale study.

Our persistence paid off, and we finally secured National Institutes of Health (NIH) grant funding to do our community-based study. Our research found that over 800,000 people in the United States had CFS (Jason, Richman, et al., 1999), a figure much higher than the 20,000 that the CDC had claimed. Our data also disproved the earlier notions about who had CFS, as we found that ethnic minorities had higher CFS rates than European Americans and that CFS rates were not greater among those with higher incomes. So much for CFS being a rare, "yuppie flu."

Eventually, the CDC endorsed our methods and published CFS prevalence rates similar to the rates our study had found (Reyes et al., 2003). We had taken on the most powerful scientific organization in America and won. By focusing on specific areas that are manageable or capable of changing—in this case estimating how many people were really ill—social activists can adopt a small-wins approach. It is easy to become overwhelmed when confronting complex problems or power holders, but by focusing on one small piece at a time, tangible change and success can be achieved (Weick, 1984).

In the late 1990s, McCleary and her CFS patient organization challenged the CDC again. This time, the CFIDS Association accused the CDC of diverting $12.9 million in congressionally appropriated CFS research funding to other projects at the CDC. After a congressional inquiry, Dr. William Reeves, the head CFS researcher at the CDC, blew the whistle on one of his associates; CFS research funds had, in fact, been diverted from 1995 to 1998 (Tuller, 2011). Many activists felt that Reeves knew of the indiscretion and only became a whistle blower to protect his job. McCleary and Reeves, who had clashed over the CDC's management of CFS research and funding for over a decade, eventually joined forces as allies.

Stigma Associated With the Term Chronic Fatigue Syndrome

In addition to changing stigmatizing myths about people with CFS, I also wanted to pursue second-order change strategies to address the name of the disease. Chronic fatigue syndrome, a name given by the CDC, belittles the seriousness of the condition (the illness was previously called myalgic encephalomyelitis [ME] before the CDC renamed it CFS in 1988). The name CFS emphasizes the symptom of fatigue when, in fact, the illness is typified by many other severe symptoms such as memory loss, flu-like symptoms, and post-exertional malaise (feeling very ill after minimal activity). Fatigue, however, is something everyone—including healthy people—experiences.

The name of a disease matters, and I knew that changing the name of CFS would be a second-order strategy to reduce the stigma and stereotyping of this disease (Watzlawick, Weakland, & Fisch, 1974). For example, multiple sclerosis (MS) was initially believed to be caused by stress linked with what Freud called "Oedipal fixations" (a Greek tragedy, Oedipus was a king who fulfilled a prophecy to kill his father and marry his mother). When the name of the disorder changed from hysterical paralysis, a term used to discredit the legitimate medical complaints of predominantly female patients, to MS, it was taken more seriously (Richman & Jason, 2001). If bronchitis or emphysema were referred to as "chronic cough syndrome," those illnesses, too, would be trivialized. Changing the name of CFS was a top priority for the CFIDS Association and other patient groups.

However, even by the late 1990s, no studies had been conducted to actually show that the name "chronic fatigue syndrome" may negatively influence others' perceptions of patients. Patient advocates wanted to better understand how the name of the illness related to stigma. Gathering data that proved or disproved a stigma may help provide patients with ammunition to officially change the name of CFS. Along with patient advocates, my DePaul team conducted several studies. In one of these, medical school students were given a description of a patient with common symptoms of CFS. The trainees were randomly assigned to several groups, and each group was given a different diagnostic label for the patient, such as CFS or ME. Results of these studies showed that the students' beliefs about CFS changed depending on which diagnostic labels were used (Jason, Taylor, Stepanek, & Plioplys, 2001). When the most serious medical-sounding term, ME, was used, the patient's condition was taken more seriously, and participants were more likely to assume the illness had a real medical cause. Name-change advocates quickly cited the study's findings that diagnostic labels can influence perceptions to justify establishing a new name for CFS.

Due to these findings and the persistence of patient advocate groups, the Department of Health and Human Services' Chronic Fatigue Syndrome Coordinating Committee established the Name Change Workgroup subcommittee in the early 2000s. Several other scientists, clinicians, McCleary (representing CFIDS), and I were appointed members to the subcommittee. The Name Change Workgroup was charged with making recommendations for the new term that would be submitted for approval to the U.S. Secretary for Health and Human Services and used by all federal officials and agencies. Early on, I made the motion to change the name back to ME and was surprised to see that I was the only one who supported this name. Even McCleary seemed hesitant to make changes, and given the CFS patient community's vociferous demand for a name change, her position was perplexing.

Shortly after, I learned that the CFIDS organization had been awarded a CDC contract of several million dollars in funding to launch a media campaign branding the term CFS (Chronic Fatigue Syndrome Advisory Committee, 2004). Many activists were furious with this close relationship between these former adversaries and about the CFS branding and public awareness campaign. Refusing to give up on a name change, other patient groups began using other names like ME/CFS, ME, and neuroendocrine immune disorder for both their organizations and the illness, even though no official name change had occurred. In 2006, the major CFS scientific organization changed its name to the International Association of CFS/ME. For the rest of this book, I will refer to CFS as ME/CFS, despite the failure of the name-change initiative in 2003.

CDC Claims Exponential Prevalence Increases

In the 1990s, the CDC had come under scrutiny for grossly underreporting the prevalence of ME/CFS. This changed dramatically in the mid-2000s, when the CDC broadened the ME/CFS definition. This new case definition (Reeves et al., 2005) was then used in a study to indicate that more than 4 million Americans suffered from ME/CFS (Reeves et al., 2007). In a relatively brief period of time, the CDC's characterization of ME/CFS had evolved from a rare disorder, affecting about 20,000 individuals, into one of the more common chronic illnesses in the United States.

In 2006, before the publication of the CDC's new prevalence data, the director of the CDC presided over a press conference in Washington, DC. The CDC and McCleary were now working closely together and enthusiastic about publicizing the new, higher prevalence data. I was concerned, however, that the broadening of the ME/CFS definition might inadvertently lead to incorrectly diagnosing people with CFS who really had psychiatric disorders, such as major depression. This diagnostic mistake would make finding biological causes or markers for the illness impossible. By 2007, both the CDC and the CFIDS Association were in favor of the new, broadened case definition, as were CFS activist groups. I felt that the new definition, as well as the media campaign, was the wrong path. Although I did not have data to support this feeling, my instincts told me that the new CDC prevalence numbers were inflated.

During this time, I served as the Vice President of the International Association of CFS/ME. Kim McCleary attended a board meeting of the association and asked the board to endorse these new prevalence numbers. My fellow board members were convinced that the larger numbers were good for the overall cause. I adamantly objected, to no avail, and uncharacteristically walked out of the meeting in protest. Walking out shook up the board as I hoped it would. The next day, rather than endorse the new prevalence numbers, the board asked me to write a position paper for the association's website. It would represent only my opinion.

The CDC's estimate that ME/CFS affected 2.5% of the population (Reeves et al., 1988), or over 4 million people, was comparable to the rate of major depressive disorder (Regier et al., 1988). My protestation at the board meeting had bought time, but I needed scientific data to back my intuition that these rates were inflated. My research team conducted a new study that collected two distinct samples, one with ME/CFS and the other with major depressive disorder. The study's outcome was that 38% of the major depressive disorder group was misdiagnosed with ME/CFS using the CDC's expanded case definition. After these findings were released (Jason, 2007), the expanded ME/CFS case definition received scrutiny (Jason, Najar, Porter, & Reh, 2009). Eventually, both the CFIDS organization and the leading scientists no longer supported the new case definition or the exaggerated prevalence numbers of the CDC. We had won another critical victory in our fight with the powerful CDC regarding the use of this inappropriate case definition.

Changes in the Leadership at the Myalgic Encephalomyelitis/ Chronic Fatigue Syndrome's CDC Program

The complex landscape of the ME/CFS movement continued to evolve. In the mid-1990s, Congress created a Chronic Fatigue Syndrome Coordinating Committee to make recommendations to the Secretary of the Department of Health and Human Services on ME/CFS policy change. After this group was disbanded, a new CFS Advisory Committee was formed (see Figure 2.1), and in

Figure 2.1 CFS Advisory Committee.
Available at: http://www.research1st.com/wp-content/uploads/2011/11/CFSAC.jpg

2006, members of the committee recommended that the CDC receive increased funding for their ME/CFS research program.

In 2007, I was appointed to this committee and was asked to serve as chair of the Research Subcommittee. Although I was encouraged by some to recommend even more CDC funding, I sensed that another action might be more effective: finding out how the CDC was using the approximately $5 million they already received annually for ME/CFS research. Many patients felt that much of this research was stigmatizing. I was now in a position of some influence and wanted to bring more transparency and public accountability for the agency that funded the largest amount of ME/CFS research in the world. Dr. William Reeves, the chief researcher for the ME/CFS's CDC program, was not willing to supply this financial data, and tensions about the organization's transparency began to rise. Finally, two of Reeves's superiors at the CDC publicly promised to grant our request for financial information, and we were able to see how the CDC was funding all of its ME/CFS research projects (Chronic Fatigue Syndrome Advisory Committee, 2007).

Around this time, McCleary and the CFIDS Association were beginning to have problems with many of the policies dictated in their contract for funding from the CDC regarding the work they were doing together. In 2008, CFIDS refused to renew a major contract with the CDC and began campaigning to have the leadership of the ME/CFS program at the CDC changed. I never learned the reasons behind this renewed antagonism between former adversaries turned allies, but I suspect that the recent disclosure of financial data, increasing criticism directed at Reeves from activists (including concerns about the broadened ME/CFS case definition), and the CDC's continued focus on psychosocial rather than biological causal factors of the illness played a role in the reevaluation of the relationship between CFIDS and the CDC.

The CFIDS organization and other researchers were publicly dissatisfied with the CDC's leadership. At the CFS Advisory Committee meetings, these disparate forces came together and grievances were aired. In meetings during 2008 and 2009, Reeves and his 20-year leadership of the ME/CFS program came under fire, and the CFIDS Association had years of CDC financial records to scrutinize. After examining them, they accused the CDC and Reeves of wasting public funds:

> Millions and millions of dollars stuck in suspended animation, if not wasted...funds that have been allocated to these projects that have not been spent, and the lack of productivity of the dollars that have been spent.... It's not a lack of resources at CDC, it's a lack of leadership, and that's really what it boils down to. Hearing the concerns of this committee over the last year has reinforced that. (McCleary, 2008)

In response to her scathing remarks, the CDC retaliated with an investigation of potential financial mismanagement of the millions of dollars in contracts awarded to the CFIDS patient organization over the past years, though charges against McCleary and her organization were eventually dropped. Amidst these accusations and counteraccusations in 2008, an external, CDC-selected committee was appointed to evaluate its CFS research program; it concluded that the CDC's ME/CFS research activities were generally positive. However, McCleary and many advocates felt the CDC had not selected impartial reviewers to ensure a fair and independent review. Nevertheless, the ME/CFS program at the CDC had a buffer from the ever-increasing criticism (putting buffers in place to deflect criticism is one of many strategies often used to maintain power; Dobson, 2012). The committee then asked Reeves to develop a 5-year research plan, which he presented at the next meeting of the CFS Advisory Committee. Senior officials within the federal government, who were overseeing the CFS Advisory Committee, told us repeatedly that Reeves would not be removed no matter what we or other activists might say. We were told rather emphatically to stop bringing up the issue at our CFS Advisory Committee meetings. We did not stop.

In 2009, the International Association of CFS/ME decided that one of its primary goals was to change the ME/CFS leadership at the CDC. In addition to CFIDS, other prominent groups (Patient Alliance for Neuroendocrineimmune Disorders Organization for Research and Advocacy and the Whitemore-Peterson Institute) joined the effort, in spite of the external review committee's positive endorsement of the CDC's ME/CFS program. The Advisory Committee then voted to submit a formal recommendation for a change in leadership. The next day, a prominent patient activist named John Herd posted the following statement on the Internet:

> Remember today. Nothing like this has ever happened in the history of ME/CFS. Never before have so many of the world's ME/CFS experts stood up to harmoniously and decisively call for the kind of research we need. Never before has the ME/CFS medical community so directly and decisively challenged the health department's flawed agenda driven programs; programs that should be driven by objective ME/CFS science.... We have been waiting a very long time for a day like today. This is our day. And it is a day the ME/CFS clinicians and investigators who spoke up today at the meeting can carry forth with pride. It was advocacy at its best. To all of those who made today possible I say thank you. (Herd, 2009)

These focused and persistent recommendations reverberated throughout the Health and Human Services Department and the CDC. Tensions rose and there was even talk of a boycott or protest against the CDC at the fall ME/CFS meeting. In January 2010, our efforts paid off: Reeves was moved to a new position at the CDC (McCleary, 2010). He would no longer be in charge of the ME/

CFS research program, bringing his approximately 20-year reign over the CDC research program to an end.

What exactly happened? In short, when the powerful CFS constituencies grew unhappy and eventually ruptured all connection with Reeves, he became vulnerable. Alienating McCleary, the CFS research community, and Advisory Committee members was the last straw. Dozens of other patient advocates and organizations were also suspicious of McCleary as the head of CFIDS, due to her opposition to the name change and her organization's history of receiving funding from the CDC. Nevertheless, it was necessary for all these groups to work together to successfully challenge decades of power abuses and inadequate leaderships at the CDC.

The coalition was hugely encouraged and strengthened by these developments, particularly the replacement of Reeves. It spurred them to organize anew to demand more research funding. One activist filed Freedom of Information requests and discovered that only a handful of studies had been funded each year in the ME/CFS area. Members of the CFS Advisory Committee also found that less than 20% of the members of the ME/CFS review group within the federal government had ever published an article on ME/CFS. These types of revelations ultimately led to the addition of more experts to the CFS review panel. In addition, in 2010, the CFS Advisory Committee voted to change the name to ME/CFS. The vote passed and was recommended to the Secretary of Health and Human Services. The CFS Advisory Committee now refers to this illness as ME/CFS (see http://www.hhs.gov/advcomcfs/cfsac-cfsa-day.html).

The replacement for Reeves, Beth Unger, has already contacted me. She wondered how she might be able to work more cooperatively with the different patient groups. Unger and I worked together in 2011 to write an article with a group of other ME/CFS scientists that outlines what information needs to be included in published research articles in the ME/CFS area (Jason et al., 2012). We believed such a document would help researchers be clearer in their publications by including certain basic information about their participants, and that this would lead to a better understanding of research articles across settings. In 2012, Unger set up a series of meetings with activists and experts in the ME/CFS area to present research and discuss issues in the field, and I was the first expert asked to be involved in this dialogue with patient activists.

In addition, over the next year, a new coalition of ME/CFS patient organizations formed, called the Coalition 4 ME/CFS. Their goal is to improve the quality of life of patients and their families. Ten patient organizations sent a joint letter to the CDC, inviting it to an open dialogue through regular meetings. The letter also included nine points of action for change in the CDC's research into ME/CFS. Replacing the ME/CFS leadership at the CDC spurred reverberating and continuing change, novel initiatives, collaboration, and a renewed momentum for change among patient organizations.

Lessons Learned

Twenty years ago, I found myself bedridden by a debilitating and bewildering fatigue. Even the slightest amount of work completely depleted me. Not long before, I had been an active, hardworking, and successful person. The next few years of my life became dictated by crippling symptoms, and I was forced to reexamine my values and priorities. In fact, the lessons in this book were forged during my illness. In spite of the bias that ME/CFS is a relatively benign condition, I learned that this illness is devastating and may even increase risks of dying from heart failure and cancer at a much younger age (Jason, Corradi, Gress, Williams, & Torres-Harding, 2006). This baffling disease also has an extraordinary economic impact: the burden to individuals and society is between $19 billion and $24 billion per year in the United States alone (Jason, Benton, Johnson, & Valentine, 2008).

My commitment to work on social justice issues relating to this illness over 20 years involved all five principles of social change. Using the first principle of developing a clear vision of possible second-order objectives, I worked to decrease stigma associated with this illness. With that vision intact, I realized that the forces that had trivialized this illness were strong. Power structures such as the CDC worked hard to maintain the status quo, and the second principle of social change helped me realize that I would need to work to change them. The third principle illustrated how coalitions must work together to take advantage of developing events and shifts in power. Obstacles to change can be overcome by collaborations between the multiple gatekeepers. We also maintained a long-term commitment to change, the fourth social change principle. During this time, I witnessed alliances emerge and crumble, but I never wavered in my commitment to change over the long run. These principles cannot and do not occur quickly, and the pace can be frustrating. It is critical to reaffirm the vision of change through measuring success. The need for feedback, our fifth principle, took the form of constant communication about research findings among important players. These five principles, and especially the focus on power abuse, were all vital to our success.

Focused attention and comprehensive evaluation are indispensable when working toward social change. It is often not easy to identify where the abuse of power exists. However, without a thorough examination and focused identification, efforts to bring about real, second-order change will be jeopardized and probably doomed to fail. Charging at ill-defined targets is ultimately futile—akin to Don Quixote's attack on windmills that he believed were giants. Even the most liberating insight into the nature of the second-order change will not work without addressing the real power source and bringing coalitions and grassroots groups together to pinpoint the most meaningful areas of intervention and work on incremental wins. All of these components and principles are necessary to achieve long-lasting change.

In reducing abuses of power, a long-term perspective, such as the ME/CFS case study in this chapter, is needed. McCleary and Reeves collaborated and battled over a period of decades. They disagreed over the prevalence and characteristics of those with ME/CFS, the name given to the illness, and the official definition of the disease. Reeves, through his position at the CDC, and McCleary, with her influence among patient groups, were both titans of power: Any second-order changes had to involve them.

In the end, McCleary moved forward and changed her positions dramatically. By 2011, the CFIDS Association changed its mission from being a patient advocacy organization to one focused on raising money to fund important and innovative ME/CFS research aimed at identifying biological markers, advancing objective diagnoses, and treating this illness. The CFIDS Association developed a biobank of information, which includes both self-report and biological data. Some of the leading clinicians/scientists across the country have been participating in this endeavor (the self-report symptom questionnaire used was developed by our research group at DePaul University). In addition, in 2012, the CFIDS Association asked our group to write an essay on postexertional malaise, which was posted to its members (Jason & Evans, 2012). By closely monitoring the complex evolution of power and the positions of key actors in a movement, we have been able to successfully collaborate with different and at times opposing groups in order to contribute to critical changes.

In this story of patients fighting to gain recognition and be taken seriously, it was clear that abuses of power were occurring at the highest levels within the CDC. Activists focused their attention on challenging the CDC, as the research funding that it controls holds the power to create a better understanding of the illness and improve outcomes for patients with ME/CFS. But the CDC is not the only source to question the legitimacy of ME/CFS as an illness and fuel stigma and myths about the disease. Books, articles, and even popular radio talk show physicians harp on the notion that ME/CFS is not a real illness. These popular forums also trivialize this serious chronic illness as hysteria (Showalter, 1997). A recent survey of 2,000-plus U.S. health care providers presented at a 2011 conference found that only 7% thought CFS was a "medical" disorder (Unger, 2011). The survey illustrates how much is left to be done in terms of how health care providers view ME/CFS. Although important strides have been made regarding the CDC, ME/CFS activists must also focus on structural, systemic redress of this type of popular discrimination.

Structural issues of power and the control of resources go beyond patient activist groups' battle with the CDC. Another concern is whether resources will be available to treat those with ME/CFS, as well as the over 60 million

Americans who suffer multiple chronic health conditions (Wu & Green, 2000). This concern speaks to a larger issue that affects not only ME/CFS funding but also resources for health care and other social services. Sixteen trillion dollars in national debt (as of August 2012) threatens our government's ability to provide the critical health services that these vulnerable groups need. An analysis of power is needed to identify what led to this massive challenge to our health care system.

Presidential decisions during the 1980s and 2000s led to expansions in defense spending (particularly when fighting two wars in Iraq and Afghanistan) while at the same time reducing taxes. Since 2001, the last time the United States had a balanced budget, spending has risen from 18.2% of gross domestic product (GDP) to 23.8% of GDP in 2010, while revenues have decreased from 19.5% of GDP to 14.9% of GDP. These imbalances cannot be sustained. The Bush tax cuts added $2 trillion to the national debt, and the wars in Iraq and Afghanistan added an additional $1.1 trillion. In addition, the recession led both to a collapse in revenue and to a sharp rise in spending on safety-net programs. Medicare and Medicaid are expected to rise from 5.3% of GDP in 2009 to 10% in 2035. David Walker (2008) has summed up our problems dealing with the budget, trade, savings, and leadership. Unless structural changes occur to redistribute resources, any attempts at reconceptualizing power on the individual level will not be successful (Riger, 1993).

Jacob Hacker and Paul Pierson's (2010) book *How Washington Made the Rich Richer—and Turned Its Back on the Middle Class* clearly shows how leading public officials made decisions over the past three decades that favored the top 1% of Americans and further increased income inequality in the United States. As the wealthy gained in influence and power, there has been a broad-base loss of faith in government. Citizens will need to organize to make structural changes in order to deal with our current and future health care challenges, just as was accomplished in the past by activists like Mother Teresa, Jane Addams, Florence Nightingale, Mahatma Gandhi, Martin Luther King, and Malcolm X. Challenging these large-scale issues of economic inequality requires an understanding of the use and abuse of power and the strategies that have proved successful in combating it.

Successful campaigns effectively mobilize community support to restructure power, as the ME/CFS movement did by organizing patient advocacy groups to challenge the CDC. The next chapter further explores the third principle, the need for grassroots, community support and coalitions to change power relationships and achieve second-order change.

Additional Resources

For more information about the ACT UP movement, see the documentary "United in Anger: A History of ACT-UP"; trailer and screening information can be found at this site: http://www.unitedinanger.com/

Other celebrities with ME/CFS include the well-known author of *Seabiscuit*, Laura Hillenbrand; singer/songwriter Stevie Nicks; and former Olympic soccer player Michelle Akers; for more information, visit this site: http://raisingawarenessforcfs.wordpress.com/2011/03/07/celebrities-with-cfsme/

David Tuller, who has written many stories for the *New York Times* on ME/CFS, provides more detailed information on the change in leadership at the CDC, as well as other issues, in this blog: http://www.virology.ws/2011/11/23/chronic-fatigue-syndrome-and-the-cdc-a-long-tangled-tale/

I provide a full discussion of events that occurred between the CDC and the CFIDS Association in this article: http://www.springerlink.com/content/c726m71k010685r8/fulltext.pdf

A patient describes what it is like to live with ME/CFS on this site: http://www.youtube.com/watch?v=B8bCLe_lN14

To view an article I wrote for the *Wall Street Journal* on ME/CFS, visit this site: http://online.wsj.com/article/SB10001424052748704507404576179031979295592.html?mod=WSJ_article_related

Two articles that appeared in the *New York Times* that quoted some of the work in this chapter can be found at these sites:
http://www.nytimes.com/2011/03/08/health/research/08fatigue.html?_r=1
http://www.nytimes.com/ref/health/healthguide/esn-chronicfatigue-expert.html

In April of 2011, the White House Chronicle PBS program aired a panel discussing ME/CFS, which can be found at this site: http://www.whchronicle.com/wp-content/plugins/simple-flash-video/video.php?height=520&width=790&file_name=http://whchronicle.net/upload/files/flv/WHC_3012.flv

A technical webinar that I conducted on problems with the diagnostic criteria for ME/CFS for the CFIDS Association can be found at this site: http://www.youtube.com/watch?v=JelwLvzW6eI

3

Navigating the Maze

In any campaign for change, the organization of like-minded allies can help build momentum for a community's cause. In some cases, community may literally refer to one's own neighborhood or town. For example, Officer Buzz Talbot focused his efforts on curbing underage smoking in one suburb. In other cases, the idea of community may be more metaphorical, such as the nationwide movement of patients with myalgic encephalomyelitis (ME)/chronic fatigue syndrome (CFS) who banded together to force changes in the Centers for Disease Control and Prevention (CDC) leadership. No matter how a group is defined, focused and collective efforts can lead to broad second-order change through the use of our third principle: identifying and mobilizing individuals and community groups to influence the cultural and political landscape affecting social change. César Chávez, one of the most prominent figures in the labor social change movement, recognized the lasting value of creating coalitions, stating in his 1986 "Wrath of Grapes Boycott" speech, "If we unite we can only triumph for ourselves, for our children and for their children" (Kent, 2012). The key is citizen participation in democratic processes that ensure that community members have meaningful involvement in decisions that affect them (Wandersman & Florin, 1990).

In our search for strategies to create alliances with other like-minded groups, we must first think about how and why people develop a psychological *sense of community* (Bishop, Chertok, & Jason, 1997; McMillan & Chavis, 1986). Psychologist Seymour Sarason (1974) originally defined this as a supportive network and a stable structure on which one can depend. Sarason felt strongly that a sense of community is a basic necessity that a person should have; in other words, developing this sense of unity and interdependence is one of life's major tasks—and it should also be the overarching goal of all collective actions. Given that a loss of connectedness lies at the root of many modern social problems, understanding its importance is integral to achieving second-order change.

Since the dawn of history, humans have always lived together in groups. For thousands of years, people living in villages helped one another, not out of charity, but for sheer survival. Although conflicts certainly existed in village life, people demonstrated mutual respect, shared goals, cooperation, and neighborliness, all of which provided a strong sense of interdependence. In his 1942 book *The Small Community,* social scientist Arthur Morgan wrote about how members of these early communities experienced interactions that grew out of mutual goals, customs, and traditions. As societies became more mechanized and urban during the Industrial Revolution, people began to organize more formally, with contracts and legislatures gradually taking the place of family and community bonds. These days, people may experience greater individual freedom, but it comes at the high cost of human connectedness and community spirit. Online forums and dating websites, for example, bring together people with shared interests or offer intimacy in our technologically advanced society, but they could also erode organic and spontaneous person-to-person interactions.

Throughout our daily lives, most of us find ourselves surrounded by others, whether it is during our daily commute or while we shop for groceries. Many people, however, lack strong connections to groups, supportive family members, or both (Etzioni, 1993). Think of the thousands of homeless, or those released from state hospitals, detox facilities, and prisons, who have no place to go. Others live in isolation suffering from chronic illnesses or disabilities. How a society treats these people—its disenfranchised members marginalized from the mainstream—is a true reflection of the society's character. A community that puts its most vulnerable members in even riskier situations can expect to be plagued by an ever-expanding array of social problems. Even when basic support programs are initiated in the community, the efforts of social service workers are sometimes compromised by the hostile or indifferent attitudes of people residing in the surrounding areas. The paradox is this: If social activists were able to address a community's lack of interdependence, they would not only help those in need but also strengthen the sense of connectedness in others.

I recently spoke with a colleague who arrived in the United States with few resources. He managed to achieve great success through hard work and determination. I felt his perceptions on these social change principles would provide great insight. As I'd suspected, he had strong opinions: He felt that many Americans had a self-defeating sense of entitlement—often without realizing it—that made them dependent on social services and government programs. As such, he firmly believed that many of those who had been incarcerated or homeless or were suffering from substance use disorders could be reintegrated into society through their own self-determination and self-reliance. For example, he thought that people addicted to drugs could—and should—stop using illegal drugs through their own strength of will, and that they should focus on finding work and becoming self-sufficient. He could accept the possibility that young people could be drawn into the world of crime and drugs through no fault of their own. Yet, older individuals had the responsibility to adopt a different lifestyle. These views are quite conservative; some would even argue that they verge on the reactionary—but they are, to our detriment, the views of many Americans and public officials.

Unfortunately, a large percentage of people dealing with addiction and mental illness are abandoned and left without any system of support. Some of the nation's largest institutions, on the other hand, are classic examples of how resources are squandered on highly dehumanizing programs. Similar to the poisonous environment of the Stanford Prison study, total institutions alone, such as mental hospitals or addiction treatment facilities, could compromise an individual's well-being. To make matters worse, many people who move from a treatment center or prison to the community are abandoned without skills that could help them function within society; it is not surprising that countless individuals become caught in a tragic cycle of entering one demoralizing setting after another. In trying to navigate the maze of failed initiatives, it is important to first understand the circumstances that create these disastrous interventions. Considering how and why these initiatives fail is the first step in understanding the creation of change strategies and how second-order change will ultimately succeed where first-order approaches have not.

Deinstitutionalization of Mental Health Facilities

After World War II, people began to recognize that mental health institutions were overcrowded, understaffed, underfunded, and inhumane and did not effectively treat people with mental illnesses. In the 1970s, after my junior year in college, I worked in a Colorado mental health facility and later worked in a New York Veterans Administration hospital as a graduate student. These experiences added to my growing anger and rejection of the way patients were being treated. Nevertheless, without a system of support or safe place to live outside of the hospital, some patients mentioned that they would regularly mislead the staff by displaying psychotic symptoms, as this was the only way they would have a place to live and receive meals. It was clear to me these institutions were exacerbating conditions and creating even more entrenched problems rather than helping to alleviate them. The hospitals needed to be closed. Truly improving the quality of life for these patients meant developing community-based care that would enable freer, more socially integrated environments.

At the time, it was unclear how we as a society could provide this type of community to those who were in such desperate need of it. Soon, health professionals and advocates of community health initiatives began to consider the process of closing mental hospitals and discharging patients into the community. This idea became known as deinstitutionalization—an initiative that exemplified potential to bring about second-order change but resulted in utter failure. A prominent psychiatrist named Dr. Robert Felix, who believed that most mental illnesses were due to stressors within particular environments, thought that state-run mental health hospitals should replace federal programs that were unable to provide patients with timely diagnoses and treatment. Felix became a primary force behind the community health movement in Washington, and in 1955, Congress called for the creation of a Joint Commission on Mental Health to analyze the human and economic problems of mental illness (Gillon, 2000). The commission recommended that, though state hospitals must still provide mental health services, the main providers should be community centers located in neighborhoods that could be easily accessed by patients living in the community.

In the early 1960s, President Kennedy set up a task force, led by Felix, to reduce the institutionalized population and create community-based treatment centers. The Mental Retardation and Community Health Centers Construction Act of 1963 (known as the Community Health Act) aimed to cut the mental hospital patient populations in half and to create a national network of community mental health centers.

In addition to this health act, the use of antipsychotic drugs accelerated the release of patients by reducing symptoms enough to justify discharge into the community. In 1955, Thorazine, the first widely used antipsychotic drug, was introduced. These types of medications contributed to a reduction from 558,239 patients living in mental hospitals to 71,619 over a 40-year period (Torrey, 1997). People were moved out of institutions by the thousands—it was one of America's most massive social experiments. But was it working?

When mental institutions closed, some families took relatives in. Community centers attempted to help others get used to life on their own. But most former patients were not prepared for discharge for a variety of reasons and received insufficient and inconsistent levels of care from community centers (Fakhoury & Priebe, 2007). Over three-quarters of those released had chronic, serious mental illness, and for them, stable, comprehensive treatment still did not exist. Most of the severely mentally ill had nowhere to turn and were quickly reinstitutionalized or, worse, sent to jail. Others remained in the community but were poor and isolated, with no hope of meaningful help (Dear & Wolch, 1987).

A nightmarish vacuum arose between the closure of hospitals and the lack of other structured care. Local governments could not match funds provided by the federal government to open the mental health centers, nor could they find adequate professionals to staff them. The biggest problem was one with which we still struggle: the "not in my backyard" mentality. Most communities did not want these services offered in their neighborhoods. Then, the Vietnam War took center stage and seized both funding and political attention. To continue funding the war, President Nixon fought against Congress's approval of community center funding and actually confiscated funds for this initiative (Gillon, 2000). In understanding the power abuses that occurred regarding deinstitutionalization, we need to look no further than to our political leaders. Nixon refused to provide funding for the care of people with mental illness when the need was dire.

Former patients found no reprieve in the mid-1980s, when President Reagan's popularity was at its height, and the United States decreased its support for mental institutions and addiction treatment centers. The Reagan administration supported the belief that everyone should be able to pull themselves up by their bootstraps. In other words, we were all responsible for our own well-being. This did not take into consideration those with few or no resources or those who did not have a family to support them. The notion that these societal problems could—or should—be solved through the good works of society was deemed a waste of taxpayer money.

Although deinstitutionalization involved the closing of one type of ineffectual system, the policy directly caused a building boom of a different type: prisons. According to a report by Human Rights Watch, prisons became the new hospital for thousands of mentally ill Americans. The Department of Justice reported that 40 mental health hospitals have closed in the past decade. During the same period, 400 new prisons have opened (Sheth, 2009). Prisons and state hospitals were forced to absorb and treat people who had formerly lived in mental institutions. Ill-equipped to treat large numbers of people with such conditions, prisons could not even begin to meet the needs of people suffering from mental illness. Additionally, without any real form of rehabilitation in these over-burdened institutions, people cycle through prisons multiple times. Half of the mentally ill inmates in state and federal facilities have been reported to have three or more prior sentences (Bureau of Justice Statistics, 2005). Compared to other countries, Figure 3.1 illustrates that the United States has the highest percentage of its population in prison or jail.

By the 1980s, the increased financial support for treatment institutions, which had been supported by Presidents Kennedy and Johnson, had been cut. The deinstitutionalization movement became one of the most shameful first-order interventions ever perpetuated on vulnerable, high-risk people. Since the 1970s, politicians have been responsible for these reprehensible policies that discharge victimized people from mental institutions. Sadly, the same failed second-order interventions were perpetuated upon people with substance use problems.

The Problem of Alcohol and Other Drug Addiction

During the late 19th century, drugs such as opium, morphine, and cocaine were legally available. Morphine, the active ingredient of opium, has been available since 1803 and was used as a painkiller during the American Civil War; unfortunately, it inadvertently caused an addiction to the drug that was so widespread that it was known as the "soldier's disease." In the early 1900s, alcohol and

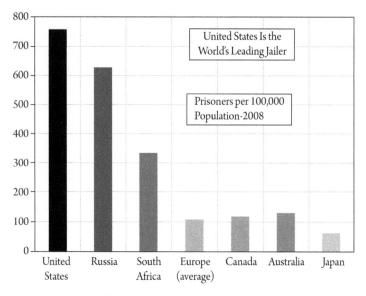

Figure 3.1 Prisoners per 100,000 in different countries.
Available at: http://proxy.baremetal.com/november.org/graphs/LeadingJailer.gif

narcotics were sold nationwide and advertised as a cure for almost any disease. Until 1929, Coca-Cola contained cocaine and was marketed as a nerve tonic.

The Eighteenth Amendment to the Constitution, however, put an end to the sale of alcohol in January 1920. While many voted for Prohibition, many others flocked to the "speakeasies" that arose in reaction to the new laws. People continued to drink behind closed doors that were opened with a password. Even worse, a whole new generation of gangsters emerged as they profited from the sale of illegal alcohol, leading to the corruption of many public officials. As these realities of Prohibition became apparent, state conventions ratified another constitutional amendment 14 years later, the Twenty-First Amendment, repealing prohibition. Alcohol was again a legal substance.

Despite the many efforts to curb illegal drug use in modern society, cocaine and morphine are more accessible now than they were in the 19th century. Steven Duke and Albert Gross (1994), authors of *America's Longest War: Rethinking Our Tragic Crusade Against Drugs*, claim that laws criminalizing drugs have not just backfired, but they've led to the polar opposite of what was intended. Instead of reducing drug abuse, these laws have directly contributed to burgeoning economic losses and criminal activity. The arguments to legalize drugs are well known: Reducing the profits of drug dealers would lead to a decrease in the supply of drugs. These benefits could reverberate through ruined communities, but there's no denying the harmful effects of drugs, which greatly complicates the argument. The 1960s generation raised awareness of many critical social and political issues; however, their reintroduction of drugs into the American middle class was a high price to pay for this awareness. Where a market was created, a supply inevitably followed, and we've been fighting the war on drugs with no end in sight. No one believes we are winning this 40-year-old war; in fact, there is a good case to be made that we have lost it, just as prohibition of alcohol in the 1920s was an outright failure. The financial toll has been unforgivably high. According to Horgan, Skwara, Strickler, Andersen, and Stein (2001), societal costs attributed to alcohol and other drug addiction in the United States alone are greater than $500 billion each year.

Substance use disorders continue to be our number one mental disorder, as addiction causes crime, homelessness, and a myriad of social ills. These problems have befuddled politicians and sociologists of the past just as much as the present. Today, alcohol and other drug problems affect over 20 million Americans (Jason, Ferrari, Davis, & Olson, 2006). Yet only about 10% manage to obtain any type of treatment for their addictions. In the best-case scenario, a person begins treatment by entering and completing the detox process and then moves through a time-limited therapeutic program; however, these programs are becoming scarce. Sources of funding—on the federal, state, and local levels—have drastically decreased (Jason, Olson, & Foli, 2008). Moreover, private and public sector inpatient treatment facilities have reduced their services dramatically.

The reality of detox is that it seldom leads to real, sustained recovery. What happens most often is that it is just the beginning of a cycle—returning from ineffectual treatment and recovery programs only to eventually land back on the street again (Richman & Neumann, 1984; Vaillant, 2003). Recidivism rates 1 year after treatment are high for both men and women, and half to three-quarters of all people with alcohol addiction drop out during treatment (Montgomery, Miller, & Tonigan, 1993). Needless to say, these programs are also costly (Schneider & Googins, 1989).

The United States can no longer afford the financial and social costs of treating people with substance use disorders that are incurred by using the expensive, revolving door programs currently in place. What happened when politicians turned their backs on funding mental institutions 50 years ago? The patients moved to prisons, nursing homes, homeless shelters, or the street. As school administrators, workplaces, and legislatures began pushing "zero tolerance" drug policies, the public began to assume that locking up the mentally ill and drug users was the solution. Such policies stigmatize people with alcohol and other drug problems and could promote practices such as insurance companies refusing coverage for people who have serious addictions. These days, 600,000 inmates are released back into communities each year, many with ongoing drug addictions (substance use within correctional facilities ranges from 74% to 82%; Keene, 1997), one of the strongest predictors of criminal recidivism (Bureau of

Justice Statistics, 2005). Most of these hundreds of thousands of people end up right back in institutional care.

Figure 3.2 illustrates the consequences of the war on drugs that began in the 1980s: an escalation of incarceration rates in our state and federal prisons. There is a better way, achieved through enduring second-order change (such as those discussed at the Drug Policy Alliance listed under Additional Resources at the end of this chapter) and creative adjustments to living environments within our communities, rather than forcing people from one institution to another.

Recovery Communities

Directly or indirectly, most of us know people who have been affected by alcohol and other drug problems. Second-order change interventions often come in the form of healing programs that promote self-help. Groups such as Alcoholics Anonymous (AA) resolutely use abstinence-only social support as a critical component in the path to recovery (Humphreys, Mankowski, Moos, & Finney, 1999). A peer-network approach, made up of abstainers and others in recovery, can be very effective at providing others with social support.

According to *Slaying the Dragon*, William White's (1998) scholarly and comprehensive book that chronicles the history of substance abuse recovery

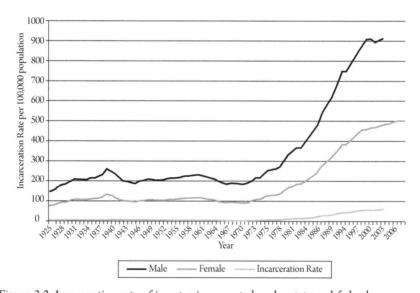

Figure 3.2 Incarceration rate of inmates incarcerated under state and federal jurisdiction per 100,000 population, 1925–2008.
Available at: http://en.wikipedia.org/wiki/File:U.S._incarceration_rates_1925_onwards.png

communities, peer-network support programs have a long history in the United States. AA, the most famous of the self-help recovery groups, was not the first of its kind. In fact, it grew out of other abstinence movements conceived by the country's original inhabitants, Native Americans. Until the 1600s, when European settlers first brought spirits to the United States, Native Americans had never experienced alcohol. The settlers used alcohol as a means to exploit and control them (Mancall, 1995). Thus, the first movement to resist alcohol and regain spiritual and mental health was born, beginning with Samson Occom, a Mohegan who recovered from alcoholism through his conversion to Christianity in the 1770s. Comparing his own experience to those of other tribe members, he wrote and spoke against the devastating effects and consequences of alcohol consumption. The abstinence movement spread in the early 1800s, when Handsome Lake, a leader of the Iroquois, organized his tribe and joined forces with the Prophet, of the Shawnee tribe, to put together a campaign that curbed alcoholism in many western tribes for years. According to White, these types of bottom-up social initiatives played a critical part in our country's history of social change.

In 1935, AA emerged in the aftermath of Prohibition, during the Great Depression. Alcoholics like Bill Wilson (Bill W.), a New York City stockbroker, desperately needed support systems and recovery options. His drinking was literally killing him, and doctors convinced his wife to commit him to a psychiatric institution. Upon having a dramatic moment of spiritual conversion that convinced him to stay sober, Bill connected with another alcoholic, Robert Halbrook Smith, MD (Dr. Bob). With Bill's support, Dr. Bob became abstinent. Bill moved in with Dr. Bob and Dr. Bob's wife to organize groups of other alcoholics who wanted to stop drinking. As the number and size of these groups began to grow, so did the need to define their group and establish rules. In the beginning, the only written directive was "don't drink," but other critical components were tried, tested, and reformed to achieve the best outcomes for members. The meetings were fervently democratic (a rare quality that is difficult to maintain), and AA's continued expansion called attention to their need for funding.

Charles Townes, the owner of a hospital in New York City, offered a permanent residence for AA within his hospital and a generous salary for Bill to run the program collaboratively. Townes further promised the longevity of the program, as it would be secure within a for-profit hospital. Although Bill was enticed, the members were hesitant to become linked to an institution and compromise the structure of their democratic, grassroots, mutual-aid organization. They believed that AA would have to make concessions if it relied on external funding. Bill reluctantly declined Townes's offer and sought funding from the oil tycoon J. D. Rockefeller. To his credit, Rockefeller knew how money could both create and destroy and did not want to disrupt the organic nature of AA. Rather than flooding the group with funding, he provided a small stipend for Bill's living expenses and a modest monthly allowance for the organization. Even publicity for AA was executed in a way that remained true to its democratic approach. Instead of having a single spokesperson, the group would issue statements from a group platform.

The early AA faced many challenges typical of transformational movements. Along with success comes temptation, but the leaders were not distracted by money or fame. They focused on the healing of members through perpetual, mutual support; the celebration of small successes; and functional improvement. There are now over 150 spin-off organizations, including Cocaine Anonymous, Narcotics Anonymous, Adult Children of Alcoholics, and Overeaters Anonymous. All of these programs share critical components, including shared stories and the study of the "Twelve Step" recovery roadmap. Performing the 12 steps religiously keeps members on task. Veteran members become sponsors to newer members after a period of substantial sobriety as they continue work on the steps. Helping another with recovery assists the sponsor in recovery as well.

Many people with addiction need more than AA meetings to maintain their abstinence. For example, some homeless individuals or people with severe mental health problems may need basic supports to be addressed before taking their first step toward recovery. A harm reduction model focuses on providing housing to reduce the hardships that people suffering from addiction face. Some believe that only after addicts gain strength and safety in their new environment can they truly begin the process of rehabilitation (Marlatt, 1996). One of these programs is called Housing First, and it targets chronically homeless populations with mental illness and provides a range of services—without requiring sobriety or alcohol or other drug use treatment.

The Housing First program, a second-order change intervention, evolved out of the needs of multiple or single families and can lead to substantial decreases in chronic homelessness (Tsemberis, Moran, Shinn, Asmussen, & Shern, 2003). The best predictor of the extent of homelessness in a community is the ratio of available affordable housing units to the number of people seeking them. Results of these programs have been promising, as more than 80% of those who were formerly homeless remained housed after 12 months (Pearson, Montgomery, & Locke, 2009). Needless to say, this model does not work for all. Some residents were incarcerated, needed more intensive treatment, or were evicted for assaulting other residents; others left voluntarily, and some died (Pearson et al., 2009).

Another alternative community recovery program is Delancey Street, a residential self-help center for former substance users and offenders newly released from prison. Hundreds reside in homes located in New Mexico, New York, North Carolina, and California. The average Delancey Street resident has been in prison four times, cannot read or write, and lacks realistic employment skills.

Many are former gang members who have been trapped in poverty for generations. Residents stay, on average, about 4 years. Before graduating from the program, they receive a high school–equivalent education and job training. They are also taught how to cope, drug-free, in their respective environments. Tenets of personal responsibility and self-reliance are stressed as necessary to thrive in mainstream society.

People assume that such an intensive program must be a drain on government resources. In fact, thousands of people have graduated from these programs at no cost to the taxpayer. The organization supports itself through additional training programs: a moving and trucking school, a restaurant and catering service, a print and copy shop, retail and wholesale services, paratransit services, advertising sales, specialty sales, Christmas tree sales and decorating, and an automotive service center. Funds garnered from these businesses provide the money to teach residents vocational skills. In San Francisco, Delancey Street residents built a 350,000-square-foot, four-story, self-managed complex, containing street-level retail stores, a public restaurant, and 177 apartments. There are also classrooms for training in purchasing, contracting, and computer and accounting services. Delancey Street has no professional staff and has never accepted any government funds. It is run entirely by residents and works more like an extended family than a treatment program. Longer term residents help newer ones, and everyone has a job.

Similar programs were creatively adapted for mental health patients. Psychologist George Fairweather (1979) developed "lodges" that allowed community-based, independent living and employment in their house's small business for people with certain forms of mental illness. Although every resident holds a work position, each house can find support in professional consultants who can train members or help with business operation. Another member-run organization and international mental health movement is GROW. One residential GROW house, located in Kankakee, Illinois, staffed by paid professionals and funded by the Illinois Department of Human Services, helps those with mental health issues learn responsibility skills and how to live independently (Jason & Perdoux, 2004). Not all of these innovations are self-sufficient and self-supporting, but at least they provide quality services to high-risk individuals within the community rather than within impersonal institutions.

Through my own experiences, I saw first-hand the effect of the abuses within large institutions and of the extent to which funding cuts can cause hardship for individuals in tremendous need. Many people who are moving from treatment settings or prisons do not have a supportive and drug-free place in which to live. Self-run sober living environments that allow for democratic participation help keep the social and financial burden of ineffective programs from being passed to others. As White (1998) has indicated, there are now recovery communities in colleges and religious and other community organizations that are providing new abstinence settings for people with alcohol and other drug problems. Some grassroots groups have been able to transform policies and organizations—as well as lives—by challenging power abuses that ignore basic rights like employment, housing, and health care. One example of such an organization is the Oxford House movement. Although the vast majority of Americans may have never heard of it, Oxford House is the largest successful residential self-help alcohol and other drug use recovery program in the nation, with a network of recovery homes in almost every state. These houses are governed and run by the people who live there—there is no external, professional staff at all. With over 10,000 residents, Oxford House, one of the largest second-order interventions and recovery-based organizations in the country, exemplifies the effort to transform our society's way of dealing with problems of addiction (Olson et al., 2002). It expands upon the AA approach by providing former addicts a place to live.

The Establishment and Growth of Oxford House

Oxford House was founded in 1975 by Paul Molloy and a group of other men in recovery from alcohol and other drug problems. Before hitting rock bottom, Molloy was once an influential congressional staffer. Alcoholism caused him to lose his job, family, and home, and he soon found himself living with about 13 others in a halfway house outside of Washington, DC. According to the rules of the halfway house, all residents had to leave at the end of their 6-month stay, whether or not they had recovered. Molloy knew that recovery would be an uphill battle; he noted that 11 of the 12 people who left his halfway house had succumbed to relapse.

In August of 1975, the residents were dealt more devastating news: They were told that funding for their house would end in just over a month. Their 6-month stays, which were already insufficient, would be cut even shorter. That evening, Molloy and several other members of the halfway house went out for coffee after attending an AA meeting. One person introduced an idea that stunned the others: They should manage the halfway house themselves. Some were so accustomed to living within a typical top-down power structure that they couldn't believe such an approach existed or was even possible. Still, they called the county office to learn how they might take over the halfway house. The county representative explained that the residents could directly lease the house from the owner for $750 a month. Soon, the concept of mutual support became tangible; a retired chief petty officer, and fellow AA member, gave Molloy and his friends a check for the first month's rent. Knowing the dilemma the residents were facing, he said that they could pay him back when they had the money.

Although Molloy had no experience creating a recovery setting, he found guidance and inspiration in Alexis de Toqueville's (1835) classic book, *Democracy in America*. It described voluntary associations and civic responsibility, such as the story of a village working together to remove a fallen tree that was blocking a trail. They did not hold meetings to decide a course of action but, instead, simply gathered enough men to collectively solve the problem. Molloy thought that such straightforward wisdom, once profound, was now lost. From that story, Molloy and his fellow residents relied on their intuition that a new model might work, and they established Oxford House. Their model stressed that each member had a responsibility to the community and that it was important to solve problems directly rather than to rely on the initiative of others. He believed that this philosophy would promote self-reliance and confidence. The first Oxford House members also turned to Orlando Cullman, a knowledgeable friend of Molloy's, for a critical perspective on the new house arrangement by asking him to stay in Oxford House for 3 days. Orlando had considerable respect in the AA movement as he had known Bill Wilson, one of the founders of AA. Every summer, Wilson and his wife would stay with Cullman and his wife in Vermont. After living with Molloy and the other residents for a short time, Cullman confirmed that the group was headed in the right direction; this confirmation provided the confidence that Molloy and his friends needed. Although Molloy and his fellow residents introduced the idea of democracy to the house, Cullman's decisive support helped solidify their proposed structure.

When Cullman left, Molloy worked to define the rules in an Oxford House manual. Once the first draft was complete, he let his fellow residents review, debate, and revise the final document. Rather than adopt oppressive halfway house rules, the members decided to implement minimal rules for the new house. For example, residents were instructed to pay an equal share of rent, perform assigned chores, and stay sober. Any deviation from the rules could lead to immediate eviction. Houses were to operate democratically with majority rule (greater than 80% approval rate) regarding admission of new members and other policies. Additionally, each Oxford House would elect a president, treasurer, comptroller, coordinator, secretary, and building maintenance person to serve 6-month terms. All members would have the opportunity to take the lead and enforce rules.

During its critical first year, Oxford House's innovative approach came under repeated attacks by critics, many of whom even tried to sabotage it. Several halfway house managers called the Environmental Protection Agency, claiming that the house's fire protection was not adequate; others made sure there would be an excessive number of building inspections at the Oxford House. Why? One explanation was that traditional halfway house organizations viewed the Oxford House resident-run style as a threat to their livelihood. If these residents could manage a house independently, then there would be no need for house managers or counselors. Their jobs would become obsolete.

Molloy and the residents held fast against the opposition. The first house thrived, even boasting a surplus of $1,200. Applicants flooded to the organization, and members quickly voted to rent another house. Just 6 months after it opened, the first Oxford House accumulated enough money to invest in renting a second house. Members of the second house, in turn, worked to rent a third house, and the cycle continued.

Nowadays, new Oxford House members are required to attend self-help meetings during their first month and have one-on-one sessions with each member of the house. These meetings build common bonds as new residents share their stories of addiction and reaffirm their plans to avoid substance use and maintain sobriety. Houses are equipped with kitchens, laundry facilities, and living rooms so that residents can meet and spend time together. Each residence is separated by gender and holds between 7 and 10 people. Depending on the number of occupants, each person is expected to share a bedroom. Houses are established in multiethnic neighborhoods with access to public transportation and employment opportunities. Groups of houses in the same geographic area are placed into chapters and share a team of elected officers.

The successes of the Oxford House movement began to gain recognition. In 1987, Ed Madigan, a Republican congressman from Lincoln, Illinois, called Molloy to inform him that a first draft of the Anti-Drug Abuse Act was coming to fruition. Madigan wondered if Molloy wanted this legislation to include seed money, which could provide loans for future Oxford House start-ups across the nation. Before giving a definitive answer, Molloy consulted with the existing 13 Oxford House presidents. True to the self-sufficient model, the presidents were strongly skeptical of any kind of government support. They knew that accepting government funds could threaten the shift in power from the residents to people outside the Oxford House. More significantly, it could compromise their vision and philosophy. Despite hesitation from the Oxford House leadership, federal representatives were so impressed with the model that they wanted to be as helpful as possible.

The following summer, Dr. Donald Ian McDonald, the top drug advisor to President Reagan, visited an Oxford House. McDonald asked the residents about when they last had a vacancy. They told him it had been several months earlier. In response to McDonald's question about how many people applied for this vacancy, he was told that out of 25 applicants, only 1 had been chosen. McDonald wondered what had happened to the 24 rejected applicants, but the residents could not give him an answer. They simply did not know.

During the visit, McDonald began to understand the primary barrier to expansion: It took approximately several years to gather enough money to open a new Oxford House. He also came to appreciate the great need in society for Oxford Houses and formulated a solution that acknowledged both the presidents' distrust of government involvement and the lack of available money to rent new houses: a revolving loan fund. It gave the presidents the first month's rent security deposit to start a new Oxford House. Because the money would be paid back by the residents, it was, therefore, *not* an entitlement program.

McDonald's loan program became part of the congressional Anti-Drug Abuse Act in 1988. This encouraged states to start up other Oxford Houses by providing them with federal funding. A group of people in recovery, for example, could request $4,000 from their state through an interest-free loan. Loans would be repaid to the state fund and then used for the start-up costs of the next Oxford Houses to be built in that state.

There was more: Several states provided separate funding to hire recruiters who could help start Oxford Houses. These recruiters, all Oxford House alumni, either worked for the state through a separate entity like an addictions agency or for the central Oxford House office located in Maryland. Recruiters work to locate homes in relatively low-crime areas, secure the leases, and make sure that each house is sufficiently furnished.

The next task for the recruiters, once a house is established, is to visit treatment centers and inform the staff and residents about the new house. As the house becomes filled, the recruiter may even stay there for the first few months to provide stability and ensure that everyone knows the rules and how to enforce policies. Then, the entire process begins anew. The recruiter will start to work on the new house while continuing to check back with the prior house members at their weekly meetings. Between 1988 and 1996, the number of Oxford Houses expanded to more than 500 residences. Today there are more than 1,500 Oxford Houses in the United States alone, with others established in Canada, Australia, England, and Africa (Ferrari, Jason, Blake, Davis, & Olson, 2006; Legler & Jason, in press). Figure 3.3 shows a picture of a typical Oxford House with its residents.

The Oxford House model has expanded to serve individuals with psychiatric problems, women and their children, those who have been homeless, people who are deaf, former soldiers, Native Americans, and former prison inmates. Countless people have found inspiration, hope, and desperately needed stability in these houses, as well as immeasurable self-confidence from functioning in leadership roles and gratification from helping others.

John is one such person. He struggled with addiction to drugs and alcohol, served jail time, and spent months without a home. Despite going through detox and several treatment programs, none made a substantial difference in his life—he would always return to his addiction. Each cycle through detox would further destroy his sense of hope and self-esteem. When John first learned of Oxford Houses, he was not sure he wanted to live with other people, but without friends, money, or familial support, his options were pretty limited. At John's entrance interview, the residents asked a lot of questions about his past to try to determine his commitment to leading a substance-free life. That

Figure 3.3 An Oxford House, called the "Henry House," and residents in Waukegan, Illinois. Photograph courtesy of Randy Ramirez. Printed with permission of the Henry House.

night, he was accepted as a member of the house, and they handed him a key. Having just shared his history of lying and stealing during his addition, he was shocked by their display of faith and said, "You can't give me a key to your house. You know that I've lied and stolen and taken from others my entire life; you can't trust me with this key. Really, this is too much for me to believe." Despite his initial resistance to accept the key, over the next 4 months, he proved the residents right: He maintained a job, paid the rent on time, did his chores, and above all, stuck to his commitment. John was slowly gaining back his confidence.

When the position of house treasurer, who oversees rent payments, opened up, members nominated John to fill the position. John again questioned friends' judgment, saying, "As a lifelong liar and thief, you can't trust me with this job. Give it to someone else. I can't believe you're asking me to do this." The house members were adamant, and John maintained secure and accurate records, fulfilling the expectations of his peers. Gradually nurtured by the support of his housemates, John developed a new notion of who he was.

Successful graduates from Oxford Houses, like John, go through a process of deep, personal transformation. Their self-concepts radically change for the better, beginning with feedback from others. Survivors of drug addiction are able to address the greatest impediment to recovery: hopelessness. As new residents spend days, weeks, and months gaining a sense of competency and control, they begin to internalize the lessons of their peers. Even more valuable, in John's case and others like his, he began to believe that the members were right in their initial judgment that he could commit to leading a substance-free life. Such dramatic conversions in mainstream, traditional treatment programs are rare and elusive. The Oxford House program grew out of a pressing need and an empowered community of former alcohol and other drug users who deeply believed in their vision. Coalition building can help create these grassroots, self-sustained programs for some of our most pressing social problems.

DePaul University and Oxford House

I first learned of Oxford Houses in 1991 when I saw Paul Molloy featured on *60 Minutes*. It surprised me that such a revolutionary departure from traditional treatment programs could exist, and that I had never heard about it. Oxford House was a radical departure from traditional hospital care or treatment programs: Not only did residents govern themselves, but also they were welcome to stay as long as they needed to recover. The latter aspect of the program—no time constraints on a resident's stay—intuitively appealed to me. During my recovery from ME/CFS, I never found a suitable residential community that would provide me with the physical, psychological, and emotional rehabilitation I needed to return to my normal lifestyle. This new, successful recovery model—with no ties to outside institutions or the government—was a revelation. Oxford House for people with ME/CFS would have been an ideal alternative solution for me.

As I thought about the Oxford House model, I considered how and why this approach would work. I turned to the work of one of the founders of social psychology, Muzafer Sherif (1966), who carried out a study exploring the interpersonal dynamics between two teams of boys that competed against each other during various summer camp events. As the study progressed, the boys started to develop negative stereotypes about the members of the other group and to behave aggressively. Sherif then tried to reverse course by creating new challenges for the boys—challenges that neither group could overcome alone. In one instance, he designed a scenario in which their bus would be stuck in mud; the only way they could move it was to combine their strengths as a team. By working together, the boys overcame the animosity they had toward each other and developed trust and friendship. Interestingly, Sherif's findings applied not only to young boys but also to all groups, regardless of age or gender. It was clear that the camaraderie among Oxford House residents—in which they worked together as a team to solve common problems—provided an inexpensive solution to foster recovery and tolerance among its members.

I needed to know more about Oxford House. I called Paul Molloy after seeing his *60 Minutes* television interview and asked him if he had an evaluator to better understand what went on at the Oxford Houses. Upon learning that he did not, I proposed a partnership with my team at DePaul University. Molloy was very receptive to the idea, and soon after, he received funding from the state of Illinois (which now also had a revolving loan program) to send Bill Lee, a former Oxford House resident, to Chicago to begin the establishment of Oxford Houses there. But the money was not sufficient to afford housing in the city. After a few days at a local shelter, all of Lee's belongings were stolen. He was ready to leave the city and give up on his mission. Our DePaul research team heard about Lee's difficulties and offered to house him—first at the home of a team member, and then at the university. With access to temporary office space, a phone, and other resources, Lee was able to focus on opening an Illinois house. Lee later named the first Chicago residence the DePaul House out of appreciation for our help.

Oxford House representatives and our research team spent a year getting to know each other by attending each other's team meetings before beginning our project. Oxford House members helped us to fashion and adapt our interview questions. After collecting pilot data, we spent several years submitting and resubmitting proposals in hopes of receiving a federal grant to more intensely study the effectiveness of Oxford Houses.

We finally received federal funding for a study, for which we recruited 150 people who were finishing addiction treatment at an alcohol and other drug use treatment facility in Illinois. Half were assigned to live in an Oxford House, while the other half received standard, traditional aftercare services. We interviewed each participant every 6 months over 2 years and found that participants assigned to a communal-living Oxford House had less substance use, were less likely to commit a crime, and found better jobs than those in traditional aftercare (Jason, Olson, & Ferrari, 2006). Oxford House participants also earned roughly $550 more per month. Over the course of a year, this difference for the 75 individuals in the Oxford House added up to additional money. The lower rate of incarceration among Oxford House residents corresponded to a yearly savings of roughly $119,000 for the Oxford House sample. Together, the productivity and incarceration benefits yield an estimated $613,000 in savings. These findings suggest that there are significant public policy benefits for these types of lower cost, nonmedical, community-based care options for individuals with alcohol and other drug problems.

Our next large-scale study, funded by the National Institute on Drug Abuse (NIDA), examined abstinence-specific social support and abstention from substance use within a sample of over 900 Oxford House residents nationwide. Results were quite positive; only 18.5% reported any substance use over the course of the 1-year study (Jason, Davis, Ferrari, & Anderson, 2007). We also found that participants' social networks increased when they were sober or in recovery.

Among Oxford House residents across the nation (Jason, Davis, et al., 2007), we found that 43% had a history of psychological medication, 30% had attempted suicide, 46% had a history of physical abuse, 35% had a history of sexual abuse, 40% had completed one or more inpatient psychiatric treatments, and 40% had done one or more outpatient treatments. While no clinical services exist on site, residents can seek out mental health professionals for support services. Of course, no one particular type of treatment setting works for everyone. Some people, particularly in their early recovery, might need more structured supervision than the freer management style in Oxford Houses.

Beyond Oxford House: Community Perceptions

Coalitions, such as the Oxford House and DePaul collaboration, create a sense of community by pooling resources, exchanging information, and supporting multiple perspectives. As groups collaborate, they share common experiences that foster trust and awareness (Davis, Jason, Ferrari, Olson, & Alvarez, 2005). The Oxford House model gained standing and influence in the world of addiction recovery. I was invited to join meetings when Paul Molloy and the Oxford House organization presented their model to the U.S. Office of National Drug Control Policy.

In early 2000s, due to budgetary problems, the governor of Illinois ended the $100,000 loan program and support of Oxford House recruiters to save money. Community psychologists Brad Olson, Josefina Alvarez, and I went to the Illinois Department of Alcohol and Substance Abuse to present some of our study findings. None of us expected the response we got. The director subsequently restarted the $100,000 loan program, allowing Oxford House alumnus Leon Venable to be hired to begin starting new houses.

People from other states became interested in the Oxford House movement, and I began talking to members of the press. For example, in 1994, the *Seattle Times* printed an in-depth article (Gelernter, 1994) detailing the success of the model. An *Associated Press* story cited our federal study: "Self-Supporting Group Homes Have High Success Rates in Helping Individuals Recover From Alcoholism and Drug Addiction, Researchers From DePaul University Reported Thursday" (Schmid, 2005). Other newspapers started to pay attention to our work and published additional articles.

Unfortunately, some communities oppose sharing their neighborhood with group homes like Oxford House. Municipalities sometimes use maximum occupancy laws in efforts to close down these homes. Cities and towns pass laws that make it illegal for more than 5 or 6 unrelated people to live in a house—this deliberately targets Oxford House, which usually needs 7 to 10 house members to make rent affordable. Most notably, our research team supplied Oxford House with preliminary research findings when they faced a lawsuit that eventually was ruled on by the Supreme Court. This lawsuit involved one of their homes in the state of Washington and was based on a zoning law that prohibited more than five unrelated people from living in one dwelling. In reality, the surrounding community feared a depreciation of their property values, and our research illustrated the baselessness of these fears. Oxford House won the suit—and the win reverberated far and wide. It set a precedent protecting other Oxford Houses, similar residences, and halfway houses. We hoped that the positive publicity would translate to greater understanding of the service Oxford House provides.

In one study, our team (Jason, Groh, et al., 2008) examined how the number of residents in Oxford House affected residents' individual outlooks for recovery. The Oxford House organization recommends that 8 to 12 individuals reside in each house, as that number helps reduce the cost per person and increases the frequency of support. Therefore, we predicted that Oxford Houses with more people would show improved outcomes compared to those with fewer people. We found that a larger house size corresponded with less criminal and aggressive behavior. These results were used in five court cases, which successfully argued against closing Oxford Houses that had more than five or six nonrelated residents. After providing several lawyers with material for their zoning case in North Carolina, I received this letter from Paul Molloy:

> Lenny—Thanks for your timely input for Scott and Greg in their efforts to resolve the zoning case in Garner, NC. You gave them the key yesterday for getting the city to agree to a consent order. Thank you. As I understand the settlement we will be able to have eight residents in the house in question. [The dispute has been ongoing for six years!] The town will pay attorney's fees, which are about $105,000 and a fine to the Department of Justice. The key to their decision appears to be your research showing that larger houses had better outcomes [less crime, more income etc.] than the smaller ones. Thanks. Once again reason and logic prevailed and more folks are able to benefit. (P. Molloy, personal communication, 2010)

People also worry that these homes will cause a spike in crime rates and make the community undesirable. We wanted to find out if there was any truth to these fears. We investigated crime rates in areas surrounding 42 Oxford Houses and 42 houses that were not Oxford Houses in a large city. A city-run Global Information Systems (GIS) website was used to gather crime data including assault, arson, burglary, larceny, robbery, sexual assault, homicide, and car theft over a calendar year. There were absolutely no significant differences between the crime rates in the areas where there was an Oxford House versus the areas where there was not an Oxford House (Deaner, Jason, Aase, & Mueller, 2009).

We next assessed how Oxford House residents interact with their neighborhoods and communities. We found that members participated in community activities for about 11 hours per month (Jason, Schober, & Olson, 2008). Most were involved in activities linked to their recovery. Sixty-three percent mentored others in recovery. Forty-four percent helped to run support groups. On a larger scale, 39% of participants helped inform or advised local agencies or leaders, and 32% were involved in community antidrug campaigns; others worked with young people and helped raise funds. Many members spoke at political events, community meetings, and public hearings. Again, the benefits of Oxford House go well beyond direct help to their members; their progress helps a community.

I recently spoke with a resident of an Illinois Oxford House named James. He mentioned that when he moved into his house after completing a 60-day treatment program, he was grateful to meet seven other people who were all employed and attending self-help group meetings. They served as James's inspiration by example—a powerful and underused motivating force. Those individuals helped James find and maintain a job and abstain from a drug dependence that had plagued him for 30 years. After a few days in the recovery house, James alerted the other residents that drug dealers were using their street as a distribution location. The house members immediately went to talk with the drug dealers and told them that their recovery home was on the block and that a school was also close by. After just one warning, the drug dealers never came back. Other community members noticed that the Oxford House members uprooted a problem that threatened everyone and were extremely grateful to them for making their neighborhood safer. This small win empowered residents and proved that a few individuals can change neighborhoods, one block at a time.

Not only do Oxford Houses help improve their communities, but also they are much less costly compared to other treatment programs. In 2007, the Oxford House organization received about $1.6 million in grants to pay outreach workers to develop and maintain networks of individual Oxford Houses in nine states and the District of Columbia. Only 6% of these costs were used for general and administrative costs. During 2007, Oxford House residents spent $48,800,000 to run the houses' operations. If these same individuals had been housed in traditional, fully staffed halfway houses, the cost to taxpayers would have been $224,388,000 (Oxford House Inc., 2007).

One of my graduate students astutely pointed out that one person's second-order change might be considered first-order change by another. For example, if advocating for mutual-help housing ignores the underlying social issues that create environments that place the individuals at risk in the first place, some might say that it is not second-order change. However, mutual-help recovery housing like Oxford Houses represents second-order change as it can affect larger issues within the community and neighborhood, by reforming the social system recovery into a more empowering one.

Lessons Learned

From my early work in the field, I came to question whether the mentally ill and those addicted to drugs and alcohol were best served in large institutions. I understand that some Americans believe that no one should be dependent upon social services, which our society cannot afford—particularly with looming budget deficits. But nearly 95% of those currently in prison will be released into the community at some point. Most of these ex-offenders are not prepared to reenter society due to a lack of realistic workforce preparation, limited education, minimal financial support, unsafe housing, substandard mental and physical health care, and alcohol and other drug use issues. Even though few adequately funded programs exist to help these people, many feel that it is their own responsibility to overcome their problems. We are clearly at a crossroads.

Allowing vulnerable people suffering from addiction to be discharged from jail or prison into a dangerous, nonsupportive, and often desperate living situation is not acceptable in a civilized society. The third principle of social change is that community coalitions can change power structures that perpetuate first-order institutional ways of treating people. Bottom-up social change movements can create alternative programs that help people in recovery integrate back into safe and supportive communities with low-cost housing options. Providing housing and job support is critical in helping them regain the skills and foundation needed to lead productive lives.

The Oxford House model and other types of programs, such as Delancey Street, dramatically suggest that alternative and creative social approaches can work—and that they can transcend the kinds of polarities that currently threaten our nation (Jason, 1997). Researchers can also challenge restrictions on recovery housing fueled by stereotypes through showing that places like Oxford House can positively affect their communities.

However, obstacles and confusion when working with partners and groups will inevitably arise. Sarason (1976), for example, suggests that government interventions for social problems can undermine the sense of community within social change movements. I've seen this occur many times. As an example, an official at the Substance Abuse Mental Health Services Administration wrote a position paper proposing an expansion of the Oxford House program, using data from our studies. When he finished, however, he complained to me that the Oxford House organization was too disorganized, lacked sufficient infrastructure, and had poor leadership. Such problems, he thought, would inhibit expansion to thousands of homes across the United States. He wanted me to train and monitor recruiters for the expansion. If I agreed, I could ensure the flow of millions of dollars into DePaul University, but it would also betray the fundamental democratic structure of Oxford House. I turned down his offer and told Paul Molloy and the Oxford House organization of this proposed plan. I wanted to preserve our current working relationship and the integrity of the Oxford House model, and in doing so, I prevented a federal department from exerting undue influence on the program. What the program really needed from the government was additional loan support, more recruiters for other states, and help with legal costs accrued by communities that were trying to prevent Oxford Houses from existing in their neighborhoods. Help from the federal government should never involve eliminating the authority or leadership of a successful grassroots organization, as the official wanted to do.

Can democracy work in total institutions or in community group home settings? The broadening self-help movement demonstrates what is possible when people are allowed the power and responsibility to make their own decisions. Yet, few of the trappings of democracy are available to the homeless, those with chronic health conditions, or those who are released from addiction treatment facilities, prisons, or mental institutions. These individuals often have no voice and are excluded from the basic rights that would empower them to create change and help themselves. They need supportive, recovery-based environments where they can participate in society and, most importantly, retain some dignity. Therefore, it is an extremely positive development that a new crop of contemporary revolutionaries, such as those involved in the Oxford House movement, is providing democratic environments to the disenfranchised in neighborhoods and communities throughout our country. Community coalitions, according to the third principle of social change, can be mobilized to transform many of the most serious problems that affect our society. These second-order interventions can revolutionize how we treat our most vulnerable citizens.

Coalition building has been used to confront homelessness, lack of safe housing, and other abuses of power in places around the world. For example, Raj Patel's (2007) book, *Stuffed and Starved*, describes a grassroots movement in Brazil. Millions from the working class have organized in one of the poorest countries in the world to fight for food sovereignty, land reform, ecological sustainability, gender and income equality, and the elimination of worker exploitation. Noam Chomsky has described it as the world's most important social movement (Patel, 2007). Brazil currently stands as the global leader of the soybean industry. For decades, the expansion of soy plantations pushed millions of families off of their land, and the country has been plagued by political upheaval, food riots, violent oppression, and workers in conditions of modern-day slavery. Since the 1960s, union members, impoverished citizens, and the Catholic Church have resisted political oppression and social corruption. These groups joined forces to become a united front in the mid-1980s to create the *Movimento dos Trabalhadores Rurais Sem Terra*, or Landless Rural Workers Movement (MST).

Millions of displaced individuals and families have peacefully occupied unused rural land to fight for agrarian reform and their civil liberties while waiting to reclaim their land. These democratic encampments, consisting of about 12 or 13 families, not only allow members to produce their own food but also provide the basic necessities that the government has not, including education and health care. Survival depends entirely on the voluntary cooperation and creative innovations of each member, as well as their ability to learn from their mistakes. These settlements represent social change within Brazil.

These kinds of models actively involve the community and, besides their primary functions, can help alleviate intractable problems and bring about second-order change. Community coalitions, such as the ones described in this chapter, address the lack of needed social services by making people aware and bringing them in to design solutions. There is a solution: inexpensive, community-based, structured programs that allow people to be reintegrated into society. Delancey Street, Oxford House, and the Brazilian MST movement are excellent examples of this second-order solution in action.

Additional Resources

For the Oxford House story on the *60 Minutes* TV program, visit this site: http://www.oxford-house.org/userfiles/file/oxfordhousevideo.html

As a result of our research with the Oxford House organization, this model was placed in SAMSHA's National Registry of Evidence-Based Programs and Practices: http://www.nrepp.samhsa.gov/ViewIntervention.aspx?id=223

Some countries have attempted an innovative albeit controversial policy. In 2001, Portugal abolished all criminal penalties for personal possession of drugs. Instead of jail time, those found guilty of possessing small amounts of drugs are provided appropriate treatment. With decriminalization, illegal drug use among teens actually declined and rates of new HIV infections dropped (Szalavitz, 2009). For more information, visit this site: http://www.time.com/time/health/article/0,8599,1893946,00.html

The Drug Policy Alliance is an organization devoted to dialoguing about alternatives (e.g., legalization of marijuana, decriminalizing the possession of small amounts of drugs, etc.) to our current drug policy. Find more information at this site: http://www.drugpolicy.org/about-drug-policy-alliance

A Frontline PBS program on deinstitutionalization can be found that this site: http://www.pbs.org/wgbh/pages/frontline/shows/asylums/special/excerpt.html

For a look inside a mental health court, where people with mental illness who are facing prison time are given probation with required mental health treatment instead, visit this site: http://www.pbs.org/wgbh/pages/frontline/released/inside/

To view the video "From Madhouse to Our House," which explores the concept of using programs such as recovery homes to support those with mental illness, visit these sites:
Part 1: http://www.youtube.com/watch?v=gnTJYtzlVkc
Part 2: http://www.youtube.com/watch?v=oZQ159HmgM0&feature=related

Beginning in about 1970, psychiatric survivor activism involved alternatives to the forced psychiatric drugging of the mental health system. For more information visit this site: http://www.mindfreedom.org/kb/act/movement-history

For an interview of community organizer George Goehl by Bill Moyers on how people can fight back against self-rewarding actions of banks and corporations, visit this site: http://billmoyers.com/segment/organizer-george-goehl-on-people-power/

Building coalitions for change is also beginning to occur in the corporate world. Seven states have passed a law that creates a new corporate class of "benefit corporations." These companies bridge the gap between the nonprofit world and traditional for-profit enterprises by including social and environmental change in their corporate mission and working not only for profits but also for a positive impact on society. Hundreds of companies have now been certified as benefit corporations, which protects them from lawsuits by shareholders who would want the companies to focus purely on maximizing profits. The certification allows these companies to pursue a broader set of interests involving how they care for their employees, the environment, and the community and is a positive step toward creating new groups dedicated to second-order change. These developments are described in a 2012 PBS NewsHour broadcast at this site: http://www.pbs.org/newshour/bb/business/jan-june12/bcorps_02–29.html

The Consumer Conscience Study has found a new activist consumer and that 76% of Americans believe that "business bears as much responsibility as government in promoting social change". Globally, 70% of consumers say they will avoid products of unethical companies. For more information visit this site: http://eurorscg.mynewsdesk.com/pressrelease/view/euro-rscg-worldwide-reveals-76-of-americans-say-business-bears-as-much-responsibility-as-government-in-driving-social-change-746361

Diamandis and Kotler's 2012 book *Abundance* makes a strong case that socially conscious entrepreneurs along with innovations in information-based technologies have the capacity to significantly improve global standards of living in the next few decades.

4

Creating Communities to Foster Success

Second-order change takes time. Progress can be gradual and uneven, and there will be setbacks along the way. We have already examined how patience and a long-term commitment—the fourth principle of social change—were critical aspects of movements to reduce tobacco use, combat stigma and myths about myalgic encephalomyelitis (ME)/chronic fatigue syndrome (CFS), and find adequate recovery housing for those dealing with addiction. The people involved in these movements maintained a long-term commitment to the cause and savored small victories along the way. When spending long periods of time in a particular campaign, activists also frequently create positive change in their own settings. Attention needs to be directed toward creating communities and organizations that encourage and support enduring commitments and provide the opportunity for second-order change. Over the course of decades of dedication to social change movements, I also employed the principles of social change within my work setting at DePaul University.

Built into this fourth principle is a reality that should be obvious but often is not: The longer the effort to bring about meaningful change, the deeper the change agents' understanding of what needs to be done. By devoting years to building a mutual relationship between partners in the community, all parties become more invested and committed. This is well illustrated by our DePaul team's deepening relationship of mutual benefits that formed over a 20-year period with Paul Molloy and the Oxford House organization.

Both patience and persistence are even more essential in opposing powerful vested interests intent on maintaining the status quo and in amassing coalitions to confront institutionalized abuses of power. Our own history provides ample examples: When George Washington faced crushing defeats at the hands of the British, his persistence and unwillingness to give up allowed his army to defeat the greatest military power of its time. Without the deep perseverance and steadfast vision of our greatest American president, Abraham Lincoln, the United States might have been splintered. Even though 2% of the U.S. population died during the Civil War, Lincoln's courage and determination led to the emancipation of one in seven Americans who were slaves. Equally brave were the passionate women who were committed to win the right to vote—another landmark victory.

The women's rights movement is an excellent example of patient, effective, second-order change here in the United States. The women's movement first took shape as a national campaign for women's suffrage in the 19th century. Although Susan B. Anthony and Elizabeth Cady Stanton are considered the movement's prominent early leaders, the struggle was, in many ways, a patchwork of local skirmishes and small wins. In small towns, state houses, and territorial legislatures across the country, women fought for what is now considered a universal right.

Once the right to vote was secured for women through the Nineteenth Amendment in 1920, a second struggle ensued. It centered on issues of equality with regard to pay, property rights, and sexual freedom. These issues, though never fully resolved, progressed slowly throughout the middle of the 20th century. With the publication of books such as the *Second Sex* by Simone de Beauvoir (1973) and the *Feminine Mystique* by Betty Friedan (1963), the second wave of American feminism rose to prominence in the early 1960s. These works and others gave voice to issues that were increasingly preoccupying a generation of educated and independent-minded women who were among the largest number of women to attend college in the country's history. Although social and professional barriers that women regularly confronted 50 years ago are unthinkable today, universal rights for women have still not been achieved, and progress has been slow. For example, the proposed Equal Rights Amendment to the U.S. Constitution, which stated, "Equality of rights under the law shall not be denied or abridged by the United States or by any State on account of sex," first proposed in 1923, has failed to be ratified after a 60-year effort. In addition, although women currently outnumber men in the workforce, women's wages still lag behind. Meg Bond, a leader in feminist community theory, has focused her work on bringing attention to issues of gender and race in the community and the workplace (Plous, 2009). Her book *Workplace Chemistry: Promoting Diversity Through Organizational Change* (2007), examines the 7-year change process that a manufacturing firm underwent to create a more diverse and accepting workplace. Through using the principles of community psychology, Bond has helped empower women and other underrepresented groups. Additionally, while the status of women has improved over the last half-century with regard to sexual and reproductive issues, the current trends in state legislatures and even in the U.S. House of Representatives threaten women's access to basic reproductive health care. Public funding of women's health programs that low-income women find essential is now seriously being threatened. Although important second-order changes have occurred within the women's rights movement by challenging those in power, more mobilized efforts over time will be needed to deal with these and other unmet needs.

History also demonstrates that patience and long-term commitment are vital when working toward political change in oppressive leadership, as it often takes decades for it to occur. Grassroots campaigns that tried to overthrow communist dictators in Hungary in 1956 and Czechoslovakia in 1968 were squashed by the Soviet Union. However, by 1989, Poland's Solidarity movement was able to win the first free election, and soon after, the foreign ministers of Austria and Hungary cut the barbed wire fence separating the two nations, which allowed thousands of East Germans to travel to Hungary in order to emigrate to the West. This movement of people opened the floodgates to the West and ultimately heralded the crumbling of the Berlin Wall and the later dissolution of the Soviet Union.

Not all social changes are grand and sweeping; some are narrow and quickly resolved. A neighborhood group might want potholes fixed at a busy intersection. This issue may be addressed quickly by an alderman or other city official. However, for most issues involving social policies that affect larger numbers of people, and in which a variety of groups hold divergent points of view, bringing about change occurs more slowly and over long periods of time.

Some people simply have more endurance to maintain a long-term commitment to social change. They are comfortable with ambiguity and able to persevere in the face of uncertainty. A coalition of neighborhood groups might strive for change on an issue for years with limited success, yet those efforts might build a social movement that is eventually able to triumph. Being willing and able to appreciate the smallest of achievements in a long path toward a larger objective is a critical trait that allows an activist to sustain enthusiasm over time. Also, well-developed interpersonal skills and resilience help create a sense of community within a group, enabling the group to sustain activism even if its cause is attacked. Activists recognize the importance of personal relationships in these movements. The connections that activists weave between individuals and organizations are often instrumental in forming or energizing new institutions or community action groups.

In his recent book *The Social Animal,* David Brooks (2011) explores the thinking that occurs below the level of awareness, within the unconscious realm, that affects our biases, genetic predispositions, character traits, and social norms. It can also influence our successes and fulfillment in powerful ways and involves traits such as being energetic, being persistent after setbacks, and accurately reading people and situations. In Malcolm Gladwell's (2005) popular book *Blink*, he describes instantaneous impressions that happen in a blink of an eye when we make snap judgments or have feelings when interacting with others. Feelings bubble up from our adaptive unconscious in seconds. Though they are not always right, they can be a powerful aid in our efforts to bring about second-order change.

Decisions that are made based on intuition can often be as good as, or even better than, ones made from a slow and deliberate process. During a psychotherapy class in graduate school, my fellow students and I listened to tapes of our therapeutic interventions with patients. My professor, Dr. Sidney Rubin, would play only about a 5- to 10-second segment of the tape and ask us what we had learned about the client or our therapeutic intervention. We would then spend an hour processing just a few seconds. We learned from cues such as silence, tone of voice, indirect verbal messages, our feelings toward the patients, and hundreds of other unconscious dimensions that constantly transpire during everyday interactions. Today, this is called "thin slicing," and some psychologists, such as John Gottman, have mastered this technique. In one study, Gottman was able to predict with 90% accuracy whether a newlywed couple would end up getting divorced after viewing a brief videotape of the couple's interaction. He coded for interpersonal issues such as criticism, defensiveness, stonewalling, and contempt by simply observing the couple's interactions (Gottman & Silver, 1999). Paying attention to these kinds of details and our intuition can be formidable tools in understanding the interpersonal dynamics among individuals, coalitions, and community groups that patiently rally to bring about social justice.

Some individuals may not be suited for the type of social policy activism described in this book. For a person who needs to perceive immediate, tangible signs of concrete success from his or her activities, participation in these types of long-term campaigns for social change could be frustrating. Although some of these individuals may not have the temperament for the protracted battles that often occur with social change, they can hold a particular role or task within an overall advocacy effort. Those who oversee and manage efforts for social change can create different roles for individuals with different aspirations and dispositions.

Having an intuition that one's vision will be fulfilled in the long run can be a sustaining and life-affirming force in the face of oppressive conditions. Social change leaders must often conjure up a dream and sustain it with hope in order to overcome discouragement and cynicism. An optimistic, can-do attitude can be invigorating and help create the perception that the hurdles an activist encounters along the way are merely obstacles to be overcome, rather than insurmountable barriers.

Leadership

A close friend recently called me and told me he had lost his job. I was stunned—my friend had worked as an administrator and teacher for a local university for almost three decades. He was one of the best-known and well-liked figures on the small campus, with a smile and a greeting for everyone: faculty members, staff members, janitorial workers, and security guards—not to mention the students. Though this man may have looked bureaucratic and conservative, dressed in his characteristic suit and tie, the hundreds of students who sought his guidance found him to be unfailingly patient, knowledgeable, and kind. One spring day, he was unexpectedly summoned to the provost's office, where he was greeted by the solemn head of the university, along with a representative from human resources. My friend was told that his job had been eliminated, and he was given a choice: sign a contract agreeing to leave the university in exchange for a paltry severance or be fired. Of course, there was no mention that a younger person would assume his position for half the pay. Upon signing, my friend joined the ranks of the unemployed and was left to wonder how he might support his family and his wife, who did not have a job. The situation was perversely ironic: The university's stated mission was to serve the poor and provide opportunities to the disenfranchised. More and more, today's society is favoring profit at the expense of honoring interpersonal connections and bonds built through years of service.

Leadership in many companies and organizations is oppressive, with rigid systems of control, stagnant bureaucracies, and few incentives for creativity (Peters & Waterman, 1982). However, putting people first and making sure their needs are met not only increases teamwork, innovation, and motivation but also revitalizes community organizations. In *The Powers to Lead*, Joseph Nye (2008) posits five leadership characteristics: emotional intelligence, vision, communication, the use of Machiavellian tactics, and contextual intelligence. By making use of these characteristics, leaders can transform schools, communities, organizations, and social change movements.

The activist leader uses emotional intelligence to build support while avoiding personal fights within the movement, as there are often passionate and differing opinions that can shatter a coalition. In other words, successful social activists need to move beyond their egos in order to dispassionately manage conflict. They need to be passionate about and attached to the larger cause, but detached from the personal issues that detract from building momentum for social justice.

Nye's second leadership quality is vision. This quality is crucial to be able to clearly distinguish and differentiate between first- and second-order change. Setting our sights on the larger structural need is the first step. Small steps are an applauded, welcome part of the process, but a social change agent who accepts these steps as final victories has lost sight of his or her broader vision. At times, leaders must dig deeply, rally, and remind fellow activists of their overriding goal, while also recognizing how far the movement has come.

A clear, accessible, and understandable vision is necessary to inspire commitment and passion; thus, communication is Nye's next leadership characteristic. In the 1990s, comprehensive health care reform failed because the Clinton administration was unable to communicate its vision to the public. This crippled them when it was time to build consensus with major constituent groups. Then, they were bombarded by negative ads from the powerful insurance and health care interests. President Obama succeeded in finally passing a comprehensive health care package due, in part, to his bottom-up approach: He communicated with multiple groups as he brought them into the evolving vision. It was their support that finally helped to pass this legislation. However, just a few years later, this landmark legislation became a major issue, both in the Supreme Court and during the 2012 presidential election, highlighting that what has broad endorsement at one point in time can very well become controversial at another time due to political reasons.

Nye's fourth leadership quality is perhaps the most controversial: the use of Machiavellian tactics in accomplishing goals. These tactics, however, are not just reserved for authoritarian types who typically want to crush democratic principles. In fact, many of the most successful change agents throughout history have used Machiavellian tactics. Basically, they are a mix of strategies that help to equalize power, and thus aid in correcting social injustices. Jeffrey Wigand, the former tobacco executive, broke confidentiality contracts when he testified against his former employer, Brown & Williamson. He maintained that executives knew that their cigarettes were addictive and contained additives that directly increased the risk of disease. Wigand used Machiavellian tactics to uncover these truths and bravely stood up to the unbridled corrupt power of the tobacco industry. This is not to say that a worthy end justifies any means; there are boundaries that simply should not be crossed.

The final leadership quality is contextual intelligence. When activists try to manage the thousands of bits of information they encounter about any social policy initiative, they must be able to separate critical issues requiring immediate attention from less pressing matters. This quality is needed to prioritize and evaluate situations and recognize that what may have been possible at one time might not be possible at another. When I was appointed to the CFS Advisory Committee in 2007, several people suggested that I recommend increasing the Centers for Disease Control and Prevention's (CDC) funding for ME/CFS research. At the time, however, I was not in any position of power to request funding or to press my concerns about how the current CDC funding was being spent. Rather, I realized that if I resisted these pressures and amassed information on how the CDC funding was spent, I would buy some time until the right opportunity arose. If a moment is not right for second-order change, smaller wins may be achievable—and should be appreciated for what they are. Waiting for the right contextual moment can make positive second-order change more likely to succeed.

I have had the good fortune over the years to have many excellent managers who were responsible for supervising staff on several university–community collaborations, all of whom demonstrated emotional intelligence, communication, and vision. For example, as they supervised their staff, they constantly assigned tasks that were concrete and achievable. Additionally, when the tasks were completed, these managers were quick to provide praise and positive feedback. These supervisors were able to create an environment in which our staff enjoyed coming to work each day as they felt both appreciated and that they were part of something important. Leadership like this can invigorate a workplace and create a space that is meaningful and satisfying to be part of; it represents what may be considered a small but important win.

Leadership and power are inherently related. According to Loomer (1976), we are more familiar with unilateral power: advancing one's own power as others lose power. In contrast, relational power mixes both the ability to affect and to be affected by power, ultimately relating to power in a way that is beneficial for both parties. Perhaps as Loomer suggests, we need a new image of power: one that no longer puts community and power at odds, but rather encourages constant interaction and a reciprocal relationship between the two.

Small Wins

In this book, I have provided many examples of how action and mobilization follow a small win. This principle is easily confused with first-order change, or Band-aid approaches to social problems, criticized in chapter 1. Small wins might not be as dramatic or compelling as working toward ending homelessness, for example, but think of it this way: If Housing First or Oxford House is able to help just one or two people find safe and affordable housing, this is a small—but resonant—win. By showing that organizations have been able to house the homeless in livable conditions, activists can push a policy agenda that may later provide all individuals who are homeless with affordable and decent housing. Karl Weick defined the concept of a small win in the following way:

> [A] small change is either a change in a relatively unimportant variable (people tend to agree on what is an important change) or a relatively unimportant change in an important variable.... Small wins often originate as solutions that single out and define as problems those specific, limited conditions for which they can serve as the complete remedy. (Weick, 1984, p. 43)

Small wins help sustain and mobilize citizen groups to continue to pursue even larger objectives. Putting up the little no-smoking sign in my office and getting people to stop blowing smoke in my face was a small win. It turned out to have very big consequences. That success energized me, and I was excited to try such steps in other places, which resulted in the first nonsmoking section in the university's cafeteria. Showing that it was possible to establish a place where non-smokers could eat their food without having to breathe in smoke was also a small win.

Saul Alinsky (1969) was one of the most famous community organizers, whose lifelong passion was motivating people to take action.

> Alinsky (1971) has noted that most American citizens do not partici-pate in the important decisions affecting their lives. He suggests that when the alienation is very severe, the community organizer needs to create conditions in which small victories can occur. Thus, in dis-cussing why he is willing to work on small problems (such as making one apartment building more inhabitable), he says: "we organize to get rid of four-legged rats so we can get on to removing two-legged rats."…(Bogat & Jason, 2000)

Alinsky knew that starting with smaller problems (and actions) and succeed-ing was a first step toward tackling larger, more intimidating social problems. Alinsky has addressed one of the most difficult questions in social change: How can activists stay committed to a cause? In the meaningful pursuit of social jus-tice, the importance of small wins cannot be overemphasized. Another core issue is emotional: how to stay calm and focused when attacked, humiliated, or unfairly criticized as a consequence of activism. At times, activists find them-selves in vicious battles among other activists—such as when the largest ME/CFS patient organization had been funded for years by the CDC to brand the term "CFS," although it was despised by the majority of other patient groups. Not only can these battles cause the splintering of needed coalitions, but also they can foster feelings of apathy or hopelessness. Whether facing attacks from former allies, challenges to their funding sources, or even threats to their per-sonal safety, social change agents must endure many assaults on their commit-ment and stamina. Dogged optimism, community support, and spiritual beliefs can provide somewhat of a shield, but there is no doubt that small wins func-tion as a life-affirming oasis for activists.

Small wins can be visible—a reduction of deaths following John Snow's removal of a London water pump to stop a cholera epidemic—or much more nuanced. A victory may be a refusal to stop protesting or the willingness to endure pain without giving in. Those who have been imprisoned can become heroic figures, and, through their victimization, they become larger than life and invoke a powerful, inspiring call to action. Imprisoned for decades, Nelson Mandela kept his hope—and that of his supporters—alive that one day the South African system of apartheid would be abolished. Aun San Suu Kyi, 1991

Nobel Peace Prize winner and leader of the New League for Democracy Party in Burma, spent 15 of the past 22 years under house arrest due to her political opposition to the ruling military junta of her country. After decades of tireless advocacy work to free political prisoners and promote democratic reform in Burma, Suu Kyi and her party may finally be reentering the political stage, supported by the international community that has followed and supported her cause. Even tragedies can spur progress when change is enacted to prevent future loss: Coal miners have been killed through negligent mining practices, but the publicity surrounding their deaths led to new laws and safety regulations.

The patience and long-term commitment that often lead to small wins are frequently influenced by the nature of the settings where we work and the people we involve in our collaborations. Some settings provide support, confidence, and resources to embark on new projects, even if they take years to accomplish. This factor is easy to overlook, but the nature of where we work can influence and contribute to the success of our second-order change efforts by increasing our fortitude to stay with an issue over time. The ideology and values of the environments in which we work also provide a shaping influence on social activists. For me, the field of community psychology has provided me the support, confidence, and resources to embark on new projects over the past four decades.

Community Psychology

The field of community psychology emerged in the late 1960s. It was born out of a desire of some psychologists to become more active in working to solve the social and community problems confronting the United States at that time (Cowen, 1973; Kloos et al., 2012; Levine & Levine, 1970). This perspective was first formulated in 1965 at a conference in Swampscott, Massachusetts (Bennett et al., 1966). Speakers stressed the need to emphasize prevention and to widen the scope of our interventions to include more environmental and structural approaches. People at this conference agreed to call this new field "community psychology." It would emphasize new roles for psychologists and mental health workers. For example, people who were affected by problems would themselves act as change agents within their communities by developing prevention programs, working for community change, consulting with community agencies, and collaborating with community members (Iscoe, Bloom, & Spielberger, 1977).

As the field evolved, certain recurring themes emerged: emphasizing prevention over treatment, highlighting competencies over weaknesses, collaborating across disciplines, exploring ecological understandings of people within their environment, promoting diversity, and focusing on community building as a mode of intervention (Kelly, 1990; Moritsugu, Wong, & Duffy, 2009). Jim Kelly, one of the founders of this movement, developed the "ecological model" during his career, which proposed theories of how people become effective and adaptive in different social environments. This model continues to be a guiding framework for understanding behavior in interaction with its social and cultural contexts. A fundamental notion with this ecological approach is the use of several different methods to increase our understanding of complex relationships and systems.

One key aspect of this ecological approach is a collaborative relationship between the researcher and participant: Concepts and hypotheses are developed and tested by both parties. Many feminists, among others, adhere to this method; they believe that, first and foremost, we listen to others from their points of view. People involved in research projects should be included as participants, not merely as subjects. For example, a graduate student and I once worked on evaluating a neighborhood antigang organization called Broader Urban Involvement and Leadership Development (BUILD). This organization, located in a high-crime area of Chicago, develops community-building efforts to discourage adolescents from joining gangs. When we first visited the office, we were introduced to several BUILD members, all of whom had multiple tattoos and had been former gang members. Their outward appearance was a bit intimidating, but they were warm and sought help in evaluating their program. The BUILD organizers were interested in having us evaluate one of their programs that dealt with school children at risk for joining gangs. We worked collaboratively with the BUILD staff on a study in which children at some schools participated only in antigang classroom information sessions while children at other schools were provided the same antigang classroom session but also after-school sports activities (Thompson & Jason, 1988). In addition, the BUILD staff made it possible for the youth in the after-school program to travel out of their neighborhoods to participate in events and activities with similar groups from other locations. About 10% of children who were only provided the antigang classroom sessions ultimately joined gangs, but none of the youth who participated in this community- and school-based intervention joined gangs. By giving these at-risk children alternative activities and a sense of fellowship and community, we were able to document that the BUILD program served as a protective buffer against joining gangs, and, in turn, the organization was able to show their supporters these important outcomes.

The ecological approach also works within long-term, collaborative relationships. By actively involving participants in planning community action, participants gain support, identify resources, and become better problem solvers for future issues. Actions that arise from active, embedded participants are more likely to endure. In using this approach, community psychologists can better appreciate the culture and unique needs of the community, which greatly increases the chance of benefiting the community. This approach analyzes and employs community traditions to respond to community problems, helps provide positive settings for people who need continued support after a formal treatment program ends, works to effect health care changes, and assesses positive and negative ripple effects of a second-order intervention.

In his book *The Power of Collaborative Solutions*, author Tom Wolff (2010) describes his own experiences using community psychology principles. They include involving the people most affected by the problem, focusing on a community's assets rather than deficits, creating a democratic process in which everyone has a voice, taking action involving social change, and engaging people at the spiritual level. Olson, Viola, and Fromm-Reed's (2011) model of community organizing and direct action also incorporates many powerful principles, similar to the principles of social change discussed in this book. Within the social work field, Rothman, Erlich, and Teresa (1976) have long promoted comparable principles, including the need for mutual respect in collaboration among researchers and practitioners in the community.

Fryer (2008) has pointed out that this field has been dominated by a U.S.-centric vision and methodology of intervention (most leading journals and textbooks are produced by U.S.-based faculty and training programs). Still, important contributions have been made to a global community psychology by psychologists from countries around the world (Reich, Riemer, Prilleltensky, & Montero, 2007; Vázquez, Pérez Jiménez, Rodríguez, & Bou, 2010).

Although internationally, activists often have to deal with societal standards and ways of doing business that differ from the context to which we are accustomed in the United States, one psychologist in Mexico has used many of the principles of community psychology, as well as Nye's leadership qualities and the principles of social change, to bring widespread improvements to health, education, and development in her country. Dr. Susan Pick founded the Mexican Institute for Family and Population Research in Mexico City (IMIFAP) in 1985 along with other psychologists who were initially interested in improving the reproductive health of Mexican women. Dr. Pick had done extensive research on the lives of women in *Ciudad Netzahualcoyotl*, a poor town on the outskirts of Mexico City, and developed her first sexuality education program, "Planning your life," based on life skills and empowerment, for these women (Pick de Weiss, 1987). The program was successful in improving the women's knowledge of contraceptives and giving them skills and a voice to negotiate family planning with their husbands. One woman said this of the program:

> We started to realize that there were many barriers: of being afraid to speak out, of being ashamed to say what we think, of not counting, of people not even seeing me.... [W]e learned that there was more than one way of doing things.... Most women who have been part of the workshops don't stay quiet anymore. Now at least they protest, and many also take action. (Pick & Sirkin, 2010)

Dr. Pick and her colleagues adapted the workshop for use as a sexuality education program for children (Pick de Weiss, Vargas Trujillo, et al., 1991) and were intent on implementing the program at a national level. At that time, nearly one of every five children in Mexico was born to a woman under the age of 20 (Pick de Weiss, Atkin, Gribble, & Andrade-Palos, 1991); it was imperative that children and youth be educated about their sexual rights and the use of contraception. You can imagine the opposition she faced in a predominantly Catholic and conservative nation in the late 1980s. Dr. Pick's program was revolutionary, and probably more progressive than many sex education programs implemented in parts of the United States today: Students would have open discussions about the facts of protecting against unwanted pregnancy and disease and about their control over their own sexual health and behaviors. Dr. Pick had a clear vision of how to implement second-order change regarding high rates of adolescent pregnancies in Mexico.

Employing the use of Nye's "contextual intelligence," Dr. Pick knew that involving the Ministry of Education was the crucial next step to scale up "Planning your life" in Mexican schools. Gaining his support, however, would not be an easy task—the current minister would not even accept an appointment to meet with Dr. Pick. She showed great patience and persistence and perhaps even started to annoy the minister's secretary when she began arriving every morning to sit on a bench outside his office and await her chance to talk to the minister. After about a month of converting the minister's lobby into her makeshift office, she was granted an appointment. This critical first step led to the minister approving a pilot run of the program with a small sample of public Mexican middle and high schools. It was a great success and a small win, but Dr. Pick still had several obstacles to overcome.

The conservative press began to smear Dr. Pick and her organization's work, and Dr. Pick realized that to make any headway, she would need to negotiate with these opposition groups (Pick & Sirkin, 2010). In particular, she needed to convince prominent conservative women, many of whom had husbands who controlled the political power in Mexico City. Dr. Pick had identified the true power holders, but her first attempt at negotiation was a failure. The women practically ran her out of the room with their cries of "sexual debauchery" that would lead to "the destruction of Mexican youth" (Pick & Sirkin, 2010).

Dr. Pick tried a second approach and, this time, used emotional intelligence, effective communication, and a bit of Machiavellian tactics. She began meeting with these women one on one for breakfast and relating to them as their peer— a fellow Mexican woman. Slowly, these women opened up to her. Many of them expressed similar marital troubles and difficulties as the women from *Ciudad Netzahualcoyotl* had expressed: a lack of control over family planning and a sense of shame and guilt about their own sexuality. By relating to these women on a personal level, not only did Dr. Pick begin to have more open conversations about her sexuality education program, but also these women even hired her to conduct the original "Planning your life" workshop for them, behind their husbands' backs (Pick & Sirkin, 2010). Dr. Pick had garnered the support she needed; she created a powerful coalition of support out of a group of women who initially had vehemently opposed her ideas. Eventually, she was able to have health and family planning education included in the national legislation.

The story of sexuality education in Mexico is just one example of how Dr. Pick used leadership skills and social change principles to bring about second-order change in her country. She then took the lessons learned and the research conducted about the sexual health program and went on to develop other workshops to promote health and education, using the same theoretical model of life skills and empowerment (Pick, Beers, & Grossman-Crist, 2011). Dr. Pick also stayed with her organization, and through achieving one small win after another over 26 years, IMIFAP has grown to be one of the most recognized and influential nongovernmental organizations in Mexico. In total, over 40 different preventative health, education, and development programs have been created, and 19 million people in Mexico, the United States, Europe, and Latin America have been reached. IMIFAP is a prime example of how starting local and creating changes in your own settings and communities can lead to broad, large-scale social change.

IMIFAP also embraces the idea of working collaboratively with the community. Every community-based "I want to, I can" workshop that is implemented is led by community members themselves who are trained beforehand by IMIFAP. Sometimes these facilitators already hold leadership positions within the community. Other times they are women who never finished high school and never felt empowered to speak up in their own families, much less lead group discussions about how to better communicate with spouses and children. The organization first instills a sense of self-worth, agency, and intrinsic motivation in community members, who then transfer these qualities to others along with practical skills and knowledge about topics like violence, addiction, or obesity prevention (Pick & Sirkin, 2010). Training a few dozen teachers or community members to replicate the program on a larger scale also ensures that the benefits to the community remain, even after the program has been conducted. The community itself has the human capital necessary to replicate the workshops for years to come, even without continued funding. The organization's success shows that applying community psychology's principles of working within your community, focusing on prevention, and involving community members as active participants can be an effective way to bring about large-scale, second-order change. Successful community psychology interventions like Dr. Pick's have demonstrated to community psychologists the importance of establishing a set of practice competencies for the field, such as community assessment and program evaluation and community organizing and coalition building; these competencies will further define and promote the capabilities of the field (e.g., Bond, Hostetler, Tran, & Haynes, 2012).

Sparks That Initiate Social Change Often Rely on Long-Term Emerging Infrastructures

Although understanding leadership and the inner qualities of principal agents of change is important, understanding the role of the community and resources within that community is equally vital. In the field of community psychology, we talk in terms of *settings*. Occasionally, change agents do operate independently, but, more often than not, they need community support—a tool that generally garners less attention than a charismatic individual agent—to truly bring about change. For example, Mother Teresa had a network of church groups that provided her with funding and personnel—she could not have had the success she enjoyed without them. Behind-the-scenes infrastructure is often critical to the long-term survivability of a social change movement. The infrastructure can even be electronic: Sites like Facebook, Twitter, and Ushahidi (a crowd-sourcing website that helps document abuse) have become essential tools for social activists to mobilize their causes. Activists around the globe have utilized these tools (often anonymously in the face of government reprisal) to organize the kind of citizen uprisings that have occurred in Iran, Libya, Tunisia, and Egypt.

In January of 2011, dramatic changes in the Arab world led to the ousting of President Zine El Abidine Ben Ali of Tunisia. Violent protests throughout the country occurred after Mohamed Al Bouazzizi, a 26-year-old university graduate, set himself on fire in protest of crippling unemployment problems. Although tragic for this young man, his defiant act helped initiate mass social movements with a vision for change throughout the Middle East. After the Tunisian revolution, throngs of young people rallied in Egypt to put an end to President Hosni Mubarak's 30-year totalitarian regime in early 2011. Like most dramatic shifts in power, success did not come quickly in Egypt. It was instead a result of the culmination of events and the development of infrastructures over the course of years of action. These events highlight the need for the fourth principle—patience and a long-term commitment—and the tenant of community psychology that emphasizes understanding the history that came before a movement for social change.

In 2008, an activist group known as the April 6 Movement uploaded images to Facebook that depicted scenes of abuse perpetrated by the Egyptian police. These photos spawned tremendous public awareness as they went viral and helped build opposition to the regime. The April 6 Egyptian activists mounted a massive protest by its young members on January 25, 2011, in Cairo's Tahrir Square. Their overwhelming demand was for second-order change in the form of democracy over President Mubarak's dictatorship. The demonstrators flooded Tahrir Square and other locations throughout the city for 18 straight days and nights. When the Egyptian army finally turned on Mubarak and joined the protestors, the writing was on the wall, and Mubarak resigned. He and his regime were overthrown by the power of the Internet, activists, and the mobilization of community forces.

Although credit went to the people working at the grassroots level, the core of this historic change actually began with the Muslim Brotherhood, a group that had been working diligently for change in Egypt since 1928—well before the April 6 activists. Although change can sometimes materialize quickly, forces generating that change in Egypt had been solidifying for decades. For the Muslim Brotherhood, the realization of their vision—the resignation of Mubarak—was an arduous and challenging journey. There were serious divisions within the organization during this critical time in January. The old guard leaders of the Muslim Brotherhood wanted to negotiate with Mubarak, while the younger members demanded his ousting. In a sense, the older Muslim Brotherhood members were out of touch with the younger leadership of the movement. Coalitions for change can often have opposing methods and visions. Nevertheless, it was their joint commitment, and the valuing of each small win, that made the final victory possible. As Egypt ushers in a new era, nothing will be easy. Ousting Mubarak, the common goal, was easy to agree upon. Now it will take hard work and negotiation to ensure that the forces of change produce a democratic state rather than another dictatorship or pseudodemocracy (Calingaert, 2012).

Changes in My Setting

Since 1975, I have been a faculty member at DePaul University, the largest Catholic university in the United States. DePaul is the setting that has sustained and grounded my social change efforts over the years. The university is named for the priest St. Vincent de Paul, who was dedicated to serving the poor in France in the early 1600s, and the university's mission and value of service is compatible with the goals of community psychology. As a community psychologist, my work within my department at DePaul has extended into the community at large. My professional and personal experience within this setting and the principles of this book have helped me achieve some of the small wins that set the stage for larger efforts within the tobacco, ME/CFS, and recovery home arenas. During this time, I made sure to make improvements to my setting, correct abusive practices, revitalize ineffective procedures, and advance the field of community psychology. I believe it is important to critically evaluate underlying assumptions and norms within one's work environment.

Early in my career at DePaul, I had an opportunity to help correct an injustice within my own setting. When I became a faculty member of the graduate clinical psychology training program at DePaul in the mid-1970s, I was alarmed to find virtually no minority students or faculty in the program. I was struck by the irony: Our graduate program focused on helping our students work with underserved populations, but our student body and faculty represented the racial majority. I realized this was an excellent opportunity for social change within my own environment. After talking to other faculty members, we were able to hire a gifted African American clinical psychologist named Dr. LaVome Robinson in 1980. Around the same time, I got to know many outstanding psychology undergraduates as faculty sponsor of the honorary psychology club. I encouraged the president of the club, an African American student, to apply to DePaul's Clinical Psychology PhD program. She had courage, heart, and a fierce determination. However, some of her formal credentials were not as high as other applicants; I knew it would not be an easy task. We strongly argued at our graduate selection committee meeting to admit her to the program because of her good grades, demonstrated leadership qualities, and good personal fit with our program. It was a battle, but we were successful. She became our first African American graduate student, and since then she has had an illustrious career.

This interaction led me to an important realization: Although many academics say they value a wide diversity of people for graduate study, that liberal rhetoric is often compromised by a rigid adherence to standardized test scores or grades. In the mid-1980s, I became the Director of the Clinical Psychology Training program. LaVome Robinson and I (along with other faculty) played a role in continuing to attract and retain other minority students, and by 1990, minorities accounted for over 25% of the clinical graduate students. I had helped bring about some changes to the racial composition of our program as an internal agent of change. By the late 1980s, I was contacted by other clinical training directors who wanted to know how DePaul University had been so successful in bringing so many bright and capable minority students to our program, as they were interested in replicating our successes at their settings.

Other changes I made within my setting dealt with the quality and types of education in the field of psychology that students would receive at DePaul. I was interested in creating classes and programs that would train effective clinical and community psychologists who would go on to do innovative, needed work in their communities. In one instance, I developed a grant-writing graduate community psychology class (Jason & Reyes, 1989). This course focused on the practical skill of writing grants to secure funding for research and community interventions.

I also made changes at the undergraduate level in the early 1980s, helping Ernie Doleys institute a new 2-year human services concentration for clinical psychology majors (Jason, 1984; Jason, Kennedy, & Taylor, 2001; Jason & Smith, 1980). Students would learn important skills for applying to a graduate school or beginning a career in human services, such as how to collect research data and interview a client. In their senior year, students would intern at a mental health agency. In this class, each student was asked to tackle two projects: one in personal self-control, such as quitting smoking, and another involving trying to bring about change to an aspect of their environment. For example, one student in this concentration studied a busy intersection near a neighborhood school and noted that even though hundreds of children crossed the street every week, only two-thirds of cars stopped before passing through. We brought the data to the elementary school's principal and a local political official, and a stop sign was soon installed. Learning through an experience like this one, a small, yet immensely gratifying win, is an invaluable lesson.

While DePaul already had a class in community psychology at the undergraduate level, I wanted to increase DePaul's community psychology focus in order to train future community advocates of social justice. I, along with Susan McMahon and Olya Rabin-Belyaev, was able to help create a community psychology concentration for undergraduates that differed from the more clinical human services concentration. Joseph Ferrari and I created the Community Psychology PhD program, which was independent of the Clinical Psychology PhD program. As a result, we now train undergraduate and graduate students in community psychology so that they can examine the bases of oppression and learn how to develop empowerment strategies for people who are marginalized from the mainstream through racism, sexism, heterosexism, or other forms of prejudice and discrimination. They also learn to conduct action research to understand and address social problems and evaluate community-based programs and nonprofit social service agencies to build organizational capacity.

Besides my work in helping create these courses and programs within DePaul, I wanted to help create support systems with a professional community psychology organization (Jason et al., 1985). The Midwestern Eco-Community Psychology conference has existed for over 30 years (Davis & Jason, 1982). Each year, the conference gives graduate students an opportunity to present their research and network with other students and faculty. Several students have landed jobs and training opportunities through the connections they developed at these annual, informal conferences. These conferences, which have now spread to other parts of the country, promote networking bases among students, faculty, and people in the field. One year, the graduate students suggested to the faculty members that, since the conference was for graduate students, the graduate students themselves, rather than the faculty, should be in charge of planning the next conference. Every conference since then has been fully planned and run by graduate students. These small wins within my professional organization and my host setting at DePaul helped sustain my energy and commitment to second-order change. As difficult as the struggle may be in the external world for social justice, I could always feel some satisfaction for the types of changes that I had helped bring about at DePaul University.

Over the last decade, I helped to create the Center for Community Research at DePaul University, which I run as director. The center has focused on three research areas that are based on an ecological perspective: youth tobacco prevention, ME/CFS stigma reduction, and recovery from alcohol and other drug use problems within the Oxford House model. Researchers and community partners collaborate in research and contribute to the process of social change. The center uses research to inform action, which may in turn enable positive change. It exists to build a connection between the world of scientific investigation and informed action. These kinds of organizations try to link research and practice. Kelly (1970) has described the role of community psychology as a bridge between the university and community action. This bridge allows the DePaul Center for Community Research to directly affect the communities with which we interact, as well as keep relevant local, state, and federal agencies informed of our mutual work. As such, we have been able to influence the policies and views held by individuals, universities, communities, and government agencies regarding our areas of research.

Our center operates on a horizontal structure: a person with a PhD oversees the graduate students, employees, and volunteers on each grant-funded project. Even the receptionist at the front desk is a research assistant. There are no individuals who do only secretarial, budget management, or administrative work; rather, we all share in these duties, and all staff and volunteers are expected to work on a research project. The shared responsibility fosters more commitment and enthusiasm for research, as jobs are rotated and do not become repetitious or monotonous. On the other hand, we are rather leanly staffed for the more prosaic work that always comes with grants. I answer my own phone and do not have a secretary, just like the rest of the staff at my center.

Closer to home, the center also provides invaluable experience to the research assistants who work here. Often, they work at the center for 1 or 2 years after completing their undergraduate studies in order to receive important preparation and guidance in applying to graduate schools in the field of psychology. Many also leave the center having developed a lifelong commitment to social justice issues. Caroline, a former research assistant at the center, was greatly affected by her work with mothers at Oxford House.

> The most difficult stories to hear were those from mothers who had lost custody of their children due to drug and alcohol abuse. Addiction had caused them to miss moments and, in some cases, years, of their children's lives. Plus, substance use during pregnancy has had deleterious effects on their children, many of which did not become apparent until the children were older. I saw women coming to grips with this reality. I hope to work with low-income, urban, at-risk children. The center gave me an invaluable insight into the lives of the mothers of this population and I will never forget it.

Over the last decade, both volunteers and staff of the center have successfully gained admission to many graduate schools, listed in Table 4.1.

Table 4.1 **Academic Programs Our Center Staff and Volunteers Have Attended Upon Leaving DePaul University**

PhD Programs

Applied Behavioral Science, University of Kansas

Behavioral and Community Health, University of Maryland

Clinical Psychology, University of Georgia

Clinical Psychology, George Washington University

Clinical Psychology, Wayne State University

Clinical Psychology, Marquette University

Clinical Psychology, Michigan State University

Clinical Psychology, Bowling Green State University

Clinical Psychology, University of Illinois-Chicago

Clinical Psychology, Illinois Institute of Technology

Clinical Psychology, University of Miami

Clinical Psychology, Northern Illinois University

Clinical Psychology, University of Kansas

Clinical Psychology, Finch Medical School

Clinical Psychology, Arizona State University

Clinical Psychology, DePaul University

Clinical Psychology, University of Missouri-St. Louis

Clinical Psychology, University of Vermont

Clinical Psychology, University of Massachusetts

Clinical Psychology, Northwestern University

Clinical Psychology, University of Pittsburgh

Clinical Psychology, Oklahoma State University

Clinical Psychology, University of North Texas

Clinical Psychology, University of Cincinnati

Clinical Psychology, Jackson State University

Clinical Psychology, University of Hawaii-Manoa

Clinical Psychology, Florida State University

Clinical Psychology, Wichita State University

Clinical Psychology, University of Alaska-Fairbanks

Clinical-Child Psychology, University of Kansas

Clinical Rehabilitation Psychology, Indiana/Purdue University at Indianapolis

Cognitive Psychology, Texas Technical University

(continued)

Table 4.1 (Continued)

Community Psychology, DePaul University

Community Psychology, Wichita State University

Community Psychology, New York University

Community Psychology, Michigan State University

Community Psychology, Vanderbilt

Community Psychology, North Carolina State

Community Psychology, National Lewis University

Community Psychology, University of Illinois-Chicago

Counseling Psychology, Virginia Commonwealth University

Counseling Psychology, Loyola University

Counseling Psychology, University of Missouri

Counseling Psychology, Texas A&M University

Department of Human Development, University of Chicago

Developmental Psychology, Loyola University

Developmental Psychology, University of Maryland

Developmental and Educational Psychology, Boston College

Developmental Psychobiology, Florida International University

Educational Psychology, University Wisconsin-Madison

Educational/School Psychology, Michigan State University

Human and Community Development, University of Illinois-Champaign

Human Development and Family Studies, University of Wisconsin

Industrial Organizational Psychology, Angelo State University

Industrial Organizational Psychology, Wayne State University

Personality and Social Contexts, University of Michigan

Psychology in the Public Interest, North Carolina State University

School Psychology, Loyola University

School Psychology, University of California-Berkeley

Social Psychology, University of Massachusetts

Social Psychology, University of Hawaii-Manoa

Social Psychology, Arizona State University

Social and Community Psychology, Portland State University

Social and Personality Psychology, City University of New York

Quantitative Psychology, University of Kansas

Women's Studies Program, Texas Women's University

(*continued*)

Table 4.1 (Continued)

Clinical Psychology PsyD Programs

Adler Institute

The Chicago School of Professional Psychology

Illinois School of Professional Psychology

Roosevelt University

Rutgers University

Master's Programs

Animals and Public Policy, School of Veterinary Medicine, Tufts University

Clinical Psychology, Benedictine University

Clinical Psychology, Southern Illinois University, Edwardsville

Community Counseling, Loyola University

Community and Regional Planning, University of Oregon

Criminal Justice, University of Illinois at Chicago

Criminal Justice, John Jay

Counseling Psychology, Northwestern University

Department of Education, Northwestern University

Forensic Psychology, Tiffin University

General Psychology, DePaul University

Gerontology Psychology, Adler School of Professional Psychology

Health Education, University of Florida

Health Psychology, National Lewis University

Human Resources and Employment Relations, Pennsylvania State University

Industrial-Organizational, Xavier University

Integrated Marketing Communications, Loyola University

Marriage and Family Therapy, Northwestern University

Marriage and Family Therapy, University of Connecticut

Master's Public Service, DePaul University

Midwest Center for the Study of Oriental Medicine

Nursing, DePaul University

Physician Assistant Program, Midwestern University

Public Health, University of Minnesota

Social Sciences, University of Chicago

Social Work, University of Pittsburgh

(continued)

Table 4.1 (Continued)

Social Work, Arizona State University
Social Work, University of Illinois Urbana-Champaign
Social Work, Washington University
Social Work, University of North Carolina-Greensboro
School Psychology Program, University of Northern Colorado
School Psychology, Loyola University in Chicago
School Psychology, Northern Illinois
School Psychology, Illinois State University

As I set up my Center for Community Research setting, I tried to keep in mind that the most important kind of learning often occurs outside of the classroom. What is often remembered over time is a revelation that came from a conversation when people spontaneously shared their opinions and ideas or met up with old friends. These informal interactions matter most to us in the long run. Why? Facts and figures that are assiduously memorized have no human connection and are easy to forget; what we remember are the special moments in which we learned something meaningful—and it almost always comes from another person.

One evening, I attended a dinner with members of a community psychology organization in Chicago. One faculty member walked up and embraced me. She said that during an earlier meeting, as members reflected on how they became community psychologists, my name came up frequently as a person who welcomed people into our field. She mentioned that after she had earned her BA over 25 years ago, she had approached four different faculty members to try to get involved in research. I was the only person to say, "Sure, you can join our research team." I was pleased to hear this. That open and welcoming attitude is at the core of being a community psychologist.

I have learned as an educator at DePaul that though the sense of community cannot be easily seen, it is felt and appreciated as a major source of inspiration in the lives of students and others who are on their way to becoming caring and effective social activists. It also serves as inspiration and an opportunity not only to revitalize myself but also to be of some service to my friends and colleagues. More than anything, I always remember the healing powers of social connections and how they provide unique and unparalleled opportunities and resources for our journey of change.

Over the years, I, along with other colleagues, helped transform DePaul University into an important educational center in the field of community psychology. These small wins within my professional organization and my host setting at DePaul helped sustain my energy and commitment to second-order change. As difficult as the struggle may be in the external world for social justice, I could always feel some satisfaction for the types of changes that I helped bring about at DePaul University. By surrounding myself with creative minds dedicated to research in pursuit of social justice, I also helped to build a solid community infrastructure from which to launch my own social change efforts.

Handling Conflict

Of course, working for the social good does not preclude occasional conflicts at the center or within social movements. How we deal with conflict in such a place takes on important implications for our work. I have always felt that my research center is not unlike a training laboratory: Our task has been to teach employees and students not only how to collect and analyze data to foster change but also how to get along with each other. Conflict helps us learn about ourselves, why and how we disagree, and the art of negotiation and compromise.

Conflict can also serve to bring about change within groups. Several years ago, I was working to secure a federal grant for a 10-year follow-up to the ME/CFS research project that my team had worked on in the mid-1990s. The federal reviewers scored it favorably and recommended funding, but my university's human subjects committee had to give its approval for the research study, indicating that adequate ethical standards would be followed. I was in a time crunch: The paperwork absolutely had to be completed during the summer in order to receive the grant, but the university human subjects review group did not meet until the fall. During a casual conversation with the chairman of the psychology department, I told him about my problem. Unbeknownst to me, the chairman of the psychology department intervened after hearing of my predicament. However, the official overseeing the human subjects review committee was annoyed: She thought this intervention was intrusive—and she let me know it. When the summer ended, the human subjects committee still had not met, and I was not awarded the $1.5 million grant. It was not only a loss for me, but also a loss for the university—and they realized it. My dilemma and the loss of the grant helped to change the university's policy: The institutional human subjects review committee began reviewing all grant proposals throughout the calendar year. Even though the university official had been upset, I was able to stay on good terms with her and did not let this incident interfere with my good standing within the university. Fortunately, the next year, I was able to secure the grant that I had lost.

Choosing which issues to fight over is a common dilemma for an activist. I decided not to fight the issue of the human subjects review committee not meeting during the summer. At the time, it seemed that the power structure was inflexible and would not allow for change. We have to pick our battles carefully. In retrospect, the incident reminded me of my experience as a graduate student—and the discontent and powerlessness the students had felt within the clinical psychology program. Facing that dilemma, I also had decided not to fight about the issue—the consequences may have been severe for a relatively powerless first-year student. Sometimes, however, it is imperative to keep fighting.

In Dr. Pick's case, she knew that she needed to meet with the Minister of Education in order to make progress toward a national sexuality education program for youth in Mexico. Despite the rejection, she continued to patiently wait outside the minister's office every day for a month until she finally was granted an appointment to discuss her program. Using one's intuition in times of uncertainty about how to proceed is critical to making these kinds of decisions.

Rules of the Game

We, as social activists, are not the only forces at work when it comes to dealing with how our professional setting or immediate environment operates: There are other players with interests and priorities of their own. But beyond this, we all act under the influence of certain rules and protocols—spoken or unspoken. Social change also involves an understanding of the rules that govern our work sites, communities, and societies. The classic French film *The Rules of the Game*, directed in 1939 by Jean Renoir, tells the story of French society just before the start of World War II. The title refers to the norms that dictate proper behavior for people of any status, but the rules apply differently to each social class. For the upper class, the rules can easily be bent, but for the lower classes, the rules call for stricter behavioral boundaries to be in place. Not surprisingly, those in power establish the rules. At times, powerful individuals who are not always visible set rules that particularly affect those who are in positions of less power and prestige.

I once knew a very gifted colleague who did not recognize some of the rules of the game at DePaul University. As an assistant professor, he had to be mindful of his relationships with those in power, especially in his department. On one occasion, a very senior psychology professor within our department gave a talk before our faculty about his research. One unspoken rule of the game was to not embarrass this faculty member, who was considered by many to be the most powerful and influential person in the department. However, my colleague asked this person a very difficult question involving statistics that he could not answer. His actions embarrassed—and angered—the senior faculty member. The next year, when his appointment was being reevaluated, he was terminated from the program. Certainly, this is another example of how knowing and adhering to the rules of the game in any setting can be very important.

Lessons Learned

We have discussed a number of lessons learned about the principles of social change. In my experience, the most important lessons learned were patience, maintaining a long-term perspective, and appreciating small wins. Attempting to bring about structural second-order change is complex and challenging. Confronting opposition in the form of powerful individuals and coalitions is unavoidable. Many people who abuse power are not intrinsically evil, and, ironically, they truly believe they are helping people who are not capable of making decisions themselves. This is true of many dictators, as well as of administrators who impose their solutions upon subordinates and, in doing so, deprive them of their due rights. When people cannot represent themselves because of this kind of power abuse, the perpetuators are often bewildered by the strident opposition and discontent that arise.

Those in power are not the only ones who need to be confronted while bringing about second-order change. Often, people agree on a goal but envision a different means of reaching it. They may have different styles and ways of working, making it difficult for coalitions to complete important tasks. Even worse, there may be high levels of antagonism among the coalitions, which can split vitally needed efforts to confront those holding real power. The change agent needs to deal with all of these complications and find a way to maintain good relationships among collaborators. For example, when the leader of the largest ME/CFS patient organization resisted a name change and wanted to expand the definition of the disease, I opposed these policies—but I also worked hard to maintain a professional working relationship with her. When she ultimately withdrew her support of the CDC, I welcomed her as an ally again. These types of mixed relationships over long periods of time are more common than most might think; however, shifting alliances pose real challenges to consistent progress on a campaign for change over the long haul.

A commitment to focus my energies on a single goal over long periods of time has defined the core of my personal success in helping to create new training settings at DePaul University. That dedication allowed me to continue to create a vibrant community of social change agents and colleagues. Patience and willingness to accept small wins helped me through the tough times, such as developing ME/CFS in the middle of my career.

In addition, I believed in myself. Along the way, I learned not to allow other people's opinions or negative evaluations affect me. For example, in the mid-1970s, I submitted a research paper about a school consultation program to a journal for publication. It was rejected and criticized. I could have accepted the reviewers' criticism of my work, but I was certain of the importance of my research. I next sent the paper to another journal, and it was published. The following year, I was invited by two distinguished psychologists to have this article published in a volume that presented the best behavioral articles of 1979 (Jason & Ferone, 1979). This was a small win and, more importantly, a vindication of my belief in myself.

This chapter focused on my host setting, DePaul University. We all work within host settings—even those who work from their homes. These settings are intertwined with social connections that can act as a protective buffer while working on social change. We can bring the same social change principles that we apply in our activism to our host settings as we work to nurture an infrastructure of support for our activities.

Since 1971, when I entered graduate school, I have been working in the field of community psychology. I am fortunate to have been a faculty member at one university for my entire career. During this time, I have had the privilege of working with hundreds of undergraduates and of serving on 78 dissertation committees and 85 master's thesis committees. We are currently the only university in the world to have both an undergraduate concentration in community psychology and a free-standing PhD program in community psychology. In addition, I created the Center for Community Research, a training site for undergraduate and graduate students, and have tried to use Nye's leadership qualities in implementing change at my center.

The creation of these training sites and the students that I successfully mentored were small wins, and I could always point with pride to these individual successes and setting changes, even in the midst of setbacks and obstacles in my efforts to bring about real second-order change in the external world. My ability to maintain a long-term commitment to social change is, in large part, due to the encouragement from these small wins at my host setting.

Additional Resources

The Collaborative for Academic, Social, and Emotional Learning (CASEL) was founded in 1994 by Daniel Goleman, the author of *Emotional Intelligence,* and educator/philanthropist Eileen Rockefeller Growal. For more than 30 years, clinical-community psychologist Roger Weissberg and other distinguished researchers and practitioners have worked with CASEL to transform our educational system by helping better understand how schools, parents, and communities work together to promote positive social and emotional outcomes in school-age children. For more information visit this site: http://casel.org/about-us/

Research for Organizing has developed a toolkit for organizations and individuals that work for social justice using participatory action research, which can be found here: http://www.researchfororganizing.org/

Gary Harper is another influential clinical-community psychologist who has created settings in collaboration with community agencies and community members to promote social justice involving prevention programs that promote the health and well-being of adolescents, with a focus on runaway/homeless youth, urban youth of color, gay/bisexual youth, and youth living with HIV. For more information visit this site: http://csh.depaul.edu/departments/psychology/faculty-and-staff/Pages/harper.aspx

During the past 30 years, Jose Antonio Abreu has founded over 100 youth orchestras that have transformed over 300,000 children's lives in Venezuela. Their involvement in his orchestras has not only cultivated a love of music within them, but it has taught them valuable life skills, such as responsibility, and increased their self-esteem. Several of his former students, despite coming from poverty, became principal musicians in world-renowned orchestras. This link tells his inspiring story of what is possible through a long-term commitment to social change: http://www.ted.com/talks/jose_abreu_on_kids_transformed_by_music. html

Khan Academy is an innovative, not-for-profit organization that provides instructional videos on thousands of math and science topics to people around the world at no charge. These videos are presented in a fashion that makes the topics interesting and easy to understand. Each video is approximately 10 minutes long and can be accessed by anyone on the internet, helping to reduce disparities in access to quality education. This link provides more information on this revolutionary way of educating and empowering individuals: http://www.khanacademy.org/

Articles on using social media and nonprofits can be found here:

http://nonprofit.about.com/od/socialmedia/tp/Tipsstartsocialnetworking.htm

http://nonprofit.about.com/od/fundraising/a/wiredyoung.htm

http://fundraisingcoach.com/free-articles/a-case-for-twitter-facebook-social-media-for-non-profit-fundraisers/

Harvard and MIT have now partnered to create a system of free online courses, known as massively open online courses, or MOOCs, which will offer certificates of mastery in lieu of college credit. The initiative allows for a much more egalitarian access to knowledge and continuing education and even has the potential to transform our higher education system. More information can be found at this site: http://www.nytimes.com/2012/05/03/education/harvard-and-mit-team-up-to-offer-free-online-courses.html?_r=3&ref=education

Gloria Levin's post on ethics and community psychology that emphasizes the importance of evaluation competencies for community psychologists can be found here: http://communitypsychologypractice.blogspot.com/2012/03/ethics-and-community-psychology.html

Other community competencies can be found here: http://www.scra27.org/practice/wiki/corecompetencies

5

Means to an End

We have seen how second-order activism can improve people's lives and bring new resources and opportunities to a community by identifying the power holders, overcoming the obstacles they create, and garnering the support of like-minded others. Our next principle, evaluating short- and long-term strategies, may sound dry. Although it lacks the glamour of hands-on social activism, it is essential to long-lasting success. Many social activists, groups, and organizations mount social justice efforts, but the activists who are effective often evaluate their methods along the way.

In some cases, the results of activism are obvious, such as the ousting of a dictator. However, the effects of social action are often not immediate or easily identifiable. Take, for instance, Rachel Carson, a scientist who compiled findings from diverse areas to bring an extremely important issue to the public's attention, leading to second-order change. After World War II, deadly pesticides were being used everywhere—in homes, in gardens, and even on commercial crops that ended up on family dinner tables—but no one was aware of their danger, least of all the public.

Carson wrote a groundbreaking book in 1962, *Silent Spring*, which detailed the widespread use and serious dangers of these poisons. A writer, scientist, and ecologist, Carson synthesized the results of hundreds of disparate scientific research articles to eloquently illustrate our society's predicament. *Silent Spring* portrayed, in graphic detail, the toll that dangerous pesticides were taking on animals, the environment, and people. Although insulated in concrete cities, we were slowly destroying the natural world with toxins. In particular, DDT, a commonly used pesticide at the time, was destroying all types of wildlife. Immediately following the publication of *Silent Spring*, Carson was viciously attacked by the chemical and pesticide industries for her outspoken views. Despite her personal struggles with cancer, her reverence for nature and determination to protect it for future generations kept her dedicated to her work. Her book moved President Kennedy to create a special panel to study the effects of pesticides. Before Carson died of cancer, she saw her theories vindicated. She testified at congressional hearings, and ultimately, her work led to the banning of DDT and the enactment of the Clean Water and the Clean Air Acts.

Carson's 4-year social change effort was a success; her work documenting abuses in the pesticide and chemical industries led to the enactment of federal policy laws. She is now hailed as one of the first environmentalists, and her book is regarded as a watershed event in the pursuit of safeguarding the environment. However, many social changes do not reach the level of national legislation—but even smaller victories can be measured when compared to both their short- and long-term goals. Activists can gauge a program's success and reassess strategies by identifying where progress is, or is not, being made.

The different principles of social change can occur concurrently or in varying orders. Vulnerabilities in any stage of the principles can put a social movement at risk. For example, if an activist has a clear vision of his or her desired social outcome but does not take into account the aspects of power that are resisting the change, he or she may fail. Failure can also occur if an activist organization has a clear idea of its desired second-order change and recognition of opposing power structures but does not have the capacity to organize and work with communities. An activist must be aware and informed of each step of the movement. While the dynamic nature of social activism campaigns may make evaluation challenging, measuring progress is vital and lies at the heart of each community strategy. Evaluations capture and help redefine the essence of each principle of social change. Program evaluations can also reveal weaknesses, identify where the weaknesses stem from, and help focus efforts on critical stages of systemic change.

Given the fluid nature of a campaign for social change, an activist may not know the best way to measure changes, or even what changes to measure. For example, a nonprofit organization might design and implement educational programs for inner-city preschoolers. Many of these types of programs frequently only focus on gains that measure academic achievement; but in fact, the real second-order changes may be the creation of new jobs for the mothers who participate as teachers in these programs. In this situation, effective evaluations can open up new realms of possibilities and can help an organization redefine itself from a first-order service provider to one capable of achieving second-order social change. The change agent must know to look out for shifts in results and be flexible with predetermined goals.

Collecting data to reveal organizational problems is a critical step toward enacting policy changes. In the fight against Big Tobacco, we sent young people into stores in Woodbridge, Illinois, to see if they would be allowed to buy cigarettes; their purpose was to gather data that would be used to gauge the rate of illegal sales to minors. This research backed the passage of the federal Synar Amendment in the 1990s that required all states to reduce illegal sales of tobacco. Before passing that milestone legislation, however, we had to first achieve smaller gains. Initially, Officer Talbot assumed that by sending storeowners in Woodbridge a written notice, tobacco sales to minors would no longer be a problem. After our data collection, we learned that the notice strategy had not worked—storeowners and their employees were still selling to minors. This information led to us creating legislation that gave police more authority to fine owners, as well as to give tickets to minors if they were smoking in public. If the Woodridge Police Department had not partnered with us to determine the extent of the problem, they would not have had a realistic picture of the situation.

After several months of fining storeowners, Officer Talbot was pleased to find that the number of illegal sales had dropped significantly and thought that enforcement was no longer needed. I, however, believed that illegal sales would increase again if the police stopped their efforts and recommended that they continue monitoring stores and fining those that continued to illegally sell tobacco to minors. After another 6 months, rates dropped to almost nothing and, because of sustained enforcement, they have remained that way for over 20 years. Data was critical in guiding the enforcement effort over time. With persistent monitoring and enforcement, we were able to set an important precedent for the entire nation regarding tobacco sales to minors and help reduce a serious public health problem.

Without consistent and widespread assessments, most of the victories described in prior chapters would not have been possible. As we discussed in chapter 2, little attention was being paid to the devastating illness of myalgic encephalomyelitis (ME)/chronic fatigue syndrome (CFS) in the early 1990s. Community-based research into the prevalence of the illness allowed us to confront the myth that it was a rare disorder. I worked with epidemiologists, research methodologists, statisticians, physicians, psychiatrists, and psychologists to challenge the Centers for Disease Control and Prevention's (CDC) unrealistic low-prevalence estimates. Our evaluations later opposed the grossly inflated prevalence estimates when the CDC broadened the definition of ME/CFS and counted people who did not have the illness. Our work benefited a coalition of patient groups and research organizations and contributed to a change in the CDC's ME/CFS leadership.

Evaluations also help to clarify accountability within organizations and identify new avenues for second-order change. In the case of Oxford House, we were able to directly assess the difference between first-order change (sending people to the same communities in which they had lived before addiction treatment) and second-order change (placing people in Oxford Houses following treatment). We learned that Oxford Houses allowed people to develop abstinent friendship networks and observe role models who successfully held jobs. In our studies, a random half of a group of people leaving treatment centers for alcohol or other drug problems were placed in Oxford Houses in order to determine whether or not the Oxford House experience would help people stay abstinent, employed, and out of jail. What we found was just that: The people who were provided an opportunity to live in an Oxford House were twice as likely to remain abstinent over the next 2 years. This second-order intervention had a powerful influence on the lives of people who were offered this empowering setting. These results garnered much attention and helped to legitimize the Oxford House model for public policy officials. More significantly, it provided support for the expansion of the model throughout the country. Based on our work with this organization, the federal government listed Oxford Houses within the National Registry of Evidenced-Based Programs and Practices (http://nrepp. samhsa.gov/ViewIntervention.aspx?id=223).

The Many Roles of Research

Participants within program communities have always played a large and critical role in my efforts for change over the years. Active participation of community members in the planning, execution, and evaluation of research is vital for any social change. Referred to as participatory approaches (Jason, Keys, et al., 2004), these markedly differ from traditional models of research in which scientists generate their own ideas about the research questions to ask or the services clients need. In other words, in traditional research, community members are often excluded from the entire process. In contrast, participatory approaches allow community members to shape the research questions and inform researchers of what services are needed by identifying the criteria or standards against which effective service should be judged. This method promotes not only collective, reciprocal, and egalitarian relationships but also a common language (Jason, Keys, et al., 2004). Participants enrich and expand the goals of the project and offer perspectives that are often overlooked. They have a unique understanding and knowledge of the issues we're trying to change; in fact, many of the best ideas come from them.

At a community intervention level, these kinds of participatory approaches often begin with a community needs assessment. For an activist planning to implement new service programs in a community, such as a health promotion or prevention program, the first step is often to conduct a community needs assessment. In this way, instead of bringing a preset program agenda to a given community, the activist allows the community to set the agenda based on its own needs. Through assessment strategies such as holding community forums or meetings with a selected group of community leaders, an activist or agency can understand the most pressing unmet needs in a community while developing rapport and collaborative relations with community members. Furthermore, with a high degree of collaboration, the program will be more consistent with the characteristics, practices, and values of the community and, thus, more likely to be adopted by community members (Rhodes & Jason, 1991).

Participatory approaches are also needed in larger social activism efforts. There are many ways to document the success rate of a change effort and just as many ways to chart its progress. When trying to analyze the nature of a social problem or find a solution for it, surveying changes in attitudes, behavior, or policies is critically important. Simple self-report methods that use rating scales and questionnaires can track these changes, such as asking open-ended questions regarding how community members feel about the social issue you hope to address. By measuring public opinion and knowledge through polls or surveys, you can identify the roots of any public opposition to your cause and develop education or awareness initiatives that target those beliefs. Likewise, you could discover that the majority of people surveyed already support the change you seek, and you could use this as powerful support to motivate lawmakers to act. When Dr. Pick hoped to introduce sexuality education in Mexican public schools on a national level, the Minister of Education asked her to provide evidence of public support for the issue. She was able to have some sexuality education questions included in a national Gallup poll, and results showed that 95% of Mexicans believed sexuality education should begin in the first grade (IMIFAP, 1993). The poll results provided Dr. Pick with the proof of public support that she needed to sway powerful opponents to her side.

On a smaller scale, it is also important to gauge how community partners feel about their involvement in the program or research project. In one instance, we assessed the attitudes of community members who worked as participant recruiters for our Oxford House research (Jason, Davis, Olson, Ferrari, & Alvarez, 2006). As the quotes below indicate, it was clear that their involvement with us had been a positive experience.

> The group of us, I would say, definitely formed into a family, similar to that of Oxford House.

> I felt that my ideas and experience were really important and valued in the shaping of this study.... It gave me self-confidence and made me realize that I had something, a lot to offer.... [B]eing part of such an open-minded, nurturing research team allowed me the opportunity to really open my mind and learn a lot of new things and different ways to look at things.

> I am now attending college full-time at age 45.... [M]y association with the DePaul students and staff has motivated me to want to earn a degree. My involvement with the Oxford Study probably will be one of the most significant milestones in my life.

Although self-reported data are essential in measuring the effects of our change efforts, it is equally as important to look for actual changes in people and their environments. Prior to analyzing these changes, however, information and feedback must be gathered. The feedback-gathering process once happened very organically for me at the end of a presentation I gave at an annual Oxford House convention. An Oxford House member approached me and suggested that we include the issue of tolerance in our future research. He explained that prior to living in an Oxford House, he had been very prejudiced against people who were different from him, such as people who were HIV positive. But while in Oxford House, he met a woman who was HIV positive; she was now his girlfriend. He wanted to point out that, for him, living in Oxford House went beyond staying clean and sober—it made him a more accepting and generous person. After hearing this information, one of our team members began a study on the development of tolerance among Oxford House members. What we learned confirmed this man's experience: Tolerance increased by living in Oxford Houses (Olson, Jason, Davidson, & Ferrari, 2009). Had we not listened to this member's feedback, we would not have known about the opportunity to study this additional, important benefit of Oxford House.

Before describing other examples of the ways in which the fifth principle contributes to the goals of social activism, a distinction should be made between the types of research and evaluation involved in this process. At times, the issue at hand requires rigorous research to uncover and expose injustices that demand public attention and correction. Like Rachel Carson's years of research and writing about DDT and other harmful chemicals, the process of conducting this research can be the primary action of the activism, and the wide dissemination of the research itself leads to second-order change. A similar process occurred with the ME/CFS research on prevalence rates and later investigation of the CDC's use of ME/CFS research funding—the research, along with the advocacy efforts that it supported, spurred change.

In other cases, research takes a supporting role to social activism. Formative research provides guidance to inform action and design and develop initiatives for change. If your aim is to improve education with a new curriculum for elementary school children, you may first do some research to determine what areas of learning your program should target. Then, once you have developed the curriculum that targets those areas, you could test the educational materials with a small group of students to see which sections to improve before introducing the program in schools. Both are examples of formative research. Formative research helps initiatives succeed by taking an informed, comprehensive approach to solve the issue before taking large-scale action.

On the other hand, summative research allows activists to evaluate the success of their actions after they have been implemented. For example, working with the Woodridge Police Department, our summative evaluations of the different approaches we took to reduce illegal tobacco sales to minors let us know which interventions worked and which needed to be altered. With each cycle of evaluation, adjustments fine-tune the interventions while providing the information needed to create fresh ways to tackle major social problems (Bogat & Jason, 2000).

Formative and summative research are conducted by academics, activists, nonprofit organizations, governments, international agencies, and others who share the common goal of developing and evaluating successful interventions. Although most of the following examples focus on research and program evaluations that I conducted as an academic researcher at DePaul University, the fifth principle of employing research techniques to measure success applies to scientists and other social activists alike. Contrary to popular belief, collecting data does not have to be boring or repetitive, nor should it be feared. Parts of the evaluation process are extremely straightforward, and community members and partner organizations can help streamline it by sharing their priorities with the appropriate people.

An Unlikely Research Topic

In the late 1970s, I once invited a representative from Martin Oberman's office, a Chicago alderman, to speak to the students of my community psychology course. After his presentation, I asked the representative which problem generated the most community dissatisfaction. I had privately pledged to work on whichever problem he mentioned. When he answered "uncollected dog feces," my jaw literally dropped.

Who was resisting change here? Not corporations or politicians. It was the citizens themselves—or rather, citizens who owned dogs. Not picking up after a dog was the most offensive and most frequently complained about type of litter in urban, residential areas, and a less-than-desirable research topic. However, I'd made a promise to the representative and agreed to collect some data on this problem. I surveyed a group of university undergraduates about their opinions on dog droppings. The students also ranked dog droppings as the most offensive type of urban litter. More importantly, dog feces were linked to several well-documented, widespread health hazards in Chicago, including the transmission of infections and parasites. And, of course, dog droppings defaced a community's beauty and attractiveness (see Figure 5.1)—not to mention the extreme aggravation experienced after stepping in them.

I needed to address this problem with a systematic approach. At that time, I had a new clinical psychology graduate student working with me. I knew he probably wouldn't be thrilled that he would be studying dog litter for his first assignment in graduate school. I wasn't sure how to introduce the idea, but I carefully

Figure 5.1 Dog being walked in Chicago.
Cha. Yang Photographer.

worked it into one of our conversations when I was asking him a bit about his hobbies and interests. He made it all too easy for me when he mentioned that he enjoyed hunting, and that to track deer he would check whether feces were fresh by sticking his finger in them, an indication that the animal was in close proximity. "Francis," I said, "you're the man to work with me on a dog litter study."

For the next few months, Francis and I worked on a study to find ways to deter dog litter. To get an initial measurement of the problem, we counted all fresh defecations in an eight-by-five-block area around DePaul and found 1,147 droppings. This large number suggested that dog litter was a serious problem within this community. We next picked a target block and, for 5 hours each day, recorded the number of dogs, the number of dogs who defecated, and the number and weight of dog defecations picked up by their owners. Unfortunately, to accomplish this, we had to pick up and weigh all defecations each morning.

We discovered that there were a few unforeseen, unpleasant consequences of this research, besides actually counting, picking up, and weighing every dog dropping. For instance, even after I left the office, I found myself counting dog droppings on walks everywhere I went. To add insult to injury, my prolonged exposure to waste and the pests that they attract caused my apartment to become infested with fleas. Several of my research assistants mentioned that they had recurring nightmares about picking up dog feces.

Our evaluation used a simple research structure: We first collected data on dog litter pickups and then introduced an action—posting anti-dog-litter signs—to see if the dog litter pickups increased (Jason, Zolik, & Matese, 1979). For activists, analyzing a behavior pre- and postintervention is a good way to determine if your action or intervention is effective; if behaviors change after the intervention, you can assume that your approach is effective. During the initial week of observations at the target block, we saw that very few people picked up after their dogs, resulting in over 19 pounds of dog defecations left in the area. Next, we posted the anti-dog-litter signs, hoping to change owners' behavior. Unfortunately, these signs were ineffective and did not change owners' behavior or reduce the amount of dog feces deposited on the block. Yet, when all dog owners were given instructions and a demonstration on how to use a plastic bag to pick up dog feces, 82% of the dog owners picked up after their dogs. Although changes in observed behavior are important to document, comments from local residents can also be valuable in data collection; we recorded some interesting reactions from dog owners:

"Dog shit isn't important. It dissolves. Why don't you do something about litter?"

"You're transient and what you are doing is kind of pissing in the wind."

"If you are such a concerned citizen, follow behind and pick up."

But there were positive responses as well:

> "I'm enthusiastic with what you are doing and am going to try to get a dog barrel on this street."

> "Leaving defecations on lawns is disgusting and I am encouraging others to carry bags."

We provided the Chicago alderman with details of the results of the study. He later invited me to testify at city hall to support an ordinance that would require dog owners to pick up after their dogs. At a televised hearing, I shared the findings of our "prompting" intervention, which effectively motivated dog owners to dispose of their dogs' waste. After this testimony, a journalist for the *Chicago Daily News* (July 12, 1977) wrote: "In what surely must be one of the most bizarre academic studies in the nation ...." Using data from our study, this reporter estimated that 382,000 pounds of dog excrement was deposited daily on city streets. When I later contacted journalist Ellen Warren regarding a few inaccuracies, she replied that "the story generated great readership interest." This story was followed by an editorial in the *Sun Times* that read:

> We're not sure what contribution this study makes to the discipline of psychology, but if it persuades the city council to pass a stronger ordinance to discipline dog owners, it will have been more than worth the effort.... The pursuit of knowledge aside, it did manage to clean up one neighborhood.

The study had hit a nerve—so much, in fact, that the police in one district began dispensing plastic bags to dog owners, and there was even a photo opinion asking residents: "Should owners clean up after their dogs?" A cartoon in the *Chicago Daily News* of July 22, 1977 (page 11), portrayed a dog wearing a diaper with the title: "Solution to a problem." I received lots of fan mail, including one that said: "This is a lost cause. The only solution is to hire out-of-work people who can clean the parks and parkways."

Following the completion of our study, several community groups contacted me about setting up their own dog-litter-removal campaigns. One group in particular eagerly wanted to work with my team in identifying which streets had the greatest accumulations of dog litter. They set up a 1-day action initiative during which community members approached dog owners to inform them of the recently passed ordinance and also offered them newspapers or plastic bags to pick up after their dogs (Jason, McCoy, Blanco, & Zolik, 1980).

For the first few days after the campaign, we learned that rates of dog litter had declined by about two pounds per day. But over the next few weeks, the dog droppings increased. The 1-day intervention was not as successful as we had anticipated. A big reason, we assumed, was the timing of the initiative: We staged the activity over a weekend when owners may have been out of town; thus, a sizeable proportion of dog owners were not reached. Furthermore, we realized that a single day was not enough to create new behavior patterns. Not every change effort will work every time, but failure is also valuable: Community members can better understand how difficult it is to change behaviors.

Rather than becoming discouraged, the locals reconvened with us to learn from the data. After reviewing it, they had renewed confidence to tenaciously launch a longer "prompting" intervention, set over a period of several weeks. Their persistence paid off—pickup rates increased nearly 90%. One unexpected benefit from the more intensive intervention was a positive ripple effect that was triggered from the target block of our intervention to the surrounding areas at a 13-month follow-up, as shown in Figure 5.2. We assumed that this ripple effect occurred because dog owners frequently walked their dogs in a wider area than just their own neighborhoods. When the pickup behaviors among owners were strengthened in the target areas, they were likely going to continue this behavior in the adjacent, nontarget blocks.

As we saw in our second attempt to educate the area about the new ordinance, community groups certainly have the power to take charge of data collection. They can then apply more refined techniques, tailored to their particular needs, to achieve documentable success. Residents first took the initiative to identify

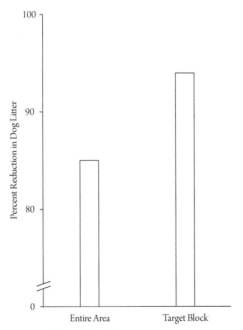

Figure 5.2 Decreases in uncollected dog feces.

the issue and then took it upon themselves to mount the dog litter pickup campaign. We, the university-based research team, were able to provide guidance, support, and expertise in planning and evaluating the interventions. Partnerships are always essential to any community effort. At a 25-month follow-up of our prompting intervention, we found an 89% reduction of dog litter in the targeted areas. The summative research we conducted allowed us to report exactly how successful our interventions had been.

The successes from these two interventions, along with my testimony at the city council hearing, helped make Chicago one of the first cities in the country to pass a "pooper-scooper" ordinance. The Chicago alderman later wrote to tell me that our project helped change politicians' attitudes toward the issue: "In the past, this problem has often been scoffed at and not taken seriously. Your comments regarding the dog defecation problem altered that perception greatly." The initiative spread to towns all over the country, and similar ordinances were adapted from the Chicago legislation.

After all of these successes, I attended a psychology convention and was eager to meet new colleagues. As I entered a room of about 100 other psychologists, Emory Cowen, my former mentor, saw me and shouted, "There's the dog shit man!" Although he was joking, it was still early in my career, and I certainly didn't want to be known as the "dog shit man" forever. It was time to pursue other areas of research and social change. Nevertheless, I still continue to receive requests from communities asking for my help in uncollected dog litter. Thirty years later, people still send me cartoons regarding the defecation habits of cats, ducks, and other animals.

I was more than ready to move on from studying dog excrement, but in 1981, a DePaul graduate student conducted a study involving different types of litter in small parks in Chicago. This project sought to improve the conditions of neighborhood parks that were sullied by trash or in need of repair. She collaborated with the Chicago Parks District, the organization Friends of the Parks, and most importantly, the Boy Scouts of America, whose young scouts played an integral role in cleaning up the parks. The graduate student's evaluation of the project showed measurable improvements in the appearance of the parks, as well as increases in the participating scouts' problem-solving skills and psychological sense of community (Bogat, 1983). The research showed that if individuals work collaboratively, even on seemingly trivial problems such as litter, they can also become more invested in their communities and more civically engaged.

Seatbelts and Child Safety

The litter projects had large effects on the aesthetics and sanitation of public spaces—bringing communities together—but other research can influence legislation that saves lives. Before states began to pass child safety restraint laws in the late 1970s, thousands of children were either injured or killed in car accidents each year, and improper restraint in a car was once the leading cause of death for children under 1 year of age. In the early 1980s, Illinois legislators considered legislation that would require infants and children to wear a seatbelt or to be placed in an equivalent type of restraint while in cars. Given the gravity of the problem, our research team wondered if legislation would effectively change citizens' behavior and enforce child restraints. We first needed to spend several months gathering relevant information. We looked inside cars to see whether or not infants and children were placed in car restraints. Then, we used telephone surveys to collect information about the public's attitude toward the child restraint bill. The goal was to use both data collection on attitudes and first-hand observations to build a more convincing case when trying to influence policy officials.

Although we were also working closely with an Illinois organization that was advocating for the passage of this bill, we were unsure if our data would persuade legislators. To see if we would achieve the desired impact, we turned to a simple technique used by many in scientific fields: We provided the information to only a random half of the legislators and then measured the difference between the informed and uninformed groups. We sent the information to only half of the Illinois state legislators prior to a vote on the child passenger restraint bill. In that letter, the senators were informed that 140 children in Illinois were killed and 25,828 injured in automobile accidents between 1975 and 1981. We also pointed out that, through our observations, 93% of Illinois children were not in adequate restraints while riding in cars. We also provided the legislators with the results of our survey, in which 78% of adults supported the child passenger restraint bill. By sending this critical information to half of the legislators, we were able to see the effect of our letter. Seventy-nine percent of senators who received the information voted for passage of the bill, whereas only 53% of senators who did not receive the letter voted for the bill. In either case, we were gratified that the majority of senators in both groups voted for the passage of legislation that would help protect children (Jason & Rose, 1984).

Based on your knowledge of your target group—in this case, senators—you may need to consider several factors to generate a positive reception. For example, we made sure that our letter was received 1 week before the vote, and that the information was clear and concise. In this way, we increased our chances that the letter would be both read and remembered. We also gave senators specific data, particularly on low rates of safety seat usage and citizen enthusiasm for the proposed legislation. Lastly, we gathered information regarding the state's share of medical care costs following debilitating car accidents. Cost-saving policies are always effective with legislators. Our intervention was a great success. Even the governor requested a copy of our findings before finally signing the legislation. As of July 1, 1983, the Illinois Child Passenger Restraint Law required children under the age of 4 to be placed in an approved child or infant car seat. Also, children aged 4 to 6 must be placed in either an approved restraint system or a secure seatbelt.

Measuring your results doesn't have to be complex; you can simply compare the data before and after your action. In the case of the new child seatbelt law, we compared our results from periods of time before and after July 1983 (the month the law went into effect). We found that the bill worked. With passage of the legislation, use of appropriate restraints increased from 49% to 74% for infants younger than 1 year of age. For children between the ages of 1 and 4, use increased from 13% to 42%. Overall, children's deaths caused by traffic accidents decreased by a startling 53% when compared to a period 2 years before the law was enacted (see Figure 5.3). This is a great example of how working collaboratively with community-based organizations can help foster solutions to serious and significant problems within a community. Our data influenced policy officials to support laws that contributed to second-order change. As a result, our children are much safer in cars today.

Passive Smoking

Much like our child restraint efforts, various campaigns and accompanying evaluations have significantly helped to reduce smoking. Smoking once dominated American culture but has now been relegated to sidewalks thanks to decades of action, evaluation, and policy. Early on in our work, we developed methods to evaluate the success of creating a nonsmoking section in a student cafeteria before there were laws restricting use (Jason & Liotta, 1982). At first, we picked a time each day to count the number of smokers in a particular section of the cafeteria. When we posted no-smoking signs, the number of smokers in the

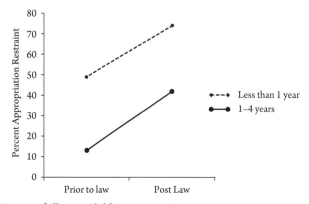

Figure 5.3 Impact of Illinois Child Passenger Restraint Law.

area did not change, so we turned to a more direct method. We began politely requesting people not to smoke. This request, along with no-smoking signs, was effective in eliminating smoking in this designated nonsmoking area. Just like with the effort to increase dog litter pickup behavior, signs alone did not change behavior, but a more direct approach was effective.

Throughout the course of our study, people were encouraged to continue asking others not to smoke in the cafeteria after seeing beneficial changes; coalitions that shared our goal also maintained the needed changes. For example, within the permanent nonsmoking section that we had established in the cafeteria, an individual who collected unreturned trays was assigned by the university management to continue politely asking smokers not to smoke. Data collected 3 months after the end of the nonsmoking section research project showed that customers had started to do the same. At one of the follow-up sessions, a student, without any prompting from us, was observed approaching smokers and asking them not to smoke in the nonsmoking section. It seemed that from the creation of this designated section, new social norms were being established; nonsmokers were becoming more comfortable and began to assert their voices. Both management and customers began to change their behaviors.

Affecting Handicapped Parking Regulations

Evaluating action in a campaign for second-order change is necessary for a number of reasons. Activists need concrete data to persuade both members of the community and policy makers to support their causes. A more subtle approach to influencing social policy concerns the ways that laws are actually implemented. Many years ago, I read in the news that handicapped parking regulations were about to be changed. The Illinois code originally required official vertical signs and pavement markings to indicate handicapped parking spaces. However, a task force recommended that the vertical signs could be optional and that ground markings would suffice.

I believed that this change was ill-advised. Without the vertical signs, nonhandicapped drivers were less likely to feel publicly shamed if they were able to obscure the ground markers by parking their cars right over them. As occurs all too frequently in policy decisions, nobody had taken the time to investigate whether the change would lead to more violations. Worse, no data had been collected to evaluate ways to keep nonhandicapped drivers from parking in reserved spaces. Many community organizations may relate to the importance of the need for this type of evaluation. Policy changes are certainly not immune to the law of unintended consequences and can inadvertently worsen conditions for a community. In this case, such a seemingly innocuous change would probably create fewer available handicapped parking spaces, making accessibility even harder for handicapped people.

To keep this obvious reality from being overlooked by the policy makers, I quickly organized a study that monitored the habits of drivers in a parking spot painted with a handicapped symbol (Jason & Jung, 1984). Often, the best way to find out whether a method is effective is to implement it for a period of time and then alternate between removing and replacing the method in the same area. By switching back and forth, you can gather data and compare the effects. In this case, we observed violations occurring 53% of the time over a 10-day period in handicapped spaces with only ground markings. When a prominent vertical sign was visible along with the ground markings, there were no violations for the next 4 days. The sign's effectiveness was very apparent: When it was taken down for several days, violations shot up to 47%. Not surprisingly, when we reposted the vertical sign for the next 5 days, illegal parking dropped back to 7%. The last time we removed the vertical signs, violations increased to 59%, and when the vertical sign was reposted, no violation observations occurred for the next 6 weeks.

This simple experiment provided us with the results I suspected—tangible evidence proving that ground markings alone were not very effective. Fortunately, before the Illinois Vehicle Code was amended, the task force chairperson told me that our study had been critical in convincing members of the need to retain vertical signs. The existing Illinois Vehicle Code was maintained. Policy evaluations do not have to be complicated, labor intensive, time consuming, or costly in order to influence regulations at the legislative level.

Nutrition and Supermarkets

Public health officials are warning us that the typical American diet has too much saturated fat, sugar, and salt. This diet has produced a generation of overweight adults and children who are at an alarming risk for serious chronic illnesses such as diabetes. Rather than waiting to implement evaluation techniques after problems have already occurred, we should be assessing what we can do to prevent them. One approach is to go to the source of people's food in the first place—the supermarkets. Despite the monopolistic features of these large stores, customers are the power holders; they have the power to influence these stores' financial bottom lines, as well as the products they carry. However, as we have seen, power holders are often reluctant to change their behaviors; if it's working, why tamper with success? Unless, of course, consumers alter that logic. A number of years ago, I worked on a study that tried to influence managers of supermarkets to stock healthier foods while simultaneously convincing consumers to buy it (Jason & Frasure, 1980).

Our initiative began with a team of DePaul researchers who went to four Chicago supermarkets. They found that, as expected, these stores did not stock the type of nutritional foods that were offered at health food stores. Once a week, we walked into the stores and talked to the store manager about carrying items such as brown rice. A separate target item was then prompted in each store for a 4-week period (using what is called a *multiple baseline design*). Our effort to increase the number of healthy foods that were stocked was successful in one store, which began stocking one of our suggested items. With that small success, we were convinced that it was possible to persuade at least some supermarkets to change what they carried.

Our next goal involved encouraging customers to buy healthier products. Much like the research on spaces for drivers who are handicapped, we counted the amount of products sold during a baseline period, posted a sign in one of the aisles, removed it, and then replaced it. The intervention involved posting an 18×14-inch sign in both English and Spanish next to the rice section, and we were able to double the purchase of the more nutritious product. The sign read:

> Buy BROWN RICE instead. It's More Nutritious.
>
> In fact, Brown Rice has more CALCIUM, POTASSIUM, IRON, SULFUR, and IODINE. And most importantly, Brown Rice contains a bran layer, which is extracted from white rice in milling processes. This bran layer is packed with protein and thiamine. And it's even easier to digest.
>
> Brown Rice has more of everything that's good for you.

These results were promising: Our in-store advertisement for brown rice was effective, and the store continued to stock the item. Rather than waiting for people to suffer weight or health problems, we can persuade supermarket managers to offer more high-quality products and encourage customers to select healthier food. Even with our recent push for fresh fruits and vegetables in inner-city convenient stores, the food desert—the availability of only processed foods—is still a fact of life for many areas of Chicago and other urban areas. If we want to protect the best interests of people in inner cities by enhancing their health and quality of life and save tax dollars spent on health care, more work needs to be done to provide fresh, unprocessed, and locally grown food to people in urban and suburban areas. Michelle Obama has been an energetic promoter in past years to change these types of lifestyle factors.

Media-Based Health Promotion Efforts

Self-report measures can also be used to evaluate campaigns that include large segments of the population who use media. About 30 years ago, I became interested in trying to decrease excessive television viewing (Jason, 1985), as well as negative advertising (Jason & Klich, 1982). In the latter study, we documented ageism, racism, sexism, and cigarette and alcohol advertisements in 24 print media sources over a 3-year period. We sent the findings to several activist organizations that used them to successfully expose these abuses to larger audiences. A key aspect of effecting social change is providing relevant details that can be presented to the public arena. Unfortunately, there was some fallout from this study that nearly affected my career. One of the media sources, the *Chicago Sun-Times*, published the results prominently on a full page. In an unfortunate coincidence, this happened on the same day that I was being evaluated for tenure at the university. It was a day that I would never forget. During my interview with members of the university tenure committee, the president of the university asked me what this study had to do with my discipline of psychology. Although I had inadvertently embarrassed a number of companies that contributed to the university, my strong publication record and endorsement from peers helped me ride out this controversy. Nevertheless, this experience served as a potent example of how even the best intentions and efforts can be risky endeavors for activists.

I next decided to design and launch a series of large-scale, community-based, preventive media interventions that targeted specific problems, such as addictive behaviors. Radio, television, social networking sites, and newspapers are the best ways to connect with the community; they can very effectively get people to participate in positive initiatives. Media outlets can reinforce the concepts and objectives of a campaign and encourage involvement. By advertising free health promotion pamphlets and materials through the media, individuals are given easy access to tools to educate themselves even further.

Health promotion interventions often use social marketing strategies to promote changes in behaviors and attitudes. Unlike commercials that bombard us with unnecessary products or socially irrelevant messages, we can educate people through the media by using the Four *P*s of marketing: a positive product (a change in behavior that improves one's health, such as giving up smoking); price (the costs and benefits of taking on this new behavior); place (the availability, or accessibility, of the new health product); and promotion (the positioning of the product in the community).

For a number of interventions, ranging from weight (Jason, Greiner, Naylor, Johnson, & Van Egeren, 1991) and stress management (Jason, Curran, Goodman, & Smith, 1989) to HIV prevention in families (Crawford et al., 1990), funding came entirely from partner organizations in Chicago. This demonstrated the power and effectiveness of community groups' resourcefulness and independence and proved that one does not have to rely on state or federal funds for assistance. These interventions can also be evaluated to ensure that the target audiences are being reached in meaningful ways. The interventions I helped to launch in the 1980s and '90s may serve as examples to guide organizers to create tailored, media-based interventions today.

Smoking Cessation Interventions

In the 1980s, after working to help establish nonsmoking sections in various settings in Chicago, I had the opportunity to begin work on creating media programs for tobacco cessation. As a member of the Smoking and Health Committee of the Chicago Lung Association, I noticed that only a minuscule number of smokers were participating in smoking cessation clinics led by the association throughout Chicago. It was obvious that the program was not serving its purpose and that a new direction was needed.

To reduce barriers of participation and reach large segments of the population, social psychologist Larry Gruder and I proposed that we begin a media-based effort that would make the program accessible to a wider audience. We launched a large-scale smoking cessation campaign on Channel 5, the NBC affiliate in Chicago, called "Freedom from Smoking in 20 Days." This self-help program aired twice in the evening for 3 weeks; its purpose was to encourage half a million viewers to pick up one of the 50,000 self-help manuals distributed in over 300 True Value Hardware stores. Biweekly support group meetings (advertised on the program) held throughout Chicago provided educational and social support. At the end of the program, 41% of those who watched the media program, received a manual, and attended self-help group meetings were able to quit smoking, compared to 21% of those who only watched the television broadcast and picked up manuals (Jason et al., 1987).

Using the momentum from our first successful effort, which put an effective structure in place, we sponsored another 20-day smoking cessation program in November of 1985. This time, we partnered with WGN-Channel 9, which allowed us to reach between approximately 286,000 and 583,000 people (about one-third of these viewers were likely to be smokers) in the Chicago area. This time, 100,000 free manuals were distributed (Jason, Tait, Goodman, Buckenberger, & Gruder, 1988).

Both of the 1985 health promotion programs were funded exclusively by the local community and potentially saved the successful quitters hundreds of millions of dollars. At the time, an estimated 150,000 smokers were involved in the media campaigns. If only 10% (a very conservative estimate) continued to abstain from cigarettes for the rest of their lives, then our programs would have helped 15,000 people quit smoking. The public health implications of these findings are profound; the lifetime health savings in preventing chronic disease, such as cancer, for each middle-aged adult who quits smoking is conservatively estimated to be $40,000. Our programs possibly saved

$600,000,000 in health care costs. This kind of cost–benefit analysis can be one of the most illustrative and compelling types of summative program evaluation.

Throughout the planning stages of each social action campaign, you gain valuable experience that prepares you for larger undertakings. With additional support from partners, you will also learn to successfully navigate through sensitive situations. To illustrate, several members of our planning group wanted to partner with McDonald's fast food restaurants to distribute our self-help manuals. Although McDonald's was willing to pay a lot of money for the increased traffic and publicity, I strongly objected, as these restaurants served fast foods with formidable health risks of their own. I believed it was important to remain true to our own values in every step of the social change process.

Tobacco and Addictions Prevention

Aside from helping smokers quit, I was also interested in preventing youth from picking up the habit in the first place (Jason, 1979; Jason, Mollica, & Ferone, 1982). My next media project in 1989 aimed specifically to change the type of exposure that African American youth received about tobacco in the media. In order to do this, we modified our media intervention approach for smoking cessation: Rather than using stores to distribute materials advertised on television, we delivered them right to participants' homes through local newspapers and popular shows.

We designed and implemented a prevention program at 472 elementary schools that combined the school-based curriculum, "Smoking Deserves a Smart Answer," from the American Lung Association and incorporated the use of media (Kaufman, Jason, Sawlski, & Halpert, 1994). Three popular media outlets partnered with us: WGCI ran eight smoking prevention public service announcements on the radio, created a call-in talk show that empowered parents to help their children resist smoking, and ran a smoking prevention rap contest, airing the winning entries. In addition, the *Chicago Defender* printed a smoking prevention curriculum on their weekly children's page, and a billboard company also promoted a prevention contest. Participants created posters, and the winning submissions were displayed on billboards in the Chicago area. These contests that promote creativity and encourage kids to express themselves through their own language and style can give the antismoking message a personal resonance for children. Our work paid off: Not only did students decrease their use of tobacco, but also they reported lower family use of cigarettes, alcohol, and marijuana.

In the spring of 1990, I helped to develop another smoking and drug prevention program for all school-age children along with the Illinois Department of Alcohol and Substance Abuse, and with the support of the *Chicago Tribune* and WGN News. We launched a statewide campaign aimed at children and parents called Kids InTouch (Jason, Pokorny, Kohner, & Bennetto, 1994). In this cross-platform approach, our InTouch daily supplement in the *Chicago Tribune* was published along with WGN news telecasts on the topics covered. Newspaper supplements provided information such as phone numbers for parent workshop sites, Chicago-area students' antidrug drawings and messages, a statewide resource guide to addiction prevention activities, and a referral for services on a national level.

By including facts about an issue and its effects on the community in your media intervention, you can build awareness, increase sensitivity to issues, and publicize support and training groups throughout the area. Our six-part news series explored topics like first-time drug use, abuse, and children of parents with substance abuse disorders. We also included individualized profiles of Chicago families who had overcome these issues. Parental involvement in the program was a significant component to bringing drug awareness to the family. More importantly, the parent–child bond strengthened the entire family and helped develop parenting skills.

We also broadcast our intervention through the time-honored kid tradition of Saturday morning cartoons. Our message aired on Chicago's Channel 32, as well as other stations on different days and times, for 6 consecutive weeks. The High Top Tower series was intended to prevent drug use and dealt with self-esteem, tactics for resisting drug use, problem solving, and alternatives to drugs. High Top Tower encouraged elementary-aged children to focus on family, health and safety concerns, and drug and alcohol awareness.

In these media efforts, we demonstrated how change agents can utilize local resources as they work to develop and implement large-scale prevention and health promotion campaigns. With the help of these resources, we strengthened the effectiveness of interventions by incorporating our efforts into participants' various "worlds"—for example, family, school, work, and community. Strong partnerships can lead to developing a network of key organizations. When planning our first media programming, we were fortunate that Donna Stein at a progressive health maintenance organization (HMO) was simultaneously seeking to launch a similar project; this helped us gain access to a number of for-profit businesses and television stations. The success of our first program was also a stepping stone to access to other media outlets and organizations.

Microcredit

Taking a step back from examples of program evaluations from my own career, the best case for the utility of measuring success is that of microcredit, a term that refers to a myriad of types of microloans and services that are provided to poor people who would otherwise be excluded from formal financial services. The microcredit model began with Grameen Bank in Bangladesh in 1976 and has been replicated around the globe, causing a revolution in the field of international development and shifting development funding priorities heavily in favor of microcredit programs. By 2009, nearly 200 million borrowers of microcredit have been served by microfinance institutions like Grameen Bank (Reed, 2011).

Although microcredit has been modified and reinvented from the Grameen framework, any variation of the model is easily evaluated. The success of microcredit programs can be measured in a number of tangible ways: microcredits granted, number of individuals receiving microcredits, repayment rates, savings or profits accrued by community bank lenders, and microcredit effectiveness indicators such as the number of houses built or small businesses started, among others. Collecting testimonies from the many beneficiaries of microcredit programs is also a compelling way to personalize the measures of success. The measurability of microcredit programs partly explains international donors' preference for these programs over other development initiatives with results that are harder to quantify. By measuring the outcomes of microcredit programs, microfinance institutions and nonprofit organizations have popularized and legitimized this model of development and are thereby able to capitalize on international funding support to expand and improve their microcredit programs.

Evaluating Unintended Consequences

If evaluations are poorly conducted or reported on, they can end up promoting unsuccessful programs. Interventions, such as youth mentoring programs, which people intuitively believe should have a positive effect, actually can have a negligible or even harmful impact depending on how they are implemented. These programs have become extremely popular in recent years—funding (primarily federal funding) has spurred a sixfold increase in the number of these kinds of programs over the past decade.

However, when the large-scale evaluation of the effectiveness of these programs was conducted, researchers found that only a handful of these programs actually had a meaningful impact on the lives of the vulnerable youth who were partnered with adult mentors (Rhodes, 2008). In research, the "effect size" is a concept that quantifies the real-world impact of an intervention; if the effect size is small, your program may have had an impact, but the "size" of this impact could be negligible. Therefore, poorly reported program evaluations will tout the fact that a statistically significant difference exists between groups of youth who participated in a mentoring program and those who did not, but will fail to mention that a very small effect size was found. In the large-scale evaluation of mentoring programs, small effect sizes across most programs were found; some programs showed negative or no effects, and the positive effects that were discovered often faded away within just a few months after the "successful" program ended (Rhodes, 2008).

As Rhodes and DuBois (2006, p. 13) point out:

> Modest findings from the evaluation of an intensive community-based approach to mentoring helped to galvanize a movement and stimulate aggressive growth goals. These goals necessitated that mentoring be delivered more efficiently, which, in turn, changed the intervention to something that bears decreasing resemblance to its inspiration.

This is not to say that all mentoring programs fail—and, in fact, the research shows that some have quite positive impacts. However, poor research, reporting, and understanding of evaluation results have resulted in millions of wasted federal funds and a push for quantity over quality of mentoring programs. It illustrates the importance of rigorous evaluation in developing new or expanding existing programs (Rhodes, 2008); researchers must even be skeptical and impartial toward programs that intuitively *seem* beneficial—the reality may surprise you.

Lessons Learned

In this chapter, I explained the importance of evaluating change efforts. Few initiatives, no matter how positive, are successful without some type of documentation to support your efforts. To this end, community activists, who may not be trained to design and evaluate a means of tracking a project's progress, may be best served by joining forces with researchers. Cooperation and flexibility among the activist and the researchers are critical, as both parties venture into unfamiliar areas of expertise. For this two-way relationship to thrive, everyone involved should respect the dignity, opinions, and needs of all of the partners. This respect will lead to trust among researchers and the community members, which will help facilitate an understanding of how each member's strengths or skills can best be utilized to achieve the mutual goal. In addition, each party must recognize and appreciate the fact that roles can evolve over time.

When trying to bring about second-order change, activists often must deal with powerful individuals and institutions. When this happens, coalitions can help challenge those who want to maintain the status quo. Because this process usually takes place over long periods of time, activists must develop the patience and persistence to see the task through. Our final principle of social change, measurement, provides the opportunity to consider the tangible short- and long-term results of our activities. Using evaluation techniques such as self-reported data and observed changes, we can determine whether or not a particular intervention or social change strategy has achieved its goals. Far from dry or lifeless, evaluation is a tremendously powerful tool that helps us discard ineffective strategies and replace them with more successful methods.

For many scholars, traditional academic practice involves publishing one's findings and then expecting the results to have a voice and influence in the public forum. I once published a study, in an obscure journal, exploring psychological damage to women who had been harassed by men (Jason, Reichler, Easton, Neal, & Wilson, 1984). After the study was published, I was contacted by a lawyer in Philadelphia who informed me that he was using the findings of my study to support his client in court against a harasser. Was this social action research? Since the findings were used in the public domain, in a sense, it was. However, from a community perspective, if publication of the findings does not lead to some second-order outcome, then the activists and researchers should try other methods to shed light on the findings and attempt to influence social policy.

The examples of evaluation that were presented in this chapter informed me that many of my interventions were ultimately successful, even if adjustments needed to be made from failures along the way. The successful results that we were able to quantify were helpful in justifying and garnering support for future interventions. The purpose of evaluation, however, is not only to point out our successes; evaluation must be an unbiased judge—able to highlight where programs have failed to produce meaningful effects.

One aspect of producing quality research is accounting for and minimizing confounding variables. For example, when we were trying to determine the effects of "no smoking" signs on smokers within a neighborhood grocery store, a security guard saw the signs and tried to help us by telling customers to "kill that cigarette." Ironically, since our research aimed to assess the effects of the signs alone in encouraging people to stop smoking in this public setting, we immediately asked him to discontinue his intervention. Counterintuitive to the overall goal of our activism, it was important to be able to accurately assess the effects of the signs alone to know if and how to alter future interventions. During our community efforts to encourage dog owners to pick up after their dogs, a girl scout troop heard of our efforts and began distributing flyers to the community that described dog owners who did not pick up after their dogs in the most unflattering ways. Although comical, the girl scouts' actions also could have altered the results of our research.

Just like these unintended confounds, researchers must also keep track of the unintended consequences that occur from our interventions (Trickett &

Mitchell, 1993); sometimes, our second-order efforts are altered in ways we do not expect. For example, a state official once asked me for advice about funding a community-based organization with which I was very familiar. Since I knew the organization's leaders and its mission, I felt confident in my recommendations. It was a relatively small and seemingly harmless intervention on my part, but when the state began funding this community organization, the push for a statewide program expansion distorted the mission and it no longer met the needs of its members. Instead, it became driven by economics; the organization's generous volunteer services were replaced with a mandated, impersonal program.

Over the years, I've seen far too many cases like this one: When state or federal funding becomes involved, it can hamper self-help groups and organizations from voluntarily contributing to community-based programs. Unforeseen issues, such as funding, can complicate the delivery of second-order types of programming and, in the process, contribute to more first-order interventions that become part of the problem. Evaluating these important types of well-intentioned failures can help guide organizations toward more successful second-order change strategies.

Unfortunately, sometimes unforeseen effects can have much more dire consequences. At the far extreme of such consequences, consider the scientists who researched the structure and properties of the atom at the beginning of the 20th century, unaware that their scientific breakthroughs eventually would lead to the creation of the atomic bomb and the unforgettable devastation at the end of World War II. While the United States' decision to drop the bomb on major Japanese cities led to Japan's surrender, the ethics of using atomic weapons on civilians was not properly examined by our government or by the scientists who developed the bomb. The discovery of these weapons also caused the ensuing 50-year atomic arms race with the Soviet Union, which has created, despite later disarmament efforts, present-day nuclear arsenals with enough power to destroy the world several times over.

Other times, the research itself, rather than its implications, goes against basic ethical and moral codes. For over 40 years (between 1932 and 1972), the U.S. Public Health Service conducted an experiment on African American men with syphilis to investigate the effects of untreated syphilis on the body. These men were never told they were suffering from syphilis and were not treated, even though by the 1940s, penicillin had been discovered as an effective treatment (Jones, 1993). Even the Surgeon General participated in the experiment by convincing the men to remain in the program. In 1972, the story finally broke in the *Washington Star*; the government was forced to end its experiment and provide the men with effective treatment, but by then, over 100 men had died and dozens of women and children had been infected.

Although this type of medical research falls into a different category than the evaluative research that is key to measuring the success of social activism, it is

important that researchers and activists alike are aware of the powerful consequences that research can have when ethical standards are not upheld. When
working for social change, we must pay close attention to the moral issues
behind our work and consider both its possible intended and possible unintended consequences in order to strive to achieve the most beneficial outcomes
of our actions.

Additional Resources

For more information on the American Lung Association's "Freedom from Smoking" program,
visit this site: http://www.ffsonline.org/program-overview.html

This link includes a video clip on the dynamics of smoking, and it shows networks from 1971
when smoking was prevalent to many years later as smoking was reduced in the general
population: http://www.nejm.org/doi/full/10.1056/NEJMsa0706154

Chris Corbett (2011) has developed excellent materials for working with legislators. He can be
contacted at chris_corbett1994@hotmail.com

Steven R. Howe (2007) also has done exemplary policy work related to housing and the transition to self-sufficiency for low-income populations.

Steve Fawcett (2011) and an international team of health care workers has developed the
Community Tool Box, which has more than 7,000 pages of free information on skills for
building healthy communities. It can be found at this site: http://ctb.ku.edu

For those with interests in qualitative analysis methods, there are a number of excellent online
websites (e.g., http://onlineqda.hud.ac.uk/Introduction/index.php) that provide a collection of learning tools for conducting these types of analyses. Mixed-methods research
involving both quantitative and qualitative methods is the topic of Jason and Glenwick's
(2012) book *Methodological Approaches to Community-Based Research.* This book provides
more advanced research strategies for understanding cutting-edge research methodologies
that analyze data in special groupings, over time, or within various contexts, which are
holistic and culturally valid and support contextually grounded community interventions.

To read a *New York Times* article that identified evidence-based programs that are happening
at various government levels, visit this link. It gives an idea of how we can help to create
policy change: http://opinionator.blogs.nytimes.com/2012/05/30/worthy-of-government-
funding-prove-it/

6

The Root of the Issue

Each principle of social change represents part of the social change journey, but they are subtly interrelated. When used tactfully in concert, they can create an unstoppable force in any movement. There is one underlying concept that influences all of the principles and should not be overlooked: historical context. When identifying power holders, one also needs to recognize how they first arrived in that position and why they have continued to maintain control; without this knowledge, tactics to thwart their efforts could be fruitless, or only first-order change could occur. Similarly, community leaders need to work with or create coalitions in order to form strategies to produce real, enduring change. Activists also need to stay committed to an issue over time and evaluate their actions. With this in mind, the five principles reviewed in this book are summarized in Table 6.1.

This last chapter examines how individual and societal values originated over time, and this context may provide us with an understanding of the underlying basis and dynamics of why some people and organizations gain and abuse power. I believe that this type of background information—knowledge of the history of the people and the power dynamics of the settings you hope to change—is vital. Through a historical perspective, we can better account for the development of many of our societal problems and understand mechanisms for creating truly effective second-order change. Having knowledge of the values and background of the individuals with whom you collaborate or challenge in an advocacy effort also allows you to be a more effective agent of change. But first, I hope to provide context into my own background and belief systems that have led to the development of these principles for social change.

My Formative Years

My dad was a man who knew how to make people laugh. As a Jewish nightclub comic in the Catskills of New York, he was good friends with many successful

Table 6.1 **The Five Principles of Social Change**

---

1. Determining the nature of the change desired: Is it a cosmetic, short-term fix or does it address the roots of the problem?

2. Identifying the power holders: Who are your influential friends and foes?

3. Creating coalitions: Identify and work with others who share your goals.

4. Learning patience and persistence: Small wins are key to attaining long-term goals.

5. Measuring your success: What have you accomplished? What is left to achieve?

---

entertainers of the 1930s through the 1990s—comics, singers, memory experts, and magicians. He played at the top night clubs in Miami Beach, Las Vegas, Hollywood, Chicago, and New York. He was a good friend of many leading entertainers, including Rodney Dangerfield and Jackie Mason. Before Woody Allen became famous, he wanted to write jokes for my father. Unfortunately, my dad thought Woody Allen's humor would not go over well in the Catskills. My dad even made appearances on the Ed Sullivan Show and Mike Wallace's Nite Beat and was on television programs that were as far away as Australia. My dad loved his work, which spanned seven decades from 1934 to 2000. I saw his passion, and I knew I had to find something like it for myself. I didn't inherit my dad's gift for standup comedy, but he did leave me with a sense of humor that helped me in my own career to build relationships, defuse tensions, and accept defeats.

Most change agents will often have many frustrating experiences before they discover the cause that will define their activism. I had become disillusioned with politics as a volunteer for the Lyndon Johnson presidential campaign, and I turned to existentialism after reading Albert Camus' *Myth of Sisyphus* (1955). Camus' main character, Sisyphus, had created meaning in the world by his personal revolt, asserting human meaning against the indifference of the universe. However, each time Sisyphus rolled a stone up the hill, it would simply roll down again. For a time, it was appealing to create my own values, but the actual tenets of the philosophy felt inherently dry, unanimated, and lifeless. Thankfully, my existentialist stint did not last long.

My undergraduate years at Brandeis University were a challenging and intellectually invigorating period of my life. The values of humanistic psychology, formulated by Abraham Maslow (1962)—the quest toward self-actualization, the ability to appreciate the mysteries of life, and a commitment to developing our human potential—deeply affected me and pulled me out of existentialism. These humanistic goals could be applied further, I realized, to build supportive relationships, enhance communications, and develop safe environments, all of which could bring about positive change. However, I also learned that people are hindered from developing positive qualities by primitive needs to dominate others and seek power.

One of my most memorable classes as an undergraduate was taught by Morrie Schwartz, who was profiled in the book *Tuesdays With Morrie* (Albom, 1997). In this fascinating course, about 15 students and I were asked to interact with one another, on a verbal and nonverbal level, and then provide feedback to each other about the interaction. It was a basic idea—simply interact—but for me it was a greatly transformative experience. I learned from Morrie that one could approach and experience the world in an alternative way—quieter, softer, more meditative, balanced, and harmonious. Around the same time, I read Somerset Maugham's novel, *The Razor's Edge* (1944), and was intrigued with the main character's spiritual journey and the peace he achieves in the end from his quest. The principles of humanism and the idea of spiritual awakening greatly broadened my belief system at the time.

At Brandeis, I also had the opportunity to learn from psychologists with diverse perspectives at a time when new approaches were emerging within the field. I learned about the principles of behaviorism—that people will respond to cues and could be conditioned to elicit certain behaviors. Although it may seem cold and contrasting to my newfound interests in humanism and spirituality, the ideas fascinated me. My undergraduate advisor, Dr. Brendon Maher, was one of the first behavioral psychopathologists. I also took a course with Dr. Mulholland, one of the creators of biofeedback therapy. He had been influenced by the behaviorist B. F. Skinner (founder of the school of radical behaviorism and the ideas of operant conditioning), with whom I had the chance to meet in the 1970s. Psychology was such a new and burgeoning field that my professors could still trace their mentorship lineage to the founder of psychology, Dr. Wilhelm Wundt. One of my professors, Dr. Krech, welcomed us to our first class by saying, "My mentor had been taught by Dr. Wundt.... You are now four generations from the founder of psychology, and by being in this class, I will pass on the mantle to you." He then shook each of our hands. It felt extremely empowering: I was personally welcomed into a field that I felt had the potential to transform lives.

For the first time in my life, thanks to my experiences at Brandeis, I understood how people develop unhealthy behaviors and, more importantly, realized that these behaviors could be learned and unlearned. I applied what I was learning to several outreach projects through tutoring disadvantaged children, teaching infants who were blind and deaf, and coteaching several psychology courses at a local high school. In one state hospital, I even talked with a psychotic patient who had been analyzed by Sigmund Freud. My encounters with all of these people helped me appreciate the history of psychology and see how people can slowly change over time. I learned then that gradual and steady progress would characterize my work, in whatever facet of psychology I chose to pursue.

During my undergraduate years, I also volunteered once a week at a nursing home where I met people outside of the classroom who also inspired me. Mrs.

Trapp was one of these residents, an elderly woman who had been an accomplished French scholar. Sadly, she was bedridden, and only a few people took the time to talk with her each day. Her life experiences gave her wisdom and valuable insights, but no one on the nursing staff appreciated that she had something to offer. I could not accept the fact that this was the end of her journey: confined to a bed, in a sterile environment, and dependent on uncaring attendants. I was deeply upset that such an inhumane place could exist for those who should be treated with honor and veneration. The treatment she received was a product of a problematic environment, and this experience awakened my sensitivity to the role of situational factors in creating second-order change.

After I finished college in 1971, I spent time on a kibbutz—a communal farm—in Israel before attending graduate school at the University of Rochester. Unlike what volunteering at the nursing home had taught me, I wanted to see how supportive environments could allow people to live and work cooperatively in a community setting. From classes like Morrie's, I had learned that simple, positive interactions among people in a group could be extremely invigorating, but I had never experienced a community setting in which these principles were put into action. The time I spent living on this communal farm reinforced my newly found beliefs in the power of community support and connection.

When my time in Israel was over, I began graduate school in clinical psychology and continued to broaden the scope of my knowledge of very different schools of psychology. During my graduate training at the University of Rochester, I learned different methods that would help me tailor my approach, depending on the situation I encountered. I worked in Dr. Stanley Sapon's Nonverbal Behavior Laboratory, where we used behaviorist approaches to teach nonverbal children to speak. One of my supervisors, Dr. Howard Friedman, however, was trained by psychoanalysts who had been trained directly by Dr. Sigmund Freud. I was able to learn several different therapy models and, from this, realized the importance of using methods from various styles to understand people and the world. For example, Dr. Friedman taught me to use certain words and phrases to help clients remember their childhood during their course of therapy. Under Dr. Sapon, I needed to use a vocabulary to describe only the behavior of people, rather than any kind of insight into their past. Another supervisor, Rita Underberg, a neo-Freudian, encouraged my therapeutic work to focus solely on the interpersonal relationship between myself and the client.

By then, I had acquired three different methods and vocabularies from different supervisors. Most of the time, I was able to use the appropriate vocabulary in each setting. If I did accidentally mix terminology, I would quickly apologize and return to the theoretical framework of which my supervisor approved. This training was invaluable in helping me interact and work with people who hold differing perspectives and ways of understanding the world.

My graduate school mentor, Dr. Emory Cowen, had an even greater impact on my career path than any of my other supervisors. Dr. Cowen was one of the founders of community psychology and strongly shaped my interest in the field of clinical-community psychology. This field emerged during the turbulent 1960s and used public health approaches to advocate for social action, prevention, and environmental change. While my academic program was focused on training me to be a clinical psychologist, my community research interests focused on prevention and social change. While I was in my first few months of graduate school, Dr. Cowen said that there would never be enough psychologists to meet the demand for mental health services. Interestingly, in stark contrast to the views of my supervisors, he noted that research showed little measurable difference in therapeutic outcome when comparing counselors who were college students with bachelor degrees to clinical psychologists with doctoral degrees for a wide variety of clinical problems. Perhaps those with less training bring more passion to their work and, therefore, were able to achieve better outcomes with some patients. Regardless, if 4 years of education to be a PhD in clinical psychology would not undoubtedly make me a better therapist than a lesser trained person, then I wanted to be a psychologist who went beyond the traditional role of providing psychotherapy. I decided to return to the issues of social change that had interested me since my youth.

To bridge my interests in social action and psychology, as a graduate student, I designed and evaluated prevention programs for underprivileged toddlers in the inner city of Rochester (Jason, Clarfield, & Cowen, 1973). These children were lagging in motor and verbal skills. We brought our infant stimulation program into the parents' homes once per week and showed family members how to encourage their children's educational and social development. We then asked parents to attend weekly support group meetings (Jason, 1977). I was proud to be a part of this program, as it was the first time that I witnessed the principles I had learned in the classroom being put to use in a community setting. Before I knew it, I was becoming a clinical-community psychologist.

In 1975, I came to Chicago to accept a teaching and research position at DePaul University, and by 1989, with grant funding, I supervised close to 20 people in my department. We launched a variety of community interventions, such as efforts to help children with school transitions (Bogat, Jones, & Jason, 1980) and to reduce prejudice among elementary children by enhancing inter-ethnic relationships (Rooney-Rebeck & Jason, 1986). Our research found that by working with the parents in addition to the children, our school transition interventions were more effective (Jason et al., 1992); this evidence further supported the strength of the ecological model of taking holistic approaches to solving community problems, and I continue to apply it in my career. The diverse training I received as a young man has shaped and informed each campaign for social change and research project of which I have been a part during my career.

But my youth and my educational background were not the only two factors that significantly impacted my professional aspirations and views on life. My struggle with myalgic encephalomyelitis (ME)/chronic fatigue syndrome (CFS) later in life also had a profound impact on the development of the principles of social change and the philosophy behind them.

Dealing With Illness

Since beginning my career at DePaul University in 1975, I have been able to investigate a number of social problems. Although all of them were important to me, none was as deeply personal as my involvement with ME/CFS research. During my trying journey of recovery from ME/CFS, I learned the importance of having spiritual, interpersonal, and environmental support structures in place.

I knew that I needed to bring balance back into my life in order to get better. Several friends brought me tapes by doctors and academics who promoted alternative and humanistic approaches to healing, such as Norman Cousins, Jerry Jampolsky, and Bernie Siegel. Siegel worked with cancer patients who, despite the fact that they were dying, had learned to live, love, and be vital. Their message moved me: While we all expect to die, what matters most is how we live before we die. I pledged that if I recovered, I would live with renewed zest and vitality. But how was I going to accomplish this, especially in my depleted state? Siegel told a story about an older man who was asked how he might have chosen to live his life differently. He said he would have had more fun, kicked up his heels, acted sillier, and behaved in a more carefree way. Also, he would have liked to have smelled more flowers, taken more risks, and opened his heart to more friends.

Inspired by Thomas Mann's novel *The Magic Mountain* (1995), I tried to first find my center, my core, where neither fear nor desire could move me. To do this, I felt that I needed to be around supportive people; perhaps my immune system would kick in. I visited friends in Montana who had a ranch where they raised sheep, bred horses, and grew crops organically. It was nestled in the pines on the side of a mountain. For the first time in many months, I was with people who knew exactly how I felt and what I needed. I started learning yoga and meditation. I felt I could be around people again and feel normal once more. This temporary community gave me the hope that I desperately needed. I then went to a farm in Wisconsin that practiced community-supported agriculture. I took day trips to nearby state parks and small country towns, watched the leaves turn, and swam in lakes. My first swim lasted only a few minutes. Gradually, I worked my way up to 10 minutes, but I paid the price—I was exhausted the next day.

In Bernie Siegel's (1990) book *Love, Medicine, and Miracles,* I read about a World War II concentration camp inmate named Wild Bill, and his story inspired me. Even in his cruel, appalling, inhumane environment, Wild Bill managed to remain positive and enthusiastic. He encouraged others—it was, he felt, the only way to survive. Before the war, his family had been rounded up by the Nazis and ruthlessly killed. As he stood and witnessed his family's execution, he realized that he had an overwhelming and almost unbearable hatred for the Nazis. However, he eventually realized that this same type of overwhelming hatred had motivated the Nazis to kill the people he loved the most. Amazingly, at that moment, he decided to end the cycle and find a way to love these people. I embraced this wonderful philosophy; no matter how wretched I felt, I would seek to find a way to appreciate every moment.

Reading Martine Rudee and Jonathan Blease's (1989) *Traveler's Guide to Healing Centers and Retreats in North America* and Corinne McLaughlin and Gordon Davidson's (1986) *Builders of the Dawn* also gave me hope. These authors described a movement in which planned communities, with varying degrees of communal living, were emerging all over the country and the world. Sometimes the communities were designed for people with special needs, but the communities were often filled with regular people who wanted to live in an environment where people worked together and cared about each other. The residents shared community goals and committed time each week or month to perform shared tasks—working in a communal garden, cleaning and maintaining their homes, or harvesting crops. This concept greatly appealed to me, and I investigated these communities more. Unfortunately, I found out that one called Gesundheit—a free, health-oriented haven in which people could recover from illness—would not be open for a couple of years. L'Arche, a community for people with mental retardation, would not accept people who did not have this disability. I needed to be sponsored to stay on the grounds of a community called "the Farm," but none of the residents would sponsor me, and with good reason: These communities were looking for members with physical and mental stamina who could help build their communities in concrete ways.

Although I was not admitted into these communities, my journey to other supportive environments made me much stronger. After traveling to several other restful oases, I regained enough strength to resume my job at DePaul on a part-time basis. Although I only had a quarter of my previous energy level, it was still a vast improvement.

Slowly, over time, I got stronger. As with the hero's journeys described by Joseph Campbell (1949) in his book on mythologies, *The Hero With a Thousand Faces*, I had to enter the darkest part of my forest, through which there was no visible path or anyone to lead me on my way. I was able to take the time I needed, and I had the financial resources to benefit from one community after another, until I regained enough strength to sustain myself. However, many patients with ME/CFS and other chronic conditions do not have even the most basic resources—such as affordable housing or health care. These situations perpetuate a vicious cycle: No one will recover without a place to live or needed medications. In fact, such deprivations exacerbate the illness. Some become so desperate that they end their lives. In a civilized society, this is simply wrong.

My own experience gave me additional insight and clarity into the urgent need for supportive environments for these and other disenfranchised people. Both caregivers and patients can mutually benefit from living together. Humanitarian and democratic values would replace economic issues as the basis for the creation of these settings. I had an intuitive belief that such communities would be cheaper to run, and they would also be substantially more effective. It was at this time, in 1991, that I learned of Oxford Houses. I decided to work with this organization as a model for people in need, whether they were homeless, suffering from chronic illnesses, or suffering from substance use disorders.

Four Vulnerabilities

During my illness, I reflected on a series of events throughout history that have created a set of vulnerabilities in our modern-day world. These vulnerabilities have contributed to the abuses of power that we see on a daily basis. They provide a historical overview of what we ultimately need to confront in our efforts to bring about social change. Inherent to these vulnerabilities are both dangers and opportunities for growth and transformation, depending on how we relate to them. Understanding these vulnerabilities will provide the social change agent with a clearer perspective of the challenges they face and knowledge of the underlying risk factors that help to identify why power abuses occur. Through a historical approach, we can also recognize the need for second-order change efforts, community support to confront power differentials, patience to uphold a movement over time, and evaluation that ensures that organizations for change are on a solid course to obtain their objectives. The characteristics of all value-based, second-order change campaigns are forged from a historical perspective (Jason, 1997).

Our First Vulnerability: Genetic Contributions to Power Abuses

Evidence of humans' innate aggressive nature in corporate America provides a glimpse of these self-serving and hostile tendencies. In *The Cheating Culture—Why More Americans Are Doing Wrong to Get Ahead*, David Callahan (2004) characterizes Enron and WorldCom's financial collapse in the early 2000s by stating:

> Simply put, we have a nastier, more cutthroat set of values than previous generations did. As the race for money and status has intensified,

it has become more acceptable for individuals to act opportunistically and dishonestly to get ahead. Notions of integrity have weakened. (p. 106)

Some of the roots of these tendencies can be traced to Adam Smith (1904), who published the first modern work in the field of economics in 1776, *An Inquiry Into the Nature and Causes of the Wealth of Nations*. He proposed that people benefit the community around them by acting solely in their own self-interest. In other words, *individual selfishness* actually produces the maximum social good (Blaug, 1985; Ross, 1995). He advocated abolishing government attempts to disrupt this *natural order*, such as restrictions on free trade. This laissez-faire doctrine had an enormous impact on Western economic thought and institutions, and his ideas became the model for capitalist societies throughout the world.

The banking and housing crisis of 1998 provides a stark example of what has gone wrong with this laissez-faire policy in our society. Twenty years ago, bankers were under no illusions about the people to whom they were giving loans. Home appraisals were legitimate, and banks owned the loans. But in the early 2000s, this all changed. Those changes led to the worst financial catastrophe since the Great Depression, in not only the United States but also the world. The corruption that we see and the abuse of power that characterized the mortgage industry in the 2000s were due in part to the repeal of the Glass Steagall Act of 1933. It had been passed to put a firewall between two types of banking activities: placing money in conservative banks versus placing money in more speculative entities such as stocks. President Clinton repealed this act in 1999 and tore down the safeguard between bank deposits (guaranteed by the federal government) and more speculative investments. President Bush later removed a variety of regulatory activities in the 2000s; those powerful few at the top of the income ladder had enormous clout to pass laws that favored the rich and ultimately created institutions that were too big to fail. There was no accountability, and the number of Americans who owed large amounts of money on their homes skyrocketed. Fraud ran rampant; loan officers, investment bankers, and pension fund managers were making outrageous returns. According to Michael Hudson's (2011) *The Monster*, almost all the subprime loans (with high interest rates) went to owners who were refinancing their homes or to first-time homeowners who had barely any money to put down.

Corruption began with the appraisal process. Business only went to those who were willing to misrepresent the value of their homes. In other words, honesty was punished. Moreover, bank telemarketers were promised $10,000 a month if they could persuade people to secure loans, but the majority of the people they persuaded had no business doing so. Wall Street financed these loans using mortgage-backed securities. It seemed that everyone connected to this scheme was making a lot of money, except for the soon-to-be victims who purchased the subprime loans. By 2008, these corrupt practices had put the entire world into a deep recession. Those who perpetuated this financial crisis were not punished, and we have learned little from these abuses of power. In fact, Wall Street's biggest banks are now even larger than they were in the mid-2000s (Morgenson & Rosner, 2011).

There is now an army of thousands of Wall Street lobbyists in Washington, and through them, powerful people in the industry contribute funds and resources to influence those who make legislative and executive decisions. Limiting financial contributions to $100 per person or organization to a political campaign would level the playing field, but our legislators have little interest in this effective solution. Isn't it interesting that the banks were rewarded for their unethical risk taking, but legislation has now been passed stating that if an individual is overwhelmed with debt and seeks relief through bankruptcy, home and student loans are never forgiven? I do believe that some of these corrupt practices and abuses of power stem from aggression that we have inherited from our genetic past.

Evolutionary tendencies have been the subject of many books by prominent psychologists and psychoanalysts, the most famous being Sigmund Freud. Konrad Lorenz's landmark book, *On Aggression* (1974), illustrated how deeply rooted these tendencies are. For 95% to 99% of our history, we have been hunters; the leap from hunter of animals to corporate predator is not a big one. Violence, in the form of highly aggressive, competitive, and libidinal tendencies, dates back to our genetic animal ancestry.

We share about 96% of the same DNA with chimpanzees, our closest animal relative. Jane Goodall's work in Gombe, Tanzania, provided groundbreaking clues about the ancestors of our species: Like us, chimpanzees instinctively live in communal groups for protection and support. They protect their children and provide them with food and safety. Like chimpanzees, our altruistic or selfless behaviors create a biochemical reward via the release of endorphins, the chemicals emitted during vigorous exercise. This natural high makes us want to continue to help others. It is also likely that chimpanzees' abundant energy, playfulness, and vitality are genetic characteristics that reside naturally within human beings, and these vibrant inner resources can supply the fuel for an animated and spirited life.

However, not all chimpanzee behavior is playful or altruistic. Dr. Goodall was disturbed when she observed tribes of chimpanzees systematically killing members of other groups and acting fiercely territorial. Often, a dominant chimpanzee displays aggression in order to show others that he is at the top of the social hierarchy. Although the genetic basis of aggression remains poorly understood (Bock & Goode, 1996), many intriguing findings have emerged. For example, after the neurotransmitter serotonin was identified in relation to offensive attacks by mice, genetically modified mice were created by manipulating a receptor for serotonin. These mutant mice showed a strong tendency to attack other mice.

Our history of continuous warfare and struggles for power alone serves as evidence that we share these aggressive biological tendencies. For some, this most primitive vulnerability manifests itself as a need for unquenchable power and status: to climb to the top of the hierarchy or to constantly assert superiority over others. While animals use these hostile inclinations as adaptive responses to territorial challenges, we often use them to exploit those with fewer resources or less power.

Our genetic history is one of the four vulnerabilities with which we are confronted: It can either reinforce self-serving, abusive expressions of power or diminish them. Ideally, we would nurture the altruistic, joyous genetic aspects of ourselves and would create communities and systems that foster these qualities. Some people manage to do this, and these kinds of environments do exist, but another part of us is also hard-wired for aggression. In the next sections, we will explore cultural and societal values that have been able to moderate this genetic aspect of ourselves and vulnerabilities that have encouraged these innate aggressive qualities and contributed to the power abuses that we see so commonly in our world today.

Our Second Vulnerability: Separation From Nature

About 2 million years ago, the first primitive human beings, known as *Homo habilis* (Latin for "handy man"), emerged. They learned to bash rocks together to create a sharp stone, the first cutting tool. Some anthropologists maintain that this development marked the dawn of human technology. With less hair on their bodies, sweating helped them to not overheat as they pursued prey for long distances. *Homo sapiens* emerged in Africa around 100,000 to 200,000 years ago and then migrated throughout the world. Our biological evolution ended, finally, 40,000 years ago with the appearance of language.

When *Homo sapiens* entered new lands about 11,000 years ago—for example, Australia, Hawaii, and the Americas—many indigenous animal species became extinct. Some indigenous cultures allowed their aggressive hunting instincts to exterminate species and rampantly destroy land (such as with cut-and-burn agriculture). Other native cultures, after these extinctions occurred, saw a balance reemerge between the remaining animals and *Homo sapiens*. This balance, and accompanying respect for nature, allowed them to live in a more respectful and interdependent world.

From 10,000 BCE onward, a great transformation occurred with the widespread development of agriculture and animal husbandry. This agricultural revolution was born out of our impulse to control nature. Horticultural agriculture became one of the earliest methods of farming because it was based on the use of a hoe or a simple digging stick. Horticultural farming soon evolved into agrarian farming that was based on animal-drawn plows, which proved to be more economical than both hunting and gathering. The production of more food helped establish an expanding population. With a larger population, not all people were needed to provide food; thus, more had the freedom and time to devote to cultural endeavors such as writing, mathematics, and metallurgy. However, these innocuous-seeming new methods had some negative consequences: Resources in the forests and fields were sometimes exhausted. Some early villages failed when their land became barren and could no longer provide food for the people, such as the Mayan civilization.

A fundamental balance with the land was a critical factor in most civilizations that began appearing throughout the world. Old Mesopotamia, for example, emerged as a partnership with the fertile banks of the Tigris and Euphrates rivers around 3500 BCE. As cities grew and flourished, so did intellectual and philosophical study, yet their traditions never strayed from their awareness and deep belief that if they did not honor and live with nature, nature would not bestow its bounty. In India around 2000 BCE, inhabitants believed that, consistent with their Hindu religion, all life—including land, plants, and animals—was sacred. Beginning around 1500 BCE, China's great civilizations were also based on a reverence for moral and natural order; they were heavily influenced by Confucius, who advocated respect for the family and the law, and by Lao Tsu's principles of honoring the forces of nature. During the period from about 2500 to 500 BCE, these Eastern philosophies spread to, and were accepted by, the planting people because they spoke to their goddesses. Through the Upanishads, the Hindu philosophical texts, the teachings of Buddha, and the writings of Lao Tsu, a way of life that emphasized living in tune with nature was strengthened. This is not to deny that there were many abuses of power that occurred with these early civilizations, such as slavery and frequent wars.

As *Homo sapiens*, we shared a deep-rooted bond with the animal kingdom. Over time, however, we began to distinguish ourselves from other animals, believing that our human world was distinct. Although some animals have the capacity, like us, to solve problems, they are intellectually limited. Our growing mastery over the natural environment began to differentiate us and led to the recognition of, and reflection upon, our unique condition. We began to exert more control over our surroundings. This increased awareness and understanding of the natural world led to our second vulnerability. Two dissimilar philosophies of relating to nature emerged: One sanctified and appreciated our interconnectedness with the land and other animals; the other simply repudiated our link with the animal world—a world seen as wild, dangerous, and in need of taming. In other words, we could either be aligned with the natural world or be separated from it.

For some, fear of nature and the broken bond between humankind and the natural world created an ever-pressing need for self-preservation and control: If we are alienated from each other and nature, then we must protect ourselves. This world becomes a threat; animals are in competition for mastery of the land and food sources. The only way to *win*—to be the highest in the animal hierarchy—was to control as many other people and species as possible. This "every man and woman for him- or herself" worldview has endured, and even been strengthened in some cultures, ever since.

Over time, Western civilization's philosophical and religious systems gradually gained dominance over many other ideologies throughout the world. In *Guns, Germs & Steel*, Jared Diamond (2005) contends that environmental circumstances gave rise to this Western dominance. He explains that Eurasians lived in areas with higher protein crops and a variety of animals that were suitable for domestication. Although the domestication of animals was partly responsible for the genesis of epidemic infectious diseases that claimed millions of lives in these areas, Europeans gradually gained some genetic and exposure resistance. However, when European explorers arrived in the New World, the diseases they brought with them ravaged the native populations and helped facilitate Europe's conquest of the Americas. The wealth of precious metals and natural resources that Europe gained through conquest further solidified its power and world influence.

The ancient Greek civilization had first proposed that knowledge could be gained only through justification through reason. But relying solely on rational thought came at a price: Rather than living in accordance with the natural world, some Greeks suggested that we were fundamentally separate from nature.

Our second vulnerability, our attempt to dominate and control nature, fundamentally changed and altered the balance among different species and within our own bodies. Even worse, our predilection for manipulating nature has destroyed entire ecosystems. However, when resources were abundant and the world was sparsely populated, attempts to control and dominate nature had few serious ecological consequences. Like the genetic polarity of aggression and altruism, when caught between dichotomous views of living harmoniously with nature or controlling it, some were headed down a destructive path. Rather than cultivate the view of nature that fosters interconnectedness and ecological diversity, consistent with traditional values, some chose the path of dominance and control over nature and the surrounding world.

Our Third Vulnerability: The Rise of Science and Repudiation of Spiritual Beliefs

In the 1300s, the Roman Catholic Church held absolute authority in Europe. From birth until death, the church established rules for anyone seeking salvation.

However, some Catholics began to notice a disconnect between the teachings of Jesus Christ and the rules and regulations imposed by the church. In 1403, Jan Huss, a Czech priest, asserted that Christ preached that anyone could drink wine from the chalice, not just priests. The Roman Catholic Church did not agree. When Huss then took issue with the purchase of gold and silver as a substitute for true repentance, he was burned at the stake. A hundred years later, Martin Luther read the sermons of Huss. He came to the stunning and dangerous realization that the scriptures did not specifically state that God and people required an intermediary. In other words, the church was simply not needed—the believer needed only faith and a Bible. Soon, serfs took up this cry, believing that they were born free in the sight of God, and caused dissention throughout Europe. The church struck back brutally. More than 120,000 peasants were slaughtered after revolts in Germany. Even though Luther eventually chose to side with the aristocracy and princes, he opened a chasm and created a great liberation during the Renaissance. Freedom of expression fueled a growing and vociferous rejection of political tyranny and introduced the world to radical, new ideas for exploration.

In the 1400s, a shift began to occur. Natural philosophers wanted to understand God's expression through nature, even though their concepts remained tied to the teachings of the Christian Church. There was an explosion of scientific curiosity to understand and explain natural phenomena—these were the first scientists and some of our greatest thinkers. From the 14th to 17th centuries, the Renaissance was a profoundly transformative period in Europe and a period of rapid expansion of the human capacity to control the natural environment. Renaissance artists looked at the world with a new perspective, and reason reigned supreme. Sir Francis Bacon, a passionate advocate for scientific discovery, urged the use of experimentation to understand nature. Descartes, a French philosopher, put forward the radical notion that the world was ruled by mechanical forces. As a result, he also believed that current and scientific instruments not yet discovered could be used to find a fundamental truth. Soon, science became the model for all intellectual activities, and groups of scientific societies began to surface all over Europe. Science was evolving into a new orthodoxy, and its adherents' near-religious worship of science troubled many critics, like the 17th-century French philosopher Blaise Pascal, who believed that truth could be grasped only by faith and the heart.

Charlene Spretnak (1991), a professor of philosophy and religion, noted that the Renaissance signaled a triumph for science and produced tension between science and the previous paradigm of harmony with the spiritual world. The Renaissance gave way to the Scientific Revolution and the Enlightenment period from the 16th to 18th centuries. According to the new science, the universe was considered to be filled with dead matter, and science continued searching for ways to control the forces of nature. Technology was also developing quickly in order to serve the new demands of commerce and industry in an emerging capitalist system.

No one can deny that scientific discoveries have saved countless lives and improved our quality of life, yet monumental scientific achievements have also contributed to the erosion of our sense of certainty and place within the universe. Ever since Copernicus revealed in *De Revolutionbus Oribum Coelestium* (1543/1995) that the universe did not revolve around the earth, our place in the cosmos has been disrupted—and subsequent discoveries have upset the equilibrium more. In 1610, Galileo expanded this study and published his discovery that the earth did, in fact, revolve around the sun. Centuries later, Charles Darwin's *The Origin of Species* (1859/1936) suggested that we had evolved from animals—a shocking and deeply disturbing proposition at the time, and one that is still not accepted in certain circles. Through the science of astronomy, we now know that there are billions of stars in our galaxy and billions of other galaxies. It's a wondrous revelation, but existentially disturbing that we are such a small and relatively insignificant part of the universe. The earth is about 4 billion years old. Before the Big Bang, all matter in the universe occupied a space less than one-tenth of a millimeter.

In the 1900s came another shocking declaration: God was dead, said German philosopher Friedrich Nietzsche. Existentialists, among others at the time, saw a world where religious metaphors had been stripped of their meaning; the only authentic values were found internally, within each person. Although science had brought great advances in medicine, quality of life, and even our basic understanding of the world, it also chipped away at religious beliefs, exposing us to a third vulnerability: a breakdown in underlying faith in religious and spiritual values.

In the 1800s and 1900s, some philosophers and scientists also proposed that organized religion had evolved into a means of controlling people, and they turned to science as their god. Others believed that the symbols and images that had once provided comfort and guidance were now erroneous and antiquated (Campbell, 1990). Many were cast into a sea of doubt without the rituals that had once given their lives meaning.

Nevertheless, these radical scientific ideas were not widely known before the late 1800s. For many, the Bible was still their primary authority concerning the origins of people and the universe, and they were unaware of the raging controversies between religion and scientific findings. Most people continued to rely on family, religion, and communities for their sense of well-being. Religion still provided relief from these existential uncertainties, as the vast majority of people, prior to the 20th century, had little exposure to these ideas.

Our Fourth Vulnerability: Separation From Land and Community

The growth of scientific advances and the capitalist class paved the way for the industrial revolution in 18th-century Europe. People left their farms and moved to impersonal, industrialized cities. The fourth vulnerability involves breaking our connections with the land and the communities that were part of this rural life. In England, there was a new labor supply for industry as modern farming techniques reduced the need for workers. Many people migrated to the cities, which had no sewage systems and unsafe water; these crowded, industrial cities were distressingly unhealthy (Upshur, Terry, Holoka, Goff, & Lowry, 1991). Markets emerged for mass quantities of goods thanks to Western imperial expansion. Surplus capital became available, allowing merchants to build factories, and politicians fell into line, passing policies that protected those willing to invest in capital enterprises. The Enlightenment had encouraged scientific inquiry and experimentation, and modern civilization began to flourish.

In the end, industrialization replaced the Old World values of connection with the land and a sense of community with neighbors with a New World determination to get ahead and increase production and consumption of goods. The growing industrial importance of urban centers continued the process of severing our ties to the land and community. The 1940s and '50s were marked by a rising standard of living, and although this change confirmed the importance of work, it slowly replaced the traditional sense of community. The unintended consequences of modern life led to alienation and isolation in depersonalized large cities, in which people moved every 5 years to find better employment and move up the ladder of success.

Previously, the simpler community life had developed rituals to protect the values and integrity of village inhabitants and their connection to each other. Life transformations such as birth, death, and the coming of age were honored in communities. People's lives were built upon a spiritual foundation and maintained a balance with and through nature; their lives were a natural and interrelated function of the community. One could not exist without the other. As more people left their villages for the city, their centuries-old bonds with the land were weakened, impacting centuries of traditions based on village life. Values naturally began to shift. With industrial jobs and higher living standards, there was a new emphasis on the individual, getting ahead (often at the expense of others), and materialism.

The media constantly reaffirms the notion that individual achievement and materialism are paramount. Often, "achievement" is defined by wealth and superficiality: Our culture reveres the rich and beautiful. The nonstop drive for more can lead to widespread poverty (and feelings of inadequacy) and is a powerful source of confusion for children's developing value systems. Our culture has failed, and many people are left to seek relief through crime, alcohol, and drugs. Modern reality TV shows have reinforced these cultural values. Although most people would say that programs such as Survivor, Big Brother, and American Idol are nothing more than a novel type of mass entertainment, and in many ways an extension of violent police dramas or choreographed spectacles such as World Wrestling Entertainment shows, I would disagree. These shows often involve participants feeling demeaned, humiliated, and betrayed. Viewers, in turn, feel superior. These shows are another sign of the profound breakdown in our sense of community.

The encounter group led by Morrie Schwartz, in which I participated as an undergrad, gave me an opportunity to experience a real-life drama session that was neither artificial nor broadcast. It allowed us to share and disclose our most private experiences in an atmosphere of respect and honesty. We were participants of an inner adventure, one that featured as much drama and excitement as any televised series. Our personas, masks, and vulnerabilities were challenged. Tearful crises were frequent in these stirring sessions, but our participation was not for fame or money. We did not come together to reveal the greed and vanity within human nature that is so often portrayed on television and the Internet. Rather, we aimed to gain insight and self-awareness into the wonder and complexity of the human condition. Through this discovery, we became true survivors. This statement is not an endorsement for encounter groups to become the next televised Survivor spin-off. Instead, each of us can create engaging and spontaneous real-life interactions that are both compelling and meaningful. Of course, not everyone in America watches reality shows, but these shows do represent symptoms of a breakdown in our sense of community, and they are connected to our vulnerabilities.

In spite of these changes, the family may have continued to offer a refuge in which to build a sense of stability and coherence. Unfortunately, social norms are passed on to the next generation: When children see competition and individual achievement glorified, they strive to gain parents' love by pursuing these values. Our separation from nature and the rise of science over religion and spirituality had already eroded our ancestors' sense of meaning and connectedness. With the loss of communal living, they began to feel even more isolated and alone. Despite the increasing globalism of today's technologically advanced and economically interdependent world, this isolation on an individual level has only deepened. By understanding this fourth vulnerability, either we can choose to maintain the dominant cultural values of consumerism and individualism or we can make strides toward redefining our relationships with each other in ways that foster a sense of community and interconnectedness.

Our Historical Legacy

In order to understand our current societal problems more clearly, we must understand their historical context and the values and vulnerabilities involved (see Table 6.2). The first vulnerability of our genetic heritage, our innate aggression, has damaged the planet and seriously wounded our psyches. It contributed to our second vulnerability: to control and dominate nature, rather than to maintain a harmonious relationship with it. A thirst for power and control has tipped the delicate balance within us. The third vulnerability was the erosion of our religious beliefs by science. Instead of embracing the mysteries of life, many individuals rejected spiritual beliefs. Likewise, some religions have hardened their belief systems, declaring the importance of specific historical events, rather than turning to their symbolic meanings and the timeless truths that they represent. When the mystery and power of these symbols were taken away, the inevitable consequence was a spiritual wasteland. Finally, the last vulnerability occurred when people moved from small communities into depersonalized cities. Our connection—our last refuge—with the land and the community was slowly eroded. We had lost our place in the universe, we were displaced from the land, and we became distanced from our small communities and families.

This bleak picture does not characterize all citizens in urban areas and industrialized countries. Some have realized and accepted their genetic predilections; found or regained a healthy balance with the forces of nature, spirituality, or religion; and built supportive and healing families and communities, even within urban areas. I also do not mean to denigrate the tremendously

Table 6.2 **Vulnerabilities: Consistent and Discordant Values**

Genetic Heritage

 Value consistent: spontaneity, joy
 Value discordant: violence, aggression

Relationship to Nature

 Value consistent: interconnectedness, diversity
 Value discordant: control, domination

Science

 Value consistent: honors spiritual traditions
 Value discordant: science worship, repudiation of religious rituals and spirituality

Connection to the Land and Community

 Value consistent: psychological sense of community
 Value discordant: individualism, consumerism

worthy contributions of Western civilization. Michael Sandel (2009) eloquently reviewed the contributions of Western moral philosophers such as Jeremy Bentham, Immanuel Kant, John Stuart Mill, Robert Nozick, and John Rawls, who offered great insights regarding our notions of right and wrong and how we might best engage in the public realm for the common good of society. Pinker (2011) claims that violence has actually decreased over time due to the increasing control of our impulses through government, literacy, trade, and cosmopolitanism. Furthermore, Diamandis and Kotler (2012) point out that over the last century, the length of the human life span has doubled, poverty has dropped over 50%, and child and infant mortality rates have been reduced by 90%. We must tap into what inspires and motivates us to take these transformative actions in order to more effectively combat the violence, poverty, and injustices that still exist throughout the world.

It is also important to point out that, in many ancient cultures, there were gross violations of basic human rights, including slavery, legal and commonly accepted child abuse, marginalization of women, and education for only the elite. In that light, one could ask if our current society is any worse. However, despite the abuses that were evident, our ancient relatives were still more connected to the land and had stronger and more enduring spiritual and community roots. Although many of the past abuses have been eliminated, the four vulnerabilities described help explain the current breakdown of community values and the pervasive abuses of power that occur in business, government, and many other sectors of our society.

Transformative Solutions to These Vulnerabilities

Some psychologists have recognized the breakdowns that have arisen from our historical vulnerabilities and have developed different approaches to fill the emotional and communal voids. For example, positive psychology is a field that borrows from the work of Maslow and other humanistic psychologists and focuses on human strengths (Seligman, 2002), such as expanding one's capacity to cope, enhancing emotional resilience, and increasing altruism (Dreher, 1995). Instead of focusing on our innate aggressive—and other negative—tendencies, it upholds and exults our strengths. One of the key tenets of this field is the notion of emotional intelligence—the awareness of emotions, emotional self-regulation, optimism, and empathy (Goldman, 1995). Emotional intelligence is also an important quality of any agent of change.

Fred Luskin (2002), another proponent of positive psychology, put forth a provocative idea, suggesting that one of the best ways to deal with anger and resentment is to be more grateful and forgiving of others. These positive psychology strategies can help people become more resilient and overcome stressors.

However, certain techniques we use to overcome stress are mechanistic and shortsighted, as when individuals are coached to only say positive statements. Many of these interventions lack recognition of the social environment, but a notable exception is the work of Ed Diener (2000), whose studies of happiness include the importance of close interpersonal ties and social support. Findings from the longitudinal Framingham Heart Study on social networks also found that our happiness depends on the happiness of others with whom we are connected (Fowler & Christakis, 2008). In general, many positive psychology theorists have not taken into account our historical vulnerabilities or the need to confront abusive powers when individuals are being exploited or environments are impoverished. We need to go beyond the person-centered focus of many of these positive psychology approaches.

Over the past decade, I have worked on developing a scale to measure wisdom, as composed of harmony (balance, self-love, good judgment, appreciation, and purpose in life), warmth (kindness, compassion, and animation), intelligence (problem-solving capacities), connection to nature (concern/reverence for the environment and a sense that all life is interconnected), and spirituality (having a fellowship/union with God; Jason, Reichler, et al., 2001). I believe that these qualities can help restore meaning to those who have lost it and are also antidotes to our four vulnerabilities. Many of us have lost at least some meaning in our lives: not only the homeless and addicted, but also those who only care about themselves and what they can acquire. By applying our historical values to promote the well-being of each other and the world, we develop and encourage the growth of community leaders. These leaders build resiliency in the face of oppression, cope with uncertainty, and help frame events in a larger context. Leaders put forth the discipline to stay on a chosen pathway for the time it takes and to accomplish their vision, even when that road is treacherous and full of distractions (Jason, Helgerson, et al., 2004).

Other approaches to solving the internal and communal breakdowns that are caused by our historical vulnerabilities draw on mythology and examining our sometimes darker unconscious realm. By keeping these vulnerabilities in mind and recognizing the darker sides of the human condition, we may account for the aggressive remnants that reside within us and explain the genesis of exploitative and abusive relationships. According to Carl Jung, archetypes occupy our collective unconscious, or the part of the unconscious mind present in all humanity, regardless of personal experience. One of Jung's archetypes is the "shadow," which represents traits that lie deep within us. Our genetic predisposition for aggression—one piece of the shadow—is just one part of this collective unconscious, residing along with other automatic psychic processes that organize and give meaning to our experiences. The archetypes, though nebulous images in the unconscious, may take shape in the form of universal myths, such as the hero who slays dragons, or they may be expressed in religious metaphors or art.

Campbell (1969) believed that these archetypes and myths provide a conduit from the unconscious to the conscious and are essential tools for confronting and understanding complexities in our lives. Rejection of these myths can alienate us from ourselves and result in power abuses and the exploitation of others.

Our first vulnerability is our innate, animalistic tendency toward aggression. From a sociological point of view, our culture and society has placed a thin veneer over our basic human physiology. To cope with these immovable realities, cultural mythologies allow us to accept these aspects of ourselves through the legacies of our primitive past. When we were confronted with the second and third vulnerabilities, many of us broke from our interconnectedness with nature and traditional reliance on religious myths and symbols. With the fourth vulnerability—the disconnection from the land and communities—we became further distanced from mythology's role in our lives. One transformative solution to these historical vulnerabilities is to reconnect with these myths and reintegrate them into our lives. Though this all may seem very abstract, a closer analysis of the functions of myths and the power they hold will allow us to understand the complex relationship among mythology, our four vulnerabilities, and the abuses of power.

Myths serve several functions, according to Campbell (1969). The first function is cosmological. These myths allow people to understand and draw conclusions about the world and humankind's beginnings, like the story of the Garden of Eden. The second function that myths serve is sociological, by which people validate their perception of the world and reinforce the social order. The third function of myths is psychological, which revolves around the development of the self, the recovery from childhood neglect, the growth of an authentic identity, and the integration of complementary aspects of the personality.

Myths teach us about the shadows within us that try to find balance in life and within ourselves. Many great philosophers and writers of the last century, such as Thomas Mann, have addressed the theme of the desire to achieve balance among the domains in one's life. In hero mythologies, the hero's task is to blend the opposing aspects of the self, even if those aspects exist in the form of a dark knight, dragon, or other dark forces. By integrating the opposite ends of one's nature and accepting the opposing paradoxes we encounter in our lives, one can embrace and love the shadow.

Campbell's *The Hero With a Thousand Faces* describes the journey of the archetypal hero that is present in a similar form in mythologies throughout the world. The hero's journey in each of these mythologies—from Moses to Hercules—serves as an eloquent metaphor for the personal journey we may take in our lives. The journey begins when the hero realizes that something is askew in nature or within himself. In these myths, the hero's recognition of this incongruence sets him on an adventure in which he must travel where no one has journeyed before. The purpose of the journey is to find what is missing—that deepest sense of harmony, the mystery that captures our imagination and holds it so that time passes without our noticing it. The hero must journey into the unknown to search for a symbol of validation. Stories of Sir Galahad and the knights of King Arthur's Court share this theme. When the knights witnessed angels carrying the Holy Grail (the cup from which Jesus Christ drank at the Last Supper) away, they embarked on a quest to find the Holy Grail. Each entered the forest alone, with no clear path, and with no one to lead the way. This search, as characterized in Western literature, is not just a hero's tale, but symbolizes an individual's journey through life. If one follows a call to action, one will encounter danger, joy, and ultimately harmony. For those involved in social activism, the call to action may be the moment when one senses that abuse is occurring or that something needs to change—a second-order remedy is needed. By personally embarking on this kind of journey, an agent of change will deviate from societal norms and roles in order to follow his or her own path toward social justice.

Myths help us understand our unconscious processes and the archetypal shadow. Often, abusive tendencies originate within these realms. Psychological myths help us make sense of the challenges we face during our development from childhood into adulthood. We have seen, from Freud (1914), Harlow (1958), and Bradshaw (1990), that development and perception of reality in childhood can be marred by parents' unrealistic expectations, intentional or unintentional abuse, and neglect. However, those who are given a positive foundation, emotional support, and confidence as children are more resilient when faced with challenges and disappointments later in life. Parental empathy is crucial. Without it, the child may develop an inadequate sense of self, low self-esteem, and an inability to make decisions and may consequently fruitlessly search for affirmation. The effects of an emotionally fractured childhood can sabotage an adult's efforts to mend. Later in life, these people might grapple with past abuses and seek to gain power and resources at the expense of others. Psychological mythologies provide the rites that help carry adolescents into the adult world. Without this guidance, the process of developing our inner traits, or self, becomes more difficult. Likewise, those who abuse power have often failed to integrate these psychological myths into their lives.

In the second part of one's life, one also relies on psychological myths to search for meaning and self-fulfillment. Those who fail to find true meaning and connection at this stage in life are more likely to seek power and become abusive. Society demands that we wear a certain mask for the sake of respect and order, but many people who abuse power mistake this mask for their true selves and let it overtake their egos. Laing (1967) has suggested that this divided self—created by the conflict between the mask we wear and our ego—will produce a disconnect that can complicate one's adjustment. For example, many people dislike their jobs and the social roles they feel obliged to play, yet they maintain their masks because they fear the unknown, a future much different from their current lives. Taking off the mask signifies a mysterious and frightening step that requires enormous courage, optimism, and faith. This journey toward authenticity can guide one to his or her inner truth and purpose, as opposed to a path prescribed by society that can lead to abuses of power—but it means giving up the mask and the security that comes with what is familiar.

Another function of myths is metaphysical, in that they allow people to develop a mystical sense of awe toward the universe. These myths help us integrate the darker or more painful sides of our lives and protect us from needing to accumulate power at the expense of others. As we approach the final stage of our lives, the metaphysical journey helps us come to terms with the universal sorrow of the world; yet evidence also suggests that growing old often brings more happiness and wisdom (Charles & Carstensen, 2010). When confronted with death, one solution—according to Joseph Campbell—is to be grounded in eternity. This means coming to the realization that eternity exists within each of us—and only once we accept this truth can we disengage from the world and then reengage as participants with the vitality of both joy and sorrow. Individuals in these mythologies may experience oneness with the universe, gain a new appreciation for the world, and be ensured protection from the surrounding terrors (Joyce, 1986).

Erikson (1959) has also described the journey into old age. The final stage of life focuses on integrity versus despair. Integrity connotes a sense of peace with and acceptance of mortality and the human life cycle. It is apparent that Western and Eastern images of the second part of life deal with somewhat similar issues: making peace with one's mortality, finding meaning in one's life, and finding the sacred within everyday experiences.

The hero of these metaphysical mythologies is also able to experience compassion and joy in the moment; the mysteries of the universe have moved the hero's soul and opened up a heightened appreciation of the wonders of life. These special experiences end at a place where one does not have to dominate and control others, where there is compassion and empathy for the suffering in this world, and where the hero is free to experience the wonders of the universe. This vision is brilliantly captured in the gospel according to Saint Thomas. In this example, the kingdom of God is described as being directly in front of us-yet, we cannot see it. It is Christ who disenchants us and opens our eyes to it. Similarly, Buddha releases people from the enchantment of Maya (or illusion). These metaphysical mythologies suggest that the world is ours to shape, formed by the images woven by our own creative egos.

On a personal level, mythology tells the stories of the kinds of journeys that we each take in our lives. Undertaking these types of journeys frees one to become whole, integrate all of the detached parts of the self, and appreciate the wonders of life. New insights or efforts to bring about second-order change, however, may receive little or no interest when shared with others. Faced with a disinterested world, people may struggle to maintain their newfound knowledge. Some, though, may guard their sacred beliefs as if the world were not ready for them. Others would persist in sharing their new knowledge, regardless of whether people were ready or able to accept their ideas, such as John Muir (1912), the activist and writer who encountered enormous obstacles in helping preserve wilderness in our natural world. The social change agent often serves this function by sharing these kinds of transformative and energizing ideas with society, regardless of how they are received. The journey for successful change agents against power abuses is similar to that of a hero's journey in mythology. Ultimately, it leads to second-order change that allows others to overcome miserable situations and creates supportive environments in which people can more completely fulfill their potential.

Relying on the principles of social change and remembering our four vulnerabilities throughout the course of one's journey will aid an activist in understanding the genesis of power abuses and the need for social campaigns to bring about second-order change. By recognizing that our genetic heritage includes aggressive tendencies, we can better understand how power abuses emerge when our vulnerabilities push us to control others, repudiate spiritual values, and separate from loving communities. Our social change efforts need to promote self-regulatory processes that allow us to recognize and channel our darker side into useful outcomes rather than let it hinder our cause. By understanding our second vulnerability, we can help correct it by creating transformational, second-order interventions that help us connect with the natural world, rather than fight or attempt to control it. Likewise, this approach would support research endeavors that validate the importance of rituals and traditions and help communities see the deep mysteries within nature and our spiritual world. Finally, reestablishing our sense of community is critical to repairing the tears in our society. As we work together toward a common goal of community, we eliminate the alienation so many of us feel. A focus on long-term and enduring involvement bonds us together to surmount obstacles and nourishes our societies and our children. These foundational values of social change sustain and enrich our personal voyages as well.

Without the road map that an understanding of our four vulnerabilities, and how mythology can help overcome them, provides, activists may fail to navigate through seemingly intractable problems and the abuses of power that condemn so many to a terrible sense of isolation. The future seems to be headed toward a world that encompasses the full spectrum of often contradictory human behavior: a desire for independence and separation, but also for interconnectedness and spirituality. As we have emerged from nature, these contradictory traits have become our greatest challenge. Yet it is possible to channel our primal instincts toward exploring the alternative ideas highlighted throughout this book—on both a community and individual level. Our planet will face many significant problems in the upcoming years: feeding a growing population, increasing poverty, the excessive wasting of resources, and environmental degradation. The principles of social change outlined in this book can be used to tackle many of these issues.

It should be mentioned that some myths have been used to perpetuate power abuse by maintaining exploitative societal structures, thus serving to justify one group's ruling authority or classify certain groups as superior to others. Some sociological myths imbedded in cultures have served to uphold subjugation and power imbalances. In India, for example, for centuries, people were severely punished for breaking the caste system, a practice that maintains the social hierarchy. In these cases, by understanding and analyzing these myths, we will have the power to expose and confront them. We should reconnect with mythology in a way that allows us to challenge and retranslate abusive myths into new forms that embrace a more peaceful, just, and balanced approach to the world.

Gandhi used native religious systems to frame his philosophies of social change. He challenged the caste system, which had been perpetuated by sociological myths for thousands of years. He returned to his most basic roots and urged his people to follow suit; all people, even the untouchables, deserved equal treatment in society. He believed that only spiritual growth based on the reinterpretations of myths could bring about change—be it economic improvement or political independence. Western-trained social activists, on the other hand, who are often less concerned with spirituality, generally do not ask whether their actions provide spiritual sustenance. Yet Gandhi, one of the most influential change agents in human history, taught that we must do more than merely provide better housing or health care to have a regenerative and lasting impact on communities; we must demonstrate that spiritual growth is the ultimate second-order change that has the power to change the world (Jason, 1997).

Morley Winograd and Michael Hais's (2011) book *Millennial Momentum* describes a new generation of social activists: those with strong, passionate beliefs about generating change to transform every institution in our society and remake America. In addition, socially conscious entrepreneurs, along with innovations in information-based technologies, have the capacity to significantly improve global standards of living (Diamandis & Kotler, 2012). The five principles of social change can create a template for this new generation to launch social movements centered on second-order change. These principles, along with an appreciation of how our four historical vulnerabilities have contributed to abuses of power, can provide the foundation for this new generation of activists to bring creative and just solutions to our society's greatest inequalities.

Additional Resources

Psychologists for Social Responsibility is an independent, nonprofit organization of psychologists, students, and other advocates for social change in the United States and around the world trying to promote peace, social justice, human rights, and sustainability. For more information visit this site: http://www.psysr.org/

Global Journal of Community Psychology Practice is an electronic journal devoted to an exchange of ideas, information, and resources for community practitioners and can be found here: http://www.gjcpp.org/en/

American Journal of Community Psychology is the official journal of SCRA and can be found here: http://www.springer.com/psychology/community+psychology/journal/10464

Journal of Community Psychology is another important journal in the field, which can be found here: http://onlinelibrary.wiley.com/journal/10.1002/(ISSN)1520–6629

Journal of Prevention and Intervention in the Community is another well-known community journal; find it here: http://www.informaworld.com/smpp/title~content=t792306944~db=all

The Community Psychologist is the newsletter of the Community Psychology Division of the American Psychological Association and can be found here: http://www.scra27.org/publications

Multicultural Pavilion is a site with information on many dimensions of human diversity; find it here: http://www.edchange.org/multicultural

The complete works of Joseph Campbell can be found at this site: http://www.jcf.org/new/index.php?categoryid=83&p9999_action=details&p9999_wid=237

Joseph Campbell's work was popularized by Bill Moyers' six-part television series on the Power of Myths in 1988, which can be found at this site: http://www.pbs.org/moyers/faithandreason/perspectives1.html

You can see a YouTube video on parts of my dad's comedy act at this site: http://www.youtube.com/watch?v=KnS-OA5zpKo

The website idealist.org is a great resource for finding or posting volunteer, internship, or job opportunities related to creating solutions to societal problems. The organization's mission is to connect people who share the common goal of creating a better world; find it here: http://www.idealist.org

In the *Citizens United v. Federal Election Commission* case (January 2010), the Supreme Court ruled that the government cannot restrict the political spending of corporations and unions. See this site for a summary of the ruling: http://www.npr.org/templates/story/story.php?storyId=122805666. Many have argued that this ruling led to a dramatic increase in political spending by corporations, as they could now donate unlimited amounts of money to Super PACs (political organizations with no spending limits), giving corporations the political power to sway election results in their favor. The following article discusses the effect of this ruling on corporate political spending: http://www.slate.com/articles/news_and_politics/politics/2012/03/the_supreme_court_s_citizens_united_decision_has_led_to_an_Explosion_of_campaign_spending_.html

To learn how Costa Ricans were able to protect their natural environment by setting aside one quarter of their land as national parks and protected areas, visit this site: http://www.smarttravels.tv/AdventuresWithPurpose/site/shows_costarica_script.html

Michael Sandel, a prominent moral philosopher at Harvard, in his provocative new book *What Money Can't Buy* speculates that we are moving toward a society where everything in our public life can be sold to the highest bidder. Sandel wrote an article sharing some highlights of his book that can be found here: http://www.theatlantic.com/magazine/archive/2012/04/what-isn-8217-t-for-sale/8902/

Many may question what I proposed as the third vulnerability, the repudiation of spiritual beliefs, particularly in the United States, which has prided itself as being one of the most religious countries in the world (certainly more religious than Europeans). However, a 2012 Pew

Research Center survey found that the United States is becoming less religious, particularly among Millennials (those born after 1980). To view Pew Research Center's commentary on its 2012 findings, go to this site: http://www.people-press.org/2012/06/04/section-6-religion-and-social-values/

Cathy Lynn Grossman has reviewed other surveys suggesting that the young in our openly secular nation do not see much influence of religion in their lives. To view her *USA Today* article, go to this site: http://www.usatoday.com/news/religion/story/2011–12–25/religion-god-atheism-so-what/52195274/1

Historian Niall Ferguson has suggested a controversial explanation of why the West has surpassed the rest of the world over the past 500 years (see http://www.avclub.com/articles/civilization-the-west-and-the-rest-with-niall-ferg,75480/). He states that there are six "killer applications" that led to the West's rise to supremacy: competition, the scientific revolution, private property rights, modern medicine, the consumer society, and Protestant work ethic. Ferguson also argues that countries in the rest of the world could surpass the West and become the next superpower by "upgrading" or "downloading" these apps. To read more about his work, visit this site: http://www.pbs.org/wnet/civilization-west-and-rest/about/#.UEYyAkbD4xc

REFERENCES

Abbey, S. E., & Garfinkel, P. E. (1991). Neurasthenia and chronic fatigue syndrome: The role of culture in the making of a diagnosis. *American Journal of Psychiatry, 148*(12), 1638–1646. Retrieved from http://ezproxy.lib.depaul.edu/login?url=http://search.proquest.com/docview/220470595?accountid=10477

Addams, J. (1930). *The second twenty years at Hull-House: September 1909 to September 1929.* New York, NY: Macmillan.

Albee, G. W. (1996). Revolutions and counterrevolutions in prevention. *American Psychologist, 51,* 1130–1133.

Albom, M. (1997). *Tuesdays With Morrie.* New York, NY: Random House.

Alinsky, S. (1969). *Reveille for radicals.* New York, NY: Vintage.

Anderson, J. S., & Ferrans, C. E. (1997). The quality of life of persons with chronic fatigue syndrome. *Journal of Nervous and Mental Disease, 185,* 359–367.

Arrien, A. (1992). *The four-fold way: Walking the paths of the warrior, teacher, healer, and visionary.* New York, NY: HarperCollins.

Barsky, A. J., & Borus, J. F. (1999). Functional somatic syndromes. *Annals of Internal Medicine, 130*(11), 910–921.

Bennett, C. C., Anderson, L. S., Cooper, S., Hassol, L., Klein, D. C., & Rosenblum, G. (1966). *Community psychology: A report of the Boston conference on the education of psychologists for community mental health.* Boston, MA: Boston University Press.

Bishop, P. D., Chertok, L., & Jason, L. A. (1997). Measuring sense of community: Beyond local boundaries. *Journal of Primary Prevention, 18,* 193–212. doi:10.1023/A:1024690424655

Blaug, M. (1985). *Economic theory in retrospect* (4th ed.). Cambridge: Cambridge University Press.

Bock, G. R., & Goode, J. A. (Eds.). (1996). *Genetics of criminal and antisocial behavior.* Chichester, England: John Wiley & Sons.

Bogat, G. A. (1983). *An environmental assessment and intervention involving small parks* (Doctoral dissertation). DePaul University, Chicago, IL.

Bogat, G. A., & Jason, L. A. (2000). Towards an integration of behaviorism and community psychology: Dogs bark at those they do not recognize. In J. Rappaport & E. Seidman (Eds.), *Handbook of community psychology* (pp. 101–114). New York, NY: Plenum Press.

Bogat, G. A., Jones, J. W., & Jason, L. A. (1980). School transitions: Preventive intervention following an elementary school closing. *Journal of Community Psychology, 8,* 343–352.

Bond, M. A. (2007). *Workplace chemistry: Promoting diversity through organizational change.* Hanover, NH: University Press of New England.

Bond, M. A., Hostetler, A. J., Tran, N., & Haynes, M. C. (2012). Practice competencies and community social psychology. *Community Psychologist, 45,* 7–11.

Bornstein, D. (2004). *How to change the world. Social entrepreneurs and the power of new ideas.* New York, NY: Oxford University Press.

Bostridge, M. (2008). *Florence Nightingale. The woman and her legend.* London: Viking.

Bowe, F. (1980). *Rehabilitating America.* New York, NY: Harper and Row.

Bradshaw, J. (1990). *Homecoming: Reclaiming and championing your inner child.* New York, NY: Bantam Books.

Brandt, A. M. (2007). *The cigarette century: The rise, fall and deadly persistence of the product that defined America.* New York, NY: Basic Books.

Brooks, D. (2011). *The social animal.* New York, NY: Random House.

Bureau of Justice Statistics. (2005). *Substance dependence, abuse, and treatment of jail inmates, 2002* (NCJ 209588). Washington, DC: Author.

Burrell, C. (1997, December 9). Pricing one step in anti-smoke war. *Associated Press.*

Calingaert, D. (2012, February 17). From bad to worse. *Wall Street Journal.* Retrieved from http://online.wsj.com/article/SB10001424052970204792404577227171522318732.html?mod=googlenews_wsj

Callahan, D. (2004). *The cheating culture—why more Americans are doing wrong to get ahead.* New York, NY: Harvest Book/Harcourt.

Campbell, J. (1949). *The hero with a thousand faces.* New York, NY: Pantheon.

Campbell, J. (1969). *The world mythology series.* Available from Dolphin Tapes (P.O. Box 71, Big Sur, CA 93920).

Campbell, J. (1990). *The flight of the wild gander.* New York, NY: Harper Perennial.

Camus, A. (1955). *The myth of Sisyphus and other essays* (J. O'Brien, Trans.). New York, NY: Knopf.

Carson, R. (1962). *Silent spring.* Boston, MA: Houghton Mifflin.

Centers for Disease Control and Prevention. (2012). Drowning – United States, 2005–2009. Retrieved from: http://www.cdc.gov/mmwr/preview/mmwrhtml/mm6119a4.htm?s_cid=mm6119a4_w

Charles, S. T., & Carstensen, L. L. (2010). Social and emotional aging. *Annual Review of Psychology, 61,* 383–409.

Chronic Fatigue Syndrome Advisory Committee. (2009, October 29–30). Chronic Fatigue Syndrome Advisory Committee meeting. Meeting minutes. Retrieved from http://www.hhs.gov/advcomcfs/meetings/minutes/cfsac102909min_pdf.pdf (videos of these meetings for Day 1: http://videocast.nih.gov/Summary.asp?File=15408 and for Day 2: http://videocast.nih.gov/Summary.asp?File=15409).

Chronic Fatigue Syndrome Advisory Committee. (2004, March 22). CFS Advisory Committee third meeting. Meeting minutes. Retrieved from http://www.hhs.gov/advcomcfs/meetings/minutes/mar_meeting_min.html

Chronic Fatigue Syndrome Advisory Committee (2007, November 28). CFS Advisory Committee meeting. Meeting minutes. Retrieved from http://www.hhs.gov/advcomcfs/meetings/minutes/cfsac071128min.html

Clemens, Master Sergeant Michael . (2010). *The secrets of Abu Ghraib revealed: American soldiers on trial.* Dulles, VA: Potomac Books.

Copernicus . (1543/1995). *On the revolutions of heavenly spheres* (C. G. Wallis, Trans.). New York, NY: Prometheus Books.

Corbett, C. (2011, June). *Doing policy work as a community psychologist.* Workshop presented at the biennial meeting of the Society for Community Research and Action, Chicago, IL.

Cowen, E. L. (1973). Social and community interventions. *Annual Review of Psychology, 24,* 423–472.

Crawford, I., Jason, L. A., Riordan, N., Kaufman, J., Salina, D. D., Sawalski, L.,…Zolik, E. S. (1990). A multi-media based approach to increasing communication and the level of AIDS knowledge within families. *Journal of Community Psychology, 18,* 361–373.

Darwin, C. A. (1859/1936). *The origin of species*. New York: Modern Library.

Davis, D. D., & Jason, L. A. (1982). Developing a support network for community psychologists. *Journal of Community Psychology, 10*, 15–22.

Davis, M. I., Jason, L. A., Ferrari, J. R., Olson, B. D., & Alvarez, J. (2005). A collaborative action approach to researching substance abuse recovery. *American Journal of Drug and Alcohol Abuse, 31*, 537–553. PMID: 16320433

Davis, R. M., & Jason, L. A. (1988). The distribution of free cigarette samples to minors. *American Journal of Preventive Medicine, 4*, 21–26. PMID: 3395486

De Beauvoir, S. (1973). *Second sex*. New York, NY: Vintage Books.

De Toqueville, A. (1835). *Democracy in America*. New York, NY: George Dearborn.

Deaner, J., Jason, L. A., Aase, D., & Mueller, D. (2009). The relationship between neighborhood criminal behavior and recovery homes. *Therapeutic Communities, 30*, 89–93.

Dear, M. J., & Wolch, J. R. (1987). *Landscapes of despair: From deinstitutionalization to homelessness*. Princeton, NJ: Princeton University Press.

Diamond, J. (2005). *Guns, germs & steel: A short history of everybody for the last 13,000 years*. London: Vintage.

Diamandis, P. H., & Kotler, S. (2012). *Abundance: The future is better than you think*. New York, NY: Free Press.

Diener, E. (2000). Subjective well-being: The science of happiness and a proposal for a national index. *American Psychology, 55*(1), 34–43.

DiFranza, J. R., Norwood, B. D., Garner, D. W., & Tye, J. B. (1987). Legislative efforts to protect children from tobacco. *Journal of the American Medical Association, 257*, 3387–3389.

DiFranza, J. R., Savageau, J. A., & Fletcher, K. E. (2009). Enforcement of underage sales laws as a predictor of daily smoking among adolescents: A national study. *BMC Public Health, 9*, 107–113.

Dobson, W. J. (2012). *The dictator's learning curve: Inside the global battle for democracy*. New York, NY: Knopf Doubleday.

Dreher, H. (1995). *The immune power personality*. New York, NY: Dutton.

Duberman, M. (1993). *Stonewall*. New York, NY: Dutton.

Duke, S. B., & Gross, A. C. (1994). *America's longest war, rethinking our tragic crusade against drugs*. New York, NY: Putnam.

Dunne, J. (1986). Sense of community in l'Arche and in the writings of Jean Vanier. *Journal of Community Psychology, 14*, 41–54.

Du Toit, B. M. (1996). The Mahatma Gandhi and South Africa. *Journal of Modern African Studies, 34*, 643–660.

Erikson, E. H. (1959). Identity and the life cycle: Selected papers. *Psychological Issues, 1*, 50–100.

Etzioni, A. (1993). *The spirit of community*. New York, NY: Crown.

Fairweather, G. W. (1979). Experimental development and dissemination of an alternative to psychiatric hospitalization: Scientific methods for social change. In R. F. Munzo, L. R. Snowden, & J. G. Kelly (Eds.), *Social and psychological research in community settings* (pp. 305–342). San Francisco, CA: Jossey-Bass.

Fakhoury, W., & Priebe, S. (2007). Deinstitutionalization and reinstitutionalization: Major changes in the provision of mental healthcare. *Psychiatry, 6*, (8), 313–316.

Falk, D. E., Yi, H., & Hiller-Sturmhöfel, S. (2006). An epidemiologic analysis of co-occurring alcohol and tobacco use and disorders. Findings from the National Epidemiologic Survey on alcohol and related conditions. *Alcohol Research & Health, 29*, 162–171.

Fawcett, S. (2011). *The community toolbox*. Retrieved from http://ctb.ku.edu/en/default.aspx

Feldman, E. A. (2004). Children and bystanders first: The ethics and politics of tobacco control in the United States. In E. A. Feldman & R. Bayer (Eds.), *Unfiltered: Conflicts over tobacco policy and public health* (pp. 9–37). Cambridge, MA: Harvard University Press.

Ferrari, J. R., Jason, L. A., Blake, R., Davis, M. I., & Olson, B. D. (2006). "This is my neighborhood": Comparing United States and Australian Oxford House neighborhoods. *Journal of Prevention & Intervention in the Community, 31*, 41–50. PMID: 16595385

Fowler, J. H., & Christakis, N. A. (2008). Dynamic spread of happiness in a large social network: Longitudinal analysis over 20 years in the Framingham Heart Study. *BMI, 337.* doi:10.1136/bmj.a2338

Freire, P. (1970). *Pedagogy of the oppressed.* New York, NY: Herder and Herder.

Freud, S. (1914). *On the history of the psycho-analytic movement* (Standard Edition, vol. 14). London, England: Hogarth Press and the Institute of Psycho-Analysis.

Friedan, B. (1963). *Feminine mystique.* New York, NY: W. W. Norton.

Fryar, C. D., Merino, M. C., Hirsch, R., & Porter, K. S. (2009, May). Smoking, alcohol use, and illicit drug use reported by adolescents aged 12–17 years: United States, 1999–2004. *National Health Statistics Reports, 15.* U.S. Department of Health and Human Services, Centers for Disease Control and Prevention. Retrieved from http://www.cdc.gov/nchs/data/nhsr/nhsr015.pdf

Fryer, D. (2008). Some questions about "the history of community psychology." *Journal of Community Psychology, 36,* 572–586.

Gelernter, C. Q. (1994). Oxford House. *Seattle Times.* Retrieved from http://community.seattletimes.nwsource.com/archive/?date=19940417&slug=1905804

Gillon, S. M. (2000). *"That's not what we meant to do": Reform and its unintended consequences in twentieth century America.* New York, NY: Norton.

Gladwell, M. (2005). *Blink: The power of thinking without thinking.* New York, NY: Little Brown & Company.

Gladwell, M. (2008). *Outliers.* New York: Little, Brown & Company—Hachette Book Group.

Glantz, S. A. (2002). Limiting youth access to tobacco: A failed intervention. *Journal of Adolescent Health, 31,* 301–302.

Goldman, D. (1995). *Emotional intelligence.* New York, NY: Bantam.

Goldstein, J. L., & Godemont, M. M. L. (2003). The legend and lessons of Geel, Belgium: A 1500-year-old legend, a 21st-century model. *Community Mental Health Journal, 39,* 441–458.

Gottman, J. M., & Silver, N. (1999). *The seven principles for making marriage.* New York, NY: Three Rivers Press.

Green, J., Romei, J., & Natelson, B. J. (1999). Stigma and chronic fatigue syndrome. *Journal of Chronic Fatigue Syndrome, 5,* 63–75.

Hacker, J. S., & Pierson, P. (2010). *How Washington made the rich richer—and turned its back on the middle class.* New York, NY: Simon & Schuster

Harlow, H. (1958). The nature of love. *American Psychologist, 13,* 673–685.

Heim, C., Wagner, D., Maloney, E., Papanicolauo, D. A., Solomon, L., Jones, J. F., . . . Reeves, W. C. (2006). Early adverse experience and risk for chronic fatigue syndrome: Results from a population-based study. *Archives of General Psychiatry, 63,* 1258–1266.

Herd, J. (2009, May 28). A day to remember. Message posted on the Co-Cure Internet.

Holton, E., & Jason, L. A. (1988). Attempts to establish nonsmoking sections in restaurants. *American Journal of Public Health, 78,* 987. PMCID: PMC1349873

Hope, A., & Timmel, S. (1985). *Training for transformation. A handbook for community workers.* Gweru, Zimbabwe: Mambo Press.

Horgan, C., Skwara, K. C., Strickler, G., Andersen, L., & Stein, J. (Eds.). (2001). *Substance abuse: The nation's number one health problem.* Princeton, NJ: Robert Wood Johnson Foundation.

Howe, S. R. (2007, October). *Foundational principles and perspectives on public policy research and intervention.* Symposia presented at the Midwest Eco Conference, Chicago, IL.

Hudson, M. W. (2011). *The monster: How a gang of predatory lenders and Wall Street bankers fleeced America—and spawned a global crisis.* New York, NY: Times Books.

Humphreys, K., Mankowski, E. S., Moos, R. H., & Finney, J. W. (1999). Do enhanced friendship networks and active coping mediate the effect of self-help groups on substance abuse? *Annals of Behavioral Medicine, 21,* 54–60.

Hwang, S. L., & Geyelin, M. (1996, February 1). Getting personal: Brown & Williamson has 500-page dossier attacking chief critic—court files, private letters, even a suspicious flood are fodder for sleuths—Ivana Trump's private eye. *Wall Street Journal* (Eastern Edition), A1. Retrieved from ABI/INFORM Global. (Document ID: 767239131)

IMIFAP (Mexican Institute for Family and Population Research). (1993). *Final report on the project: Development of support for national sex education in Mexico.* Mexico City: Author.

Iscoe, I., Bloom, B., & Spielberger, C. (Eds.). (1977). *Community psychology in transition.* New York, NY: John Wiley & Sons.

Jason, L. A. (1976, December). *Eliminating smoking through stimulus control.* Paper presented at Association for Advancement of Behavior Therapy annual convention, New York, NY.

Jason, L. A. (1977). A behavioral approach in enhancing disadvantaged children's academic abilities. *American Journal of Community Psychology, 5,* 413–421.

Jason, L. A. (1979). Preventive community interventions: Reducing school children's smoking and decreasing smoke exposure. *Professional Psychology, 10,* 744–752. doi:10.1037/0735-7028.10.5.744

Jason, L. A. (1984). Developing undergraduates' skills in behavioral interventions. *Journal of Community Psychology, 12,* 130–139.

Jason, L. A. (1985). Using a token-actuated timer to reduce television viewing. *Journal of Applied Behavior Analysis, 18,* 269–272.

Jason, L. A. (1996, August 23). Politics vs. science: Do we really care about kids who light up? *Chicago Tribune, 123.* (Document ID: 10166551)

Jason, L. A. (1997). *Community building: Values for a sustainable future.* Westport, CT: Praeger.

Jason, L. A. (2007, January). *Epidemiology session summary: State-of-the-art with a CFS-perspective.* Paper presented at the International Association of Chronic Fatigue Syndrome Conference, Ft. Lauderdale, Florida.

Jason, L. A. (2011). Small wins matter in advocacy movements: Giving voice to patients. *American Journal of Community Research, 49,* 307–316. PMID: 21858612

Jason, L. A., Benton, M., Johnson, A., & Valentine, L. (2008). The economic impact of ME/CFS: Individual and societal level costs. *Dynamic Medicine, 7,* 6. PMCID: PMC2324078

Jason, L. A., Berk, M., Schnopp-Wyatt, D. L., & Talbot, B. (1999). Effects of enforcement of youth access laws on smoking prevalence. *American Journal of Community Psychology, 27,* 143–160.

Jason, L. A., Clarfield, S., & Cowen, E. L. (1973). Preventive intervention with young disadvantaged children. *American Journal of Community Psychology, 1,* 50–61.

Jason, L. A., & Clay, R. (1978). Modifying smoking behaviors in a barber shop. *Man-Environment Systems, 8,* 38–40.

Jason, L. A., Clay, R., & Martin, M. (1979–1980). Reducing cigarette smoke in supermarkets and elevators. *Journal of Environmental Systems, 9,* 57–66.

Jason, L. A., Corradi, K., Gress, S., Williams, S., & Torres-Harding, S. (2006). Causes of death among patients with chronic fatigue syndrome. *Health Care for Women International, 27,* 615–626.

Jason, L. A., Curran, T., Goodman, D., & Smith. M. (1989). A media-based stress management intervention. *Journal of Community Psychology, 17,* 155–165. doi:10.1002/1520–6629

Jason, L. A., Davis, M. I., Ferrari, J. R., & Anderson, E. (2007). The need for substance abuse after-care: Longitudinal analysis of Oxford House. *Addictive Behaviors, 32,* 803–818.

Jason, L. A., Davis, M. I., Olson, B. D., Ferrari, J. R., & Alvarez, J. (2006). Attitudes of community members as a function of participatory research with Oxford Houses. *Journal of Prevention & Intervention in the Community, 31,* 13–26.

Jason, L. A., & Evans, M. (2012). To PEM or not to PEM? That is the question for case definition. *Research 1st.* Retrieved from http://www.research1st.com/2012/04/27/pem-case-def/

Jason, L. A., & Ferone, L. (1979). Behavioral versus process consultation interventions in school settings. In C. M. Franks & G. T. Wilson (Eds.), *Annual review of behavior therapy, theory and practice* (pp. 327–340). New York, NY: Brunner/Mazel.

Jason, L. A., Ferrari, J. R., Davis, M. I., & Olson, B. D. (2006). *Creating communities for addiction recovery: The Oxford House model*. New York, NY: Haworth.

Jason, L. A., & Frasure, S. (1980). Monitoring and changing behaviors in supermarket managers and consumers. *Man-Environment Systems, 10*, 288–290.

Jason, L. A., & Fricano, G. (1999). Testifying at a congressional hearing on the tobacco settlement. *Professional Psychology: Research and Practice, 30*, 372–377.

Jason, L. A., & Glenwick, D. S. (Eds.). (2012). *Methodological approaches to community-based research*. Washington, DC: American Psychological Association.

Jason, L. A., Greiner, B. J., Naylor, K., Johnson, S. P., & Van Egeren, L. (1991). A large-scale, short-term, media-based weight loss program. *American Journal of Health Promotion, 5*, 432–437.

Jason, L. A., Groh, D. R., Durocher, M., Alvarez, J., Aase, D. M., & Ferrari, J. R. (2008). Counteracting "not in my backyard": The positive effects of greater occupancy within mutual-help recovery homes. *Journal of Community Psychology, 36*, 947–958.

Jason, L. A., Gruder, C. L., Martino, S., Flay, B. R., Warnecke, R., & Thomas, N. (1987). Worksite group meetings and the effectiveness of a televised smoking cessation intervention. *American Journal of Community Psychology, 15*, 57–72.

Jason, L. A., Helgerson, J. L., Torres-Harding, S., Fries, M., Carrico, A., & Chimata, R. (2004). A scale to measure wisdom: Socio-demographic and psychological characteristics. *Humanistic Psychologist, 32*, 284–306.

Jason, L. A., Hunt, Y. M., Adams, M. L., Pokorny, S. B., & Gadiraju, P. B. (2007). Strengthening communities' youth access policies may facilitate clean indoor air Action [Letter]. *Preventing Chronic Disease, 4*(4). Retrieved from http://www.cdc.gov/pcd/issues/2007/oct/07_0127.htm

Jason, L. A., Ji, P. Y., Anes, M., & Birkhead, S. H. (1991). Active enforcement of cigarette control laws in the prevention of cigarette sales to minors. *Journal of American Medical Association, 266*(22), 3159–3161.

Jason, L. A., & Jung, R. (1984). Stimulus control techniques applied to handicapped-designated parking spaces. Deterring unauthorized use by the nonhandicapped. *Environment and Behavior, 16*, 675–686.

Jason, L. A., Kennedy, C., & Taylor, R. R. (2001). Development and evaluation of a web based classroom. *Journal of Instructional Psychology, 28*, 155–160.

Jason, L. A., Keys, C. B., Suarez-Balcazar, Y., Taylor, R. R., Davis, M., Durlak, J., & Isenberg, D. (Eds.). (2004). *Participatory community research: Theories and methods in action*. Washington, DC: American Psychological Association.

Jason, L. A., & Klich, M. (1982). Intervening to alter inappropriate advertising in the mass media. *Behavioral Community Psychology, 1*, 9–16.

Jason, L. A., & Liotta, R. (1982). Reducing cigarette smoking in a university cafeteria. *Journal of Applied Behavior Analysis, 15*, 573–577.

Jason, L. A., McCoy, K., Blanco, D., & Zolik, E. S. (1980). Decreasing dog litter: Behavioral consultation to help a community group. *Evaluation Review, 4*, 355–369.

Jason, L. A., Mollica, M., & Ferone, L. (1982). Evaluating an early secondary smoking prevention intervention. *Preventive Medicine, 11*, 96–102.

Jason, L. A., Moritsugu, J. N., Albino, J., Abbott, M., Anderson, J., Cameron, L.,…Zarit, J. (1985). Facilitating social support among community psychologists. *Journal of Community Psychology, 13*, 83–89.

Jason, L. A., Najar, N., Porter, N., & Reh, C. (2009). Evaluating the Centers for Disease Control's empirical chronic fatigue syndrome case definition. *Journal of Disability Policy Studies, 20*, 93–100.

Jason, L. A., Olson, B., & Ferrari, J. R. (2006). An evaluation of communal housing settings for substance abuse recovery. *American Journal of Public Health, 91*, 1727–1729.

Jason, L. A., Olson, B. D., & Foli, K. (2008). *Rescued lives: The Oxford House approach to substance abuse*. New York, NY: Routledge.

Jason, L. A., & Perdoux, M. (2004). *Havens: True stories of community healing.* Westport, CT: Praeger Publishers.

Jason, L. A., Pokorny, S., Kohner, K., & Bennetto, L. (1994). An evaluation of the short-term impact of a media-based substance abuse prevention program. *Journal of Community and Applied Social Psychology, 4,* 63–69.

Jason, L. A., Pokorny, S. B., Adams, M., & Hunt, Y. (2008). A randomized trial evaluating tobacco possession-use-purchase laws. *Social Science & Medicine, 67,* 1700–1707. PMID: 18947913

Jason, L. A., Pokorny, S. B., Adams, M., Nihls, A., Kim, H. Y., & Hunt, Y. (2009). Cracking down on youth tobacco may influence drug use. *Journal of Community Psychology, 38,* 1–15. doi:10.1002/jcop.20347

Jason, L. A., Pokorny, S. B., Adams, M., Topliff, A., Harris, C., & Hunt, Y. (2009). Youth tobacco access and possession policy interventions: Effects on observed and perceived tobacco use. *American Journal on Addictions, 18,* 367–374. PMID: 19874155

Jason, L. A., Reichler, A., Easton, J., Neal, A., & Wilson, M. (1984). Female harassment after ending a relationship: A preliminary study. *Alternative Lifestyles, 6,* 259–269.

Jason, L. A., Reichler, A., King, C., Madsen, D., Camacho, J., & Marchese, W. (2001). The measurement of wisdom: A preliminary effort. *Journal of Community Psychology, 29,* 585–598.

Jason, L. A., & Reyes, O. (1989). Developing grant writing skills within a community psychology course. *Community Psychologist, 22,* 6–7.

Jason, L. A., Richman, J. A., Friedberg, F., Wagner, L., Taylor, R. R., & Jordan, K. M. (1997). Politics, science, and the emergence of a new disease: The case of chronic fatigue syndrome. *American Psychologist, 52,* 973–983.

Jason, L. A., Richman, J. A., Rademaker, A. W., Jordan, K. M., Plioplys, A. V., Taylor, R. R.,...Plioplys, S. (1999). A community-based study of chronic fatigue syndrome. *Archives of Internal Medicine, 159,* 2129–2137.

Jason, L. A., & Rose, T. (1984). Influencing the passage of child passenger restraint legislation. *American Journal of Community Psychology, 12,* 485–495.

Jason, L. A., Schober, D., & Olson, B. D. (2008). Community involvement among second-order change recovery homes. *Australian Community Psychologist, 20,* 73–83. Retrieved from http://www.groups.psychology.org.au/Assets/Files/20(1)-08-Jason-etal.pdf

Jason, L. A., & Smith, T. (1980). The behavioral ecological matchmaker. *Teaching of Psychology, 7,* 116–117.

Jason, L. A., Tait, E., Goodman, D., Buckenberger, L., & Gruder, C. L. (1988). Effects of a televised smoking cessation intervention among low income and minority smokers. *American Journal of Community Psychology, 16,* 863–876.

Jason, L. A., Taylor, R. R., Stepanek, Z., & Plioplys, S. (2001). Attitudes regarding chronic fatigue syndrome: The importance of a name. *Journal of Health Psychology, 6,* 61–71.

Jason, L. A., Taylor, R. R., Wagner, L., Holden, J., Ferrari, J. R., Plioplys, A. V.,...Papernik, M. (1995). Estimating rates of chronic fatigue syndrome from a community based sample: A pilot study. *American Journal of Community Psychology, 23,* 557–568.

Jason, L. A., Unger, E. R., Dimitrakoff, J. D., Fagin, A. P., Houghton, M., Cook, D.,...Snell, C. (2012). Minimum data elements for research reports on CFS. *Brain, Behavior and Immunity, 26*(3), 401–406. PMID: 22306456

Jason, L. A., Weine, A. M., Johnson, J. H., Warren- Sohlberg, L., Filippelli, L. A., Turner, E. Y., & Lardon, C. (1992). *Helping transfer students: Strategies for educational and social readjustment.* San Francisco, CA: Jossey-Bass.

Jason, L. A., Zolik, E. S., & Matese, F. (1979). Prompting dog owners to pick-up dog droppings. *American Journal of Community Psychology, 7,* 339–351.

Johnson, H. (1996). *Osler's web: Inside the labyrinth of the chronic fatigue syndrome epidemic.* New York, NY: Crown Publishers.

Jones, J. H. (1993). *Bad blood: The Tuskegee syphilis experiment.* New York, NY: Free Press.

Joyce, J. (1986). *Ulysses.* New York, NY: Vintage Books.

Kagan, R. A., & Nelson, W. P. (2001). The politics of tobacco regulation in the United States. In R. L. Rabin & S. D. Sugerman (Eds.), *Regulating tobacco* (pp. 11–38). New York, NY: Oxford University Press.

Kaufman, J., Jason, L. A., Sawlski, L. M., & Halpert, J. A. (1994). A comprehensive multi-media program to prevent smoking among black students. *Journal of Drug Education, 24,* 95–108.

Keene, J. (1997). Drug use among prisoners before, during and after custody. *Addiction Research, 4,* 343–353.

Kelly, J. G. (1970) Antidotes to arrogance: Training for community psychology. *American Psychologist, 25*(6), 524.

Kelly, J. G. (1979). *Adolescent boys in high school: A psychological study of coping and adaptation.* Hillsdale, NJ: L. Erlbaum Associates.

Kelly, J. G. (1990). Changing contexts and the field of community psychology. *American Journal of Community Psychology, 18*(6), 769–792.

Kendall, N. (2008). The state(s) of sexuality education in America. *Sexuality Research & Social Policy, 5*(2), 1–11.

Kent, E. (2012). Wrath of Grapes boycott. Retrieved from http://www.emersonkent.com/speeches/wrath_of_grapes_boycott.htm

Kloos, B., Hill, J., Thomas, E., Wandersman, A., Elias, M. J., & Dalton, J. H. (2012). *Community psychology: Linking individuals and communities* (3rd ed., pp. 360–363). Stamford, CT: Wadsworth.

Kroll-Smith, S., & Gunter, V. J. (Eds.). (2000). *Illness and the environment: A reader in contested medicine.* New York, NY: New York University Press.

Laing, R. D. (1967). *The politics of experience.* New York, NY: Pantheon.

Langan, P. A., & Levin, D. J. (2002). *Recidivism of prisoners released in 1994.* Washington, DC: Bureau of Justice Statistics.

Legler, R., & Jason, L. A. (in press). Formative evaluation of a community-based recovery home in Ghana, Africa. *Annals of Research.*

Levine, M., & Levine, A. (1970). *A social history of helping services: Clinic, court, school, and community.* New York, NY: Appleton-Century-Crofts.

Lewis, G., & Wessely, S. (1992). The epidemiology of fatigue: More questions than answers. *Journal of Epidemiology and Community Health, 46,* 92–97.

Loomer, B. (1976). Two conceptions of power. *Process Studies, 6,* 5–32.

Lorenz, K. (1974). *On aggression* (M. Kerr Wilson, Trans.). New York, NY: Harcourt Brace Jovanovich.

Lost Voices. (2008). *Invest in ME.* Mabe, Cornwall, United Kingdom: Wild Conversations Press.

Low, D. A. (1997). *Britain and Indian nationalism: The imprint of ambiguity 1929–1942.* Cambridge: Cambridge University Press.

Luskin, F. (2002). *Forgive for good.* New York, NY: HarperCollins.

Malcolm X. (1965). *The autobiography of Malcolm X* (with the assistance of A. Haley). New York, NY: Grove.

Mancall, P. C. (1995). *Deadly medicine: Indians and alcohol in early America.* Ithaca, NY: Cornell University Press.

Mann, T. (1995). *The magic mountain: A novel* (J. E. Woods, Trans.). New York, NY: Knopf.

Marlatt, G. A. (1996). Harm reduction: Come as you are. *Addictive Behaviors, 21*(6), 779–788.

Maslow, A. (1962). *Toward a psychology of being.* Princeton, NJ: Van Nostrand.

Maugham, S. (1944). *The razor's edge.* New York, NY: Doubleday.

McCann, D. P. (1991). Hinduism. In J. D. Crossan (Ed.), *Religious worlds. Primary readings in comparative perspective* (pp. 13–68). Dubuque, IA: Kendall/Hunt Pub.

McCleary, K. (2010, January 29). CDC announces leadership change for CFS research program. Retrieved from http://www.cfids.org/cfidslink/2010/020303.asp

McCleary, K. K. (2008, October 28). Testimony to the DHHS Chronic Fatigue Syndrome Advisory Committee. Retrieved from http://www.cfids.org/advocacy/testimony-mccleary-oct2008.pdf

McClelland, D. C. (1979). Inhibited power motivation and high blood pressure in men. *Journal of Abnormal Psychology, 88*, 182–190.

McLaughlin, C., & Davidson, G. (1986). *Builders of the dawn. Community lifestyles in a changing world.* Shutesbury, MA: Sirius.

McMillan, D. W., & Chavis, D. M. (1986). Sense of community: A definition and theory. *Journal of Community Psychology, 14*, 6–23.

Michaels, D., & Bryan-Low, C. (2010, February 6). BAE to settle bribery cases for more than $400 million. *Wall Street Journal.* Retrieved from http://www.stwr.org/multinational-corporations/bae-systems-has-justice-been-done.html#WSJ

Miles, R. H. (1982). *Coffin nails and corporate strategies.* Englewood Cliffs, NJ: Prentice-Hall.

Montgomery, H. A., Miller, W. R., & Tonigan, J. S. (1993). Differences among AA groups: Implications for research. *Journal of Studies on Alcohol, 54*, 502–504.

Morgan, A. E. (1942). *The small community.* Yellow Springs, OH: Community Service.

Morgenson, G., & Rosner, J. (2011). *Reckless endangerment.* New York, NY: Times Books/Henry Holt & Company.

Moritsugu, J., Wong, F. W., & Duffy, K. G. (2009). *Community psychology* (4th ed.). Upper Saddle River, NJ: Pearson.

Muir, J. (1912). *The Yosemite.* Retrieved from http://www.gutenberg.org/ebooks/7091

Murphy, H. B. M. (1982). Culture and schizophrenia. In I. Al-Issa (Ed.), *Culture and psychopathology* (pp. 49–82). Baltimore, MD: University Park Press.

Murphy, H. B. M. (1983). *Comparative psychiatry.* Berlin: Springer-Verlag.

Nye, J. S. (2008). *The powers to lead.* New York, NY: Oxford University Press.

Olson, B. D., Jason, L. A., d'Arlach, L., Ferrari, J. R., Alvarez, J., Davis, M. I., ... Viola, J. (2002). Oxford House, second-order thinking, and the diffusion of systems-based innovations. *Community Psychologist, 35*, 21–22.

Olson, B. D., Jason, L. A., Davidson, M., & Ferrari, J. R. (2009). Increases in tolerance within naturalistic, self-help recovery homes. *American Journal of Community Psychology, 44*, 188–195. doi:10.1007/s10464-009-9275-3

Olson, B., Viola, J., & Fromm-Reed, S. (2011). A temporal model of community organizing and direct action. *Peace Review, 23*(1), 52–60.

Oxford House Inc. (2007). *Annual Report, 2007.* Retrieved from http://www.oxfordhouse.org/userfiles/file/doc/ar2007.pdf

Patel, R. (2007). *Stuffed and starved.* New York, NY: Melville House Publishing.

PBS NewsHour. (2012, February 29). Benefit corporations aim to make a profit—and a positive impact. *Public Broadcast Station.* Retrieved from http://www.pbs.org/newshour/bb/business/jan-june12/bcorps_02-29.html

Pearson, C., Montgomery, A. E., & Locke, G. (2009). Housing stability among homeless individuals with serious mental illness participating in Housing First programs. *Journal of Community Psychology, 37*, 404–417.

Peters, T., & Waterman, B. (1982). *In search of excellence: Lessons from American's best-run companies.* New York, NY: Warner Books.

Peterson, A. V., Jr., Kealey, K. A., Mann, S. L., Marek, P. M., & Sarason, I. G. (2000). Hutchinson smoking prevention project: Long-term randomized trial in school-based tobacco use prevention: Results on smoking. *Journal of the National Cancer Institute, 92*, 1979–1991.

Peto, R., Lopez, A. D., Boreham, J., Thun, M., Heath, C., Jr., & Doll, R. (1996). Mortality from smoking worldwide. *British Medical Bulletin, 52*, 12–21.

Pick de Weiss, S. (1987). Actitudes, conocimientos y conductas de planificación familiar en México: Una década de investigación psicosocial (1975–1985). *Revista Mexicana de Psicología, 3*(2), 155–160.

Pick de Weiss, S., Atkin, L. C., Gribble, J., & Andrade-Palos, P. (1991). Sex, contraception and pregnancy among adolescents in Mexico City. *Studies in Family Planning, 22*(2), 74–82.

Pick de Weiss, S., Vargas Trujillo, E., Solano Flores, G., Rubio, M. L., López Velasco, A. L., Pier, D., ... Galdos, S. (1991). *Serie Planeando tu vida (serie de 76 libros para la vida familiar y educación para la salud de niños de 2 a 12 años de edad).* México: Editorial LIMUSA.

Pick, S., & Sirkin, J. (2010). *Breaking the poverty cycle: The human basis for sustainable development.* New York, NY: Oxford University Press.

Pick, S., Beers, K., & Grossman-Crist, S. (2011). A human basis for sustainable development: How psychosocial change at the individual level promotes development. *Poverty and Public Policy, 3*(3). doi:10.2202/1944-2858.1174

Pinker, S. (2011). *The better angels of our nature.* New York, NY: Viking.

Plous, S. (2009). Meg Bond. Retrieved from http://meg.bond.socialpsychology.org/

Pokorny, S. B., Jason, L. A., & Schoeny, M. (2006). Youth supplying tobacco to other minors: Evaluating individual and town-level correlates. *Journal of Youth and Adolescence, 35*, 705–715.

Prilleltensky, I. (2008). The role of power in wellness, oppression, and liberation: The promise of psychopolitical validity. *Journal of Community Psychology, 36*, 232–237.

Prison Policy Initiative. (2005). Incarceration is not an equal opportunity punishment. Retrieved from http://www.prisonpolicy.org/articles/notequal.html

Purpel, D. E. (1989). *The moral and spiritual crisis in education: A curriculum for justice and compassion in education.* Granby, MA: Bergin & Garvey Publishers.

Putnam, R. D. (1993). *Making democracy work. Civic traditions in modern Italy.* Princeton, NJ: Princeton University Press.

Reed, L. R. (2011). *State of the Microcredit Summit Campaign Report 2011.* Washington, DC: Microcredit Summit Campaign. Retrieved from http://www.microcreditsummit.org/pubs/reports/socr/2011/SOCR_2011_EN_web.pdf

Reeves, W. C., Jones, J. J., Maloney, E., Heim, C., Hoaglin, D. C., Boneva, R., ... Devlin, R. (2007). New study on the prevalence of CFS in metro, urban and rural Georgia populations. *Population Health Metrics, 5*, 5. doi:10.1186/1478-7954-5-5. Retrieved from http://www.pophealthmetrics.com/content/5/1/5

Reeves, W., Wagner, D., Nisenbaum, R., Jones, J., Gurbaxani, B., Papanicolaou, D., ... Heim, C. (2005). Chronic fatigue syndrome—a clinical empirical approach to its definition and study. *BMC Medicine, 3*, 19. doi:10.1186/1741-7015-3-19. Retrieved from http://www.ncbi.nlm.nih.gov/pmc/articles/PMC1334212/

Reeves, W. C., Wagner, D., Nisenbaum, R., Jones, J. F., Gurbaxani, B., Solomon, L., ... Locke, B. Z. (1988). One-month prevalence of mental disorders in the United States: Based on five epidemiological catchment area sites. *Archives of General Psychiatry, 45*, 977–986.

Regier, D. A., Boyd, J. H., Burke, J. D., Jr., Rae, D. S., Myers, J. K., Kramer, M., ... Locke, B. Z. (1988). One-month prevalence of mental disorders in the United States: Based on five Epidemiological Catchment area sites. *Archives of General Psychiatry, 45*, 977–986.

Reich, S. M., Riemer, M., Prilleltensky, I., & Montero, M. (Eds.). (2007). *International community psychology: History and theories.* New York, NY: Springer Science + Business Media.

Reyes, M., Gary, H. E., Jr., Dobbins, J. G., Randall, B., Steele, L., Fukuda, K., ... Reeves, W. C. (1997, February 21). Descriptive epidemiology of chronic fatigue syndrome: CDC surveillance in four cities. *Morbidity and Mortality Weekly Report Surveillance Summaries, 46*(SS2), 113.

Reyes, M., Nisenbaum, R., Hoaglin, D. C., Unger, E. R., Emmons, C., Randall, B., ... Reeves, W. C. (2003). Prevalence and incidence of chronic fatigue syndrome in Wichita, Kansas. *Archives of Internal Medicine, 163*, 1530–1536.

Rhodes, J. (2008). Improving youth mentoring through research-based practice. *American Journal of Community Psychology, 41*, 35–42.

Rhodes, J., & DuBois, D. (2006). Understanding and facilitating the youth mentoring movement. *Social Policy Report, XX*, 3–19.

Rhodes, J. E., & Jason, L. A. (1991). Community health assessment. In H. Schroeder (Ed.), *New directions in health psychology: Assessment* (pp. 159–173). New York, NY: Hemisphere Press.

Richman, A., & Neumann, B. (1984). Breaking the "detox-loop" for alcoholics with social detoxification. *Drug and Alcohol Dependence, 13*, 65–73.

Richman, J. A., & Jason, L. A. (2001). Gender biases underlying the social construction of illness states: The case of chronic fatigue syndrome. *Current Sociology, 49*, 15–29.

Riger, S. (1993). What's wrong with empowerment. *American Journal of Community Psychology, 21*, 279–292.

Rimmerman, C. A. (1998). ACT UP. The body. The complete HIV/AIDS resource. Retrieved from http://www.thebody.com/content/art14001.html

Rooney-Rebeck, P., & Jason, L. A. (1986). Prevention of prejudice in elementary school students. *Journal of Primary Prevention, 7*(2), 63–73.

Ross, I. S. (1995). *The life of Adam Smith.* Oxford, England: Clarendon Press.

Rothman, J., Erlich, J. L., & Teresa, J. G. (1976). *Promoting innovation and change in organizations and communities.* New York, NY: John Wiley & Sons.

Rudee, M., & Blease, J. (1989). *Traveler's guide to healing centers and retreats in North America.* Santa Fe, NM: John Muir.

Ryan Baldwin returned home. (2010). *Prohealth.* Retrieved from http://www.prohealth.com/me-cfs/blog/boardDetail.cfm?id=1384763

Sameroff, A. J., & Chandler, M. J. (1975). Reproductive risk and the continuum of caretaking casualty. In F. D. Horowitz, M. Hetherington, S. Scarr-Salapatek, & G. Siegel (Eds.), *Review of child development research* (Vol. 4., pp. 187–244). Chicago, IL: University of Chicago Press.

Sandel, M. (2009). *Justice: What's the right thing to do?* New York, NY: Farrar, Straus, Giroux.

Sandler, I. N., Gensheimer, L., & Braver, S. (2000). Stress: Theory, research, and action. In J. Rappaport & E. Seidman (Eds.), *Handbook of community psychology* (pp. 187–214). New York, NY: Kluwer/Plenum.

Sarason, S. B. (1974). *The psychological sense of community: Prospects for a community psychology.* San Francisco, CA: Jossey Bass.

Sarason, S. B. (1976). Community psychology and the anarchist insight. *American Journal of Community Psychology, 4*, 243–261.

Schmid, R. (2005, August 18). Community-based homes seem to help addicts. *Associated Press.* Retrieved from http://www.oxfordhouse.org/userfiles/file/doc/ap_depaul.pdf

Schneider, R., & Googins, B. (1989). Alcoholism day treatment: Rationale, research, and resistance. *Journal of Drug Issues, 19*, 437–449.

Schnupp, J. M. (2003). Despite serious consequences, teens still start smoking. The Children's Rights of New York. *Hotline, 23*(2), 1–4. Retrieved from http://www.northeaglecorp.com/HotlineFall03.pdf

Seidman, E. (1988). Back to the future, community psychology: Unfolding a theory of social intervention. *American Journal of Community Psychology, 16*, 3–24.

Seligman, M. (2002). *Authentic happiness: Using the new positive psychology to realize your potential for lasting fulfillment.* New York, NY: Simon and Schuster.

Shapiro, W. (1997, December 10). Tobacco deal means money to burn. *USA Today.*

Sherif, M. (1966). *In common predicament: Social psychology of intergroup conflict and cooperation.* Boston, MA: Houghton-Mifflin.

Sheth, H. C. (2009). Deinstitutionalization or disowning responsibility? *International Journal of Psychosocial Rehabilitation, 13*(2), 11–20.

Shinn, M., & Toohey, S. (2003). Community contexts of human welfare. *Annual Review of Psychology, 54*, 427–459.

Showalter, E. (1997). *Hystories: Hysterical epidemics and modern media.* New York, NY: Columbia University Press.

Siegel, B. (1990). *Love, medicine, and miracles.* New York, NY: HarperCollins.

Smith, A. (1904). *An inquiry into the nature and causes of the wealth of nations* (5th ed.). London: Methuen & Co.

Smith, G. D. (2002, October). Behind the broad street pump: Aetiology, epidemiology and prevention of cholera in mid-19th century Britain. *International Journal of Epidemiology, 31*(5), 920–932. Retrieved from http://www.ph.ucla.edu/epi/snow/injepidemiology31_920_932_2002.pdf

Spink, K. (1997). *Mother Teresa: A complete authorized biography.* New York, NY: HarperCollins.

Spretnak, C. (1991). *States of grace.* New York, NY: HarperCollins.

Stephan, J. J. (2004). *State prison expenditures, 2001.* Washington, DC: Bureau of Justice Statistics.

Szalavitz, M. (2009, April 26). Drugs in Portugal: Did decriminalization work? *Time.* Retrieved from http://www.time.com/time/health/article/0,8599,1893946,00.html

Teens and tobacco. (1991, December 12). *Chicago Daily Herald.*

Thompson, D. W., & Jason, L. A. (1988). Street gangs and preventive interventions. *Criminal Justice and Behavior, 15,* 323–333.

Torrey, E. F. (1997). *Out of the shadows: Confronting America's mental illness crisis.* New York, NY: John Wiley & Sons.

Trickett, E. J., & Mitchell, R. E. (1993). An ecological metaphor for research and intervention in community psychology. In M. S. Gibbs, J. R. Lachenmeyer, & J. Sigal (Eds.), *Community psychology: Theoretical and empirical approaches* (2nd ed.). New York, NY: Wiley.

Tsemberis, S., Moran, L., Shinn, M., Asmussen, S., & Shern, D. (2003). Consumer preference programs for individuals who are homeless and have psychiatric disabilities: A drop-in center and a supported housing program. *American Journal of Community Psychology, 32,* 305–318.

Tuller, D. (2011, November 23). Chronic fatigue syndrome and the CDC: A long, tangled tale. Virology Blog. About viruses and viral disease. Retrieved from http://www.virology.ws/2011/11/23/chronic-fatigue-syndrome-and-the-cdc-a-long-tangled-tale/

Unger, E. R. (2011). *CFS knowledge and illness management behavior among U.S. healthcare providers and the public.* Paper presented at the IACFS/ME Conference, Ottawa, Canada.

Upshur, J-H. L., Terry, J. J., Holoka, J. P., Goff, R. D., & Lowry, B. (1991). *World history* (Vol. II). New York, NY: West.

Vaillant, G. E. (2003). A 60-year follow-up of alcoholic men. *Addiction, 98,* 1043–1051.

Vázquez, C., Pérez Jiménez, D., Rodríguez, M. F., & Bou, W. P. (Eds.). (2010). *International community psychology: Shared agendas in diversity* (pp. 315–340). Puerto Rico: Actividades d Formación Comunitaria.

Vercoulen, J. H., Swanink, C. M., Galama, J. M., Fennis, J. F., Jongen, P. J., Hommes, O. R.,…Bleijenberg, G. (1998). The persistence of fatigue in chronic fatigue syndrome and multiple sclerosis: Development of a model. *Journal of Psychosomatic Research, 45,* 507–517.

Vogeli, C., Shields, A. E., Lee, T. A., Gibson, T. B., Marder, W. D., Weiss, K. B., & Blumenthal, D. (2007). Multiple chronic conditions: Prevalence, health consequences, and implications for quality, care management, and costs. *Journal of General Internal Medicine, 22*(3), 391–395.

Walker, D. (2008). GAO-U.S. financial condition and fiscal future briefing-David Walker-January 2008. Retrieved from http://www.gao.gov/cghome/d08446cg.pdf

Wandersman, A., & Florin, P. (1990). Citizen participation, voluntary organizations and community development: Insights for empowerment and research [Special Issue]. *American Journal of Community Psychology, 18,* 41–177.

Warner, K. E. (2006). Tobacco control policy research: Insights and contributions to public health policy. In S. Isaacs & J. Knickman (Eds.), *Series on health policy: Tobacco control policy* (pp. 3–86). San Francisco, CA: Jossey-Bass.

Watts, R. J., & Abdul- Adil, J. (1994). Psychological aspects of oppression and sociopolitical development. In R. Newby & T. Manley (Eds.), *The poverty of inclusion, innovation and interventions: The dilemma of the African-American underclass.* Rutgers, NJ: Rutgers University Press.

Watzlawick, P., Weakland, J. H., & Fisch, R. (1974). *Change: Principles of problem formation and problem resolution.* New York, NY: W. W. Norton.

Weick, K. E. (1984). Small wins: Redefining the scale of social problems. *American Psychologist, 39,* 40–49.

White, W. (1998). *Slaying the dragon: A history of addiction treatment and recovery in America.* Bloomington, IL: Chestnut Health Systems.

WHO Framework Convention on Tobacco Control. (2003). Retrieved from http://www.who.int/fctc/text_download/en/index.html

Wiehe, S. E., Garrison, M. M., Christakis, D. A., Ebel, B. E., & Rivara, F. P. (2005). A systematic review of school-based smoking prevention trials with long-term follow-up. *Journal of Adolescent Health, 36,* 162–169.

Wilkinson, R., & Pickett, K. (2009). *The spirit level: Why more equal societies almost always do better.* Essex, England: Allen Lane.

Winograd, M., & Hais, M. (2011). *Millennium momentum: How a generation is remaking America.* Piscataway, NJ: Rutgers University Press.

Wolff, T. (2010). *The power of collaborative solutions: Six principles and effective tools for building healthy communities.* San Francisco, CA: Jossey-Bass.

World Health Organization. (2010, April 13). Alcohol facts and figures. Retrieved from http://www.who.int/substance_abuse/facts/alcohol/en/index.html

Wu, S. Y., & Green, A. (2000). *Projection of chronic illness prevalence and cost inflation.* Prepared for Partnership for Solutions by the Rand Corporation. Baltimore, MD: Johns Hopkins University.

Yach, D. (2010). From Framingham to the framework convention on tobacco control. *Progress in Cardiovascular Diseases, 53,* 52–54.

Zimbardo, P. G. (1971). The power and pathology of imprisonment. Congressional Record (Serial No. 15, 1971–10–25). Hearings before Subcommittee No. 3 of the Committee on the Judiciary, House of Representatives, Ninety-Second Congress. *First Session on Corrections, Part II, prisons, prison reform and prisoner's rights: California.* Washington, DC: U.S. Government Printing Office.

Zimbardo, P. G. (2007). *The Lucifer effect.* New York, NY: Random House.

ABOUT THE AUTHOR

Dr. Leonard A. Jason is a Professor of Psychology and the Director of the Center for Community Research at DePaul University, in Chicago. He is well respected for his concern for social issues, tackling diverse and interesting subjects with real-world implications. He took a number of nontraditional paths in his thought-provoking work throughout his career and has remained consistent with the ideals of community psychology. He has received more than $26 million in federal grants and published 588 articles, 77 book chapters, and 24 books. Dr. Jason has investigated topics such as the prevention of alcohol and substance use disorders within recovery homes, youth tobacco prevention programs, school-based preventive interventions, and the prevalence and treatment of myalgic encephalomyelitis (ME)/chronic fatigue syndrome (CFS). For his research on media interventions, the American Psychological Association honored him with three awards, and he continues to be asked to comment on policy issues for media outlets. He has been on the editorial boards of seven peer-reviewed psychology journals and served on review committees for the National Institute of Drug Abuse and the National Institute of Mental Health.

Dr. Jason received the 1997 Distinguished Contributions to Theory and Research Award, and in 1998, DePaul University acknowledged his ground-breaking work with the prestigious Cortelyou-Lowery Award for Excellence. The Society for Community Research and Action (Division 27 of the American Psychological Association) presented him with the 2007 Special Contribution to Public Policy award, and the Oxford House organization recognized his outstanding contributions to the field of addiction with the prestigious Tom Fellows Award in 2011. He has previously functioned as President of the Division of Community Psychology of the American Psychological Association, a past Editor of *The Community Psychologist,* and a former Director of the Clinical Training program at DePaul University. Over the past three and a half decades, he has served on 85 master's thesis and 78 dissertation Committees.

His pioneering work on ME/CFS earned him the 2003 Dutch ME-Foundation International ME-Award. He is the recipient of the International Association for CFS/ME's 2011 Perpich Award for distinguished service to the ME/CFS community. In addition to serving as Vice President and member of the Board of Directors of the International Association of ME/CFS, he presided as Chairperson of the Research Subcommittee of the Chronic Fatigue Syndrome Advisory Committee, which has advised the U.S. Secretary of Health and Human Services on policy issues involving ME/CFS.

INDEX

CPSIA information can be obtained
at www.ICGtesting.com
Printed in the USA
BVHW030450070219
539569BV00006B/148/P